Positive Public Relations
2nd Edition

Carl Hausman
and
Philip Benoit

LIBERTY HALL
PRESS™

This publication is designed to provide accurate and authoritative information in regard to the subject matter covered. It is sold with the understanding that the publisher is not engaged in rendering legal, accounting or other professional service. If legal advice or other expert assistance is required, the services of a competent professional person should be sought.

—From a declaration of principles jointly adopted by a committee of the American Bar Association and a committee of publishers.

LIBERTY HALL PRESS books are published by LIBERTY HALL PRESS, a division of TAB BOOKS. Its trademark, consisting of the words "LIBERTY HALL PRESS" and the portrayal of Benjamin Franklin, is registered in the United States Patent and Trademark Office.

Second Edition
First Printing

©1990 by TAB BOOKS

Printed in the United States of America

Reproduction or publication of the content in any manner, without express permission of the publisher, is prohibited. No liability is assumed with respect to the use of the information herein.

Library of Congress Cataloging-in-Publication Data

Hausman, Carl, 1953-
Positive public relations / by Carl Hausman and Philip Benoit.
p. cm.
ISBN 0-8306-3095-3
1. Public Relations. I. Benoit, Philip, 1944- . II. Title.
HD59.H292 1990
659.2—dc20
89-13443
CIP

TAB BOOKS offers software for sale.
For information and a catalog, please contact:
TAB Software Department
Blue Ridge Summit, PA 17294-0850

Questions regarding the content of this book
should be addressed to:
Reader Inquiry Branch
TAB BOOKS
Blue Ridge Summit, PA 17294-0214

Acquisitions Editor: Kimberly Tabor
Book Editor: Karen R. Bitner
Book Design: Jaclyn J. Boone
Cover Design: Lori E. Schlosser
Production: Katherine Brown

Contents

Acknowledgments	ix
Introduction	xi

1 What Is Public Relations? — 1
What Does Public Relations Involve? *1*
What Kind of PR Do You Need? *4*
A PR Checklist *5*
Going after Your Goals *7*
Dealing with the Media *9*

2 Getting Along with the Written Word — 11
Tips for Clear, Concise Writing *12*
Lively and Interesting Writing *19*
Demonstrate Instead of Describe *19*
One More Note *21*

3 Newspapers — 22
The Workings of a Modern Newspaper *22*
What Do Newspapers Want to Print? *27*
Getting Your Stories in the Newspaper *31*

4 Television — 34
How a TV Station Operates *34*
How to Set Up a TV News Event *41*
Public Service Announcements *44*
TV Talk Shows *44*

5 Radio — 48
How a Radio Station Operates *48*
Types of Radio News *50*
Public Service Announcements *53*
Radio Talk Shows *53*
Producing Your Own Radio *54*

6 The Press Release   58
    The Purpose of a Press Release   *58*
    Press Release Formats   *59*
    Categories of Press Releases   *59*
    How to Write a Press Release   *63*
    Keeping Your Press Releases Out of the Wastebasket   *70*
    How to Distribute Press Releases   *70*
    Models for Press Releases   *74*

7 Photography   75
    The Camera   *76*
    The Lens   *76*
    The F-Stop   *82*
    Shutter Speed   *84*
    Depth of Field   *85*
    Exposure Meters   *87*
    Film Speed   *89*
    Selecting Film for PR Work   *90*
    Equipping and Using a Darkroom   *96*
    Photo Composition   *106*
    How to Use Your Photos   *117*

8 Producing Publications   122
    Type   *122*
    Layout   *126*
    Newsletters   *138*
    Brochures   *140*
    Other Publications   *144*
    The Printing Process   *144*

9 Desktop Publishing   151
    What Is Desktop Publishing?   *152*
    Graphic Design with Desktop Publishing   *157*
    Using Desktop Publishing in Public Relations   *158*

10 Fund Raising   164
    Getting Started   *165*
    Organizing   *165*
    How to Reach Donors   *167*
    Appeals: How to Ask for Money   *170*

11 Public Relations for the Entrepreneur   173
    Cost-Effective Public Relations for the Entrepreneur   *175*
    Marketing for the Entrepreneur   *175*
    Advertising for the Entrepreneur   *178*

12	**How Much Does All This Cost?**	**182**
	Money-Saving Tips *182*	
	Prices of Products and Services *185*	
13	**National Media**	**188**
	Types of National Media *188*	
	Efforts Versus Results *189*	
	Tough and Easy Markets *190*	
	Consumer and Trade Magazines *191*	
	Approaching Magazines *192*	
	Elements of a National-Interest Story *194*	
14	**Feature News**	**196**
	The Structure of a Feature Story *196*	
	50 Feature Ideas *206*	
15	**Other Things You'll Need to Know**	**212**
	Slide Shows *212*	
	Speaking Engagements *218*	
	Promotional Gimmicks *218*	
	Events *218*	
	Displays *219*	
	Buying Advertising *219*	
	Choosing Media *222*	
	How to Contact and Deal with a Reporter *224*	
	Preparing a Press Kit *226*	
	Using Reprints *228*	
	Final Thoughts *228*	

Appendices

A	**Sample Press Releases**	**229**
B	**Broadcast Style**	**241**
C	**Model Release**	**242**
D	**Put It in the Paper!**	**243**

Index

Acknowledgments

Several people helped in the writing of this book, and they are credited where appropriate within the text. Other people we wish to thank are Susan Rezen, Candy Benoit, Bruce Arnold, Jan VanLiew, Brian Higgins, Todd Benson, Carl Hausman, Sr., Carol Dumas, Ken Botty, and Fred Broad.

Introduction

It's been said that you can tell a great deal about people from their choice of reading material. Well, we can tell a lot about you. By virtue of the fact that you've picked up this book, we know that you're someone who needs to get a message across to the public. To hazard a guess, we'd say that you are one of the following:

- A businessperson who wants to publicize a product or service.
- A volunteer for a cause or organization.
- An entrepreneur who needs to generate publicity on a tight budget.
- An employee whose job responsibilities have been expanded to include public relations.

Pretty close, aren't we? Guessing wasn't all that difficult because there is a perceptible trend in public relations, a need that this book was written to meet. Every day, more people are becoming involved in public relations, either for a business they're starting, an existing firm, or a cause in which they believe. Many PR jobs are part-time because startup firms need PR but don't have much in the way of financial resources. In other cases, companies or organizations perceiving the need for better PR are assigning those duties (production of a newsletter, perhaps) to someone currently in sales, marketing, or personnel.

Regardless of the motivation, you've picked up this book because you want to do a professional job of public relations—and that's exactly what we intend to show you how to do. *Positive Public Relations—2nd Edition* has been revised and expanded to provide step-by-step, explicit instructions on how to do PR for any firm, group, or organization. We've updated this second edition to cover the relationship of PR to such current trends as desktop publishing and entrepreneurship.

We've written this book for a number of reasons. Primarily, of course, we wrote it because we knew it would sell. There are so many people entering public relations that the market is enormous. But given the state of current instructional resources, getting started in PR might not be easy. After surveying some of the other books on the market, we wondered how anyone would be able to pick up the necessary skills. Some books, for example, were wordy texts that exploded every possible permutation of public relations except actually doing it. Other books focused on an extremely narrow range, such as product news or high-level corporate theory.

Positive Public Relations is a practical and complete guidebook to actually doing the job. Chapter 1, for example, will help you determine exactly what kind of PR you want and need. Chapter 2 is a comprehensive writing course that will help you develop the skills needed to tackle releases, publications, and correspondence.

Chapters 3, 4, and 5 are devoted to the workings of various media. Understanding how the media operate is probably the most important facet of PR, but it is glossed over in many of the references currently available.

Chapter 6 tells all you'll need to know about press releases. Chapter 7 gives a basic introduction to photography. Photographs are something with which PR people deal virtually every day, but often without any real understanding of the process or the product. In chapter 7 we take the mystery out of f-stops and shutter speeds.

Would you like to put together a newsletter or brochure, or just learn about the principles of graphic design? Chapter 8 spells them out in a concise, readable format. Chapter 9 continues this exploration of publications design with an introduction to the fascinating new technology of desktop publishing.

Many PR people in nonprofit institutions are at least partly responsible for fund-raising operations, the subject of chapter 10.

Chapter 11 specifically addresses the techniques of effective public relations for the entrepreneur, the start-up businessperson who needs good PR but has limited funds. Along the same lines, chapter 12 gives you some guidance on getting the most for your money in the PR marketplace. Cash-saving tips are provided, along with a general guide to products and services.

For the truly ambitious, chapter 13 suggests some strategies for gaining nationwide exposure. A detailed section discusses the various types of national publications and the most effective strategies for cracking them.

Chapter 14 is a complete guide to writing a feature story—one of the most productive, but least understood, PR tools. Chapter 15 deals with various details you'll need to know, such as choosing media; speaking with a reporter; preparing a press kit, doing slide shows, advertising, and more.

Positive Public Relations is the kind of book we wish had been around when we started doing PR. To be honest, though, you really don't need this book. All the information can be picked up easily through trial and error, along with a few years of working for newspapers, radio, and television. And of course, you can learn from a few ghastly mistakes here and there.

Or would you rather do it the easy way? Then let's start with chapter 1 and figure out what, exactly, this whole public relations business is all about.

1

What Is Public Relations?

IT'S NOT UNHEARD OF FOR A NEWCOMER TO PUBLIC RELATIONS TO THUMB through the dictionary to find out exactly what it is that he's supposed to be doing. *Promoting a favorable relationship with the public?* Yes, that's certainly a part of it. *Increase profits by earning public good will?* That certainly has a nice ring to it.

In 1978, the First World Assembly of Public Relations Associations defined the field as: "the art and social science of analyzing trends, predicting their consequences, counseling organization leaders, and implementing planned programs of action which serve both the organization's and the public interest."

Not bad, but not the whole answer either. Public relations means different things to different people. Although it's not our aim to get involved in a pseudo-scholarly survey of the meaning of public relations, it really is important to understand the various aspects of the field.

WHAT DOES PUBLIC RELATIONS INVOLVE?

Public relations involves a number of functions. Please bear with us as we examine some of these categories. Understanding the various public relations functions will help you determine what you want to accomplish as you do your own public relations. Remember, these categories don't necessarily describe specific jobs. Often, someone doing public relations will be responsible for several of the following tasks. We'll show you how to carry out these functions in appropriate sections of this book.

Promoting Goodwill

Ever notice how many companies run advertisements that have no direct sales pitch? Highway safety messages or grants for public television documentaries might not sell much gasoline, but they do promote *goodwill*, which is vital to any industry in need of some image-building.

The need for goodwill is vitally important to organizations who are dependent on support from the community, such as charities or foundations. Organizations that rely on the public for licensing or authorization to purchase equipment or build new facilities also live and die on goodwill.

Releasing Information to the Public

Some organizations, such as police departments, retain public relations specialists to fulfill an obligation to pass along information the news media—and therefore the public—is entitled to receive. These specialists are often referred to as *public information officers* or *PIOs*. Managing the release of information will become a part of a publication relations person's job in the event of a crisis such as a fire at company headquarters. Quick release of accurate information is often crucial.

Creating or Reinforcing an Image

Colleges and universities often seek general publicity about faculty research or the accomplishments of students. There's no direct product pitch here, but the publicity does serve a purpose: it reinforces an image of a particular trait the institution would like the public to be aware of. Naturally, the college would like to be considered a center for research. The college public relations office (often called a *news bureau* or *public affairs office*) is well aware that this kind of publicity—even though it probably won't generate massive enrollments the day the story appears—will pay in the long run.

Directly Promoting a Product or Service

One enterprising businessman, who sold a book designed to keep household records, did very well using a *press release* describing the product. The press release was his only sales tool. Most of his releases were sent to women's magazines. Although only a fraction of the magazines ran the release as a story, a couple mentioned the item in "new product news" sections. This assured the businessman of a profitable number of orders.

Don't expect a press release to always work this well. The book seller enjoyed a good measure of luck and another factor that is absolutely essential: editorial interest in his product. The only reason an editor will run a release on a product (remember, we're referring to a news release, not a paid advertisement) is if the editor feels his readers will be interested.

Issuing Propaganda

Although few like to be thought of as propagandists, many of us have been forced to wear that label. In Vietnam, for example, each time an alleged incident by the North Vietnamese or Viet Cong paralleling My Lai hit the news, an American photo unit would be sent out to take gruesome photos of dead South Vietnamese. The message was "we're not the only ones who do this kind of thing."

It's not easy to draw the line that separates public relations from propaganda. Perhaps the best definition is that *propaganda* is usually designed to injure a person or a cause, or to convert followers to your cause without much regard to the finer points of truth in advertising. At worst, this type of persuasion amounts to *brainwashing*.

Incidentally, much communications theory actually grew out of the Allied propaganda efforts of World War II. Many of the principles of persuasion used during that war formed the basis for modern advertising.

Let's hope you don't have to assume the role of a propagandist. Although your message might be valid, it's a mistake to assume that the end justifies the means.

Counteracting Negative Publicity

Every business, organization, or political candidate will face some adverse press eventually. When the worst happens, the public relations person will be in charge of damage control. The function of public relations in this case will be to present the story in the best possible light. This does not mean covering up. Watergate taught most of us how well the stonewall approach works.

Handling Internal Communications

Employee newsletters are a good example of in-house publications. The goal of most such newsletters is to create a feeling of goodwill and community among employees or members of an organization. The theory is that higher morale will increase productivity. Another important function of internal newsletters is to inform workers of company policy.

Promoting and Planning Events

Promoting events can be as simple as issuing a press release describing the event and giving the time and date. But planning the entire event can be complex and nervewracking. Press parties, conferences, open houses, testimonial dinners, and celebrity golf tournaments are proven methods of promotion that require a great deal of work and attention to detail.

Achieving mention in the press is one obvious benefit attached to an event, Another, more subtle benefit involves the sense of identification people attain after attending an event. This is especially the case if it involves touring your facilities. NOTE the number of firms that sponsor tours of their plants, and the frequency with which institutions concerned with public sentiment hold open houses.

WHAT KIND OF PR DO YOU NEED?

With the exception (we hope) of propaganda, you will probably want to use public relations strategies from all the preceding categories. Depending on what you want to accomplish, the formula will be varied—a little of this, and a lot of that.

What do you want to accomplish? That's not such an obvious question as it might seem. First of all, let's consider the position you're in. Because you have taken the initiative to buy a book on public relations, you are probably one of the following:

The Owner or Manager of a Small Business. You are concerned with getting news of your product or service before the public.

A Volunteer Worker for an Organization, Club, or Cause. Your goal is to get your message across and possibly to recruit volunteers or raise funds.

A Part-Time Worker for an Institution or Program. You might work for a museum, hospital, cultural organization, or community program. You are concerned with getting news of your place of employment into the media for direct or indirect benefit. PR might be your primary responsibility.

An Employee of a Small or Medium-Size Firm. You might recently have been assigned the responsibility of PR. You might be an executive assistant, a marketing director, or a development officer. You want to do PR effectively and to advance your career.

Regardless of the category into which you fall, the practices and techniques will be the same. If you are getting paid for your work or if you work under the supervision of someone whose opinion matters to you, finding out what's expected of you right from the start can save a lot of wheelspinning and frustration. Even if you are your own boss, setting clear objectives now will avoid the time-wasting process of going through motions that might or might not be useful.

A PR CHECKLIST

There's no magic formula for figuring out what kinds and what proportions of these kinds of PR you need. Because there are so many avenue open—and because time and budget limitations will always prevent you from pursuing all of them—it makes sense to set your priorities before dipping both oars in the water.

The following checklist will help you determine what you want and what other people will want from you. If you're the boss, sit down with some staff members who are knowledgeable about marketing and run through the items in this checklist.

If you are reporting to someone, this checklist will also help determine what is expected of you. There's no point in chasing after goals that might turn out to have no importance at all to the person who signs your paycheck. So sit down with the boss or prime mover in the organization and tactfully find out what is expected of you as an employee.

- *Do you want local publicity, regional publicity, national publicity, or a little of each?*

    A ski resort, for instance, would benefit from regional and national publicity, but local publicity might not be of any help in increasing customers. Presumably, most of the people in town will know of the ski center, and if they haven't patronized it by now they probably never will.

- *Is it important that we reach a certain group?*

    The ski resort owner will want to reach skiers in other localities rather than local nonskiers. He might be very interested in placing a release in the recreation sections of newspapers in neighboring cities.

    If there is a membership or marketing specialist in your organization, it's likely that he or she will have access to some sort of research that reflects the kind of potential customers you want to reach.

- *How important is goodwill to us?*

    Goodwill never hurts, but pursuing it is more important to some organizations than to others. Hospitals, for instance, might have to have some of their purchases or services approved by public boards. In such a case, goodwill can be especially important.

- *What kind of information do we want to communicate?*

    Another consideration is, *"How will it help us?"* Colleges want to show that their faculty is accomplishing great things. Oil companies want to communicate the idea that they are friends of the environment.

Organizations that depend on membership will want to focus on the benefits of being a member.

☞ *Is it important that I appease someone's ego?*

It might be a tacit priority to get your chief executive officer in the limelight. Find a tactful way to learn if this will be part of your job.

If it turns out that it is, indeed, important for you to get exposure for the CEO, don't chafe under this requirement. After all, it's a legitimate function of public relations. It might be the reason you were hired. If this is an important part of your duties, you're cutting your own throat by not recognizing it.

☞ *Are there specific programs or services we want to stress?*

Colleges want to emphasize their computer science department or other high-revenue departments. Businesses might have a particular product or service they believe will be of particular significance in the current market. Also, consider if there are any programs in your organization that will create goodwill. Do you have the city's only day-care service for employees?

☞ *To whom must my work ultimately appeal?*

This requires some delicacy. If you are being paid for what you do, it's important to find out who sets the tempo of the band. In short, be aware that your immediate supervisor might not have a handle on what the boss wants in terms of PR. Keep your eyes and ears open.

☞ *Are we trying to offset a bad image?*

This is usually the reason why someone is suddenly assigned the job of public relations. Often, however, no one is willing to come right out and admit it in so many words.

☞ *Is it more important for me to do a good job or prove I'm doing a good job?*

Everybody spends a little time proving how well the job is being done, but in some cases it's more important than others. There are PR staffs that might spend 10 percent of their time putting out publicity and 90 percent putting together scrapbooks, applying for awards, and writing reports documenting what a great job they are doing. Find out what the situation is from the start and you won't have to spend time mopping up later.

☞ *Do people confuse us with some other organization?*

Confusion with another company is a common reason that someone decides that the company needs some image building. The image-building might take the form of increased publicity or a frontal attack such as that waged by B.F. Goodrich; who told the public in no uncertain terms that it does not own a blimp.

GOING AFTER YOUR GOALS

Now that you've reviewed the different kinds of public relations and determined what goals you or your organization want to pursue, it's time to set up a system to achieve your objectives.

Facilities and Equipment

For starters, equipment you'll need includes a typewriter or a computer with a good word-processing program, a telephone, and access to a good photocopy machine. If at all possible, buy a 35mm single-lens reflex camera and some interchangeable lenses. See chapter 7 for more information.

Develop Familiarity with the Media

Begin by becoming a consumer of the media in your local area. Be an aware consumer; read the newspapers with an eye toward determining editorial slant and content. Find the masthead—the statement of ownership and management—and make a note of the names of the editors.

The next step in becoming familiar with the media is to obtain media directories. These list and briefly describe the media in various locations. Here are some you might want to consider:

- *The All in One Directory*, from Gebbie Press.
- *Writers' Market*, published by Writer's Digest Books.
- *State-by-state directories*, published by Burrelle's.
- Ayer's *Directory of Publications*.
- Editor and Publisher *International Yearbook*.
- *Broadcasting/Cable Yearbook*, from Broadcasting Publications, Inc.

Don't rush out and buy or order any of these directories until you visit the local public library and look them over. They might not fit your needs. Your local library is sure to have them its reference section.

Public relations journals and newsletters are often an excellent way to pick up useful hints and stay abreast of trends. Some useful ones are:

Communication Briefings
806 Westminster Blvd.
Blackwood, NJ 08012

Impact
203 N. Wabash Ave.
Chicago, IL 60601

Publicist
221 Park Ave. S.
New York, NY 10003

The Ragan Report
Lawrence Ragan Communications, Inc.
407 S. Dearborn St.
Chicago, IL 60605

More public relations publications can be found listed in the media directories you will be researching. Other reference books you can benefit from include style books and dictionaries. Familiarizing yourself with the medias also includes contacting reporters and editors.

Understanding the People You Want to Reach

Find out whom you want to reach, their interests, their education level, their religion, and their age group. The best way to do this is through research, but this can be costly. Informally, you can survey people in your organization who are familiar with the market. If you are doing public relations for a small college, talk to the admissions officer to get an idea of the prospective students. Sales executives in your firm should be able to give you an extremely accurate idea of the public you want to reach.

Within the local community, there will be all sorts of resources available to you. The local chamber of commerce will most likely have reams of research that define the local constituencies. The local government will have a glut of material, such as census reports, that will be available to you. Is there an advertising agency connected with your firm? If so, it will have some accurate insights into your audience. Poke around your organization. If you keep at it long enough, an image will emerge.

Assess the Skills Needed for the Job

If you don't possess the skills needed for the job, develop them or find people who you can hire or convince to volunteer. You'll need certain skills to do some or all of the following functions:

Writing Press Releases. Press releases are basic units of information in public relations. They are generally duplicated and sent to the media. (See chapter 6.)

Preparing Newsletters, Annual Reports, or Other Publications. Such publications can be anything from a mimeographed sheet to a bound, full-color booklet. (See chapter 8.)

Taking and Developing Photographs. Photos will often be used as an adjunct to a press release or as part of a publication. In some cases, photos are required simply for display or archival purposes. (See chapter 7.)

Being a Spokesman and a Liaison with the Community. Liaison involves contact with the media and speaking before groups. For information on contacting the media, see the chapters on newspapers, television and radio. For a discussion of special events and speaking engagements, refer to chapter 15.

DEALING WITH THE MEDIA

There are some important points to remember when you have contact with a reporter or an editor. Because this is where you are immediately on the firing line, it's essential to be prepared. Here are some pitfalls to avoid:

- *Don't lie.* This can do irreparable harm to your relationship with the press and your organization's image. Experience shows that if the press has you dead to rights with some unfavorable information, you are probably better off admitting it and taking your lumps.
- *Don't stonewall if you can possibly avoid it.* You might be put in the position where people in your organization are trying to pressure you into not releasing some information. If you can't convince them, or yourself, of the need for releasing the information, probably the best way to deal with the press is to say, "I can't discuss that."
- *Don't feel that you are obligated to volunteer damaging information.* This is a difficult line to tread and it will be a judgment call. Keep in mind that you aren't expected to bare your soul every time you talk to a reporter.
- *Don't think you can get away with amateurish attempts to bury negative information.* And *don't* let second-guessers in your organization convince you that you can.

    "We can't come out and say we're laying off 50 people," the second-guesser will implore. "Lead the press release with 'productive new management goals' and mention the layoff at the end."

    All this approach will get is a good chuckle down at the local newspaper. You have a perfect right to present any information that will mitigate the bad news, and to present it in the proper context. If layoffs at your firm are below the average number made in similar firms, say so. But don't try to bury the news. If news people have to make an effort to uncover negative news, they are likely to publicize it with considerably more zeal.
- *Don't demand coverage.* A surly attitude with an editor will help about as much as trying to get out of a traffic ticket by haranguing the cop. You

probably won't get anywhere by bringing up the amount of advertising you buy. News people are quickly offended by this approach.

- *Don't try to overplay a story by misleading the media about its importance.* If you are under pressure to get good coverage on a particular story, you'll be better off coming right out and asking for a favor instead of overselling the story.
- *Don't complicate things.* This is one of the biggest failings of a newcomer to PR. Reporters and editors are busy people. If they must sit through your endless descriptions of all the possible permutations of the program or event you are promoting, they likely will never want to deal with you again. By the same token, don't make things difficult by unnecessarily referring a reporter's questions to other people.

"How many employees do we have? . . . well, that's really a question for our personnel director. Oh, yes, I know the number of employees, but I think it's really the place of our personnel director to answer that question."

This list of don'ts isn't comprehensive, but it should help you gain some insight that is usually picked up by hard, sad experience. Experience is also a factor in what might be the most important of a public relations person's skills: good, clear writing. Because you probably don't have the time or inclination to spend the next couple of years learning by trial and error, the next chapter offers some time-tested suggestions and techniques.

2

Getting Along with the Written Word

If I can't figure it out in three sentences, I throw it away.
—A veteran editor who throws away a lot of press releases.

PUBLIC RELATIONS INVOLVES WRITING—A LOT OF IT. YOU'LL BE WRITING press releases, letters, copy for brochures, advertisements, invitations, newspapers, and reports. If you don't write clearly, your efforts will largely be wasted.

But even perfectly understandable writing might not completely make the grade. Because you are trying to captivate and persuade, your writing must also be interesting and lively.

This chapter passes along some suggestions for making your writing readable and interesting. Because writing is the foundation of almost all aspects of public relations, we'll deal with it here before moving on to a detailed study of the press release in chapter 6.

This chapter takes an approach that is different from most writing guides. Outlined are what we feel are the most important pointers, and there are illustrations where appropriate. You won't be overloaded with information, but you will be able to use the examples to recognize typical problems. Some of the suggestions cover areas other than how to write. We also show how and why to proofread and we give an introduction to essential reference books.

TIPS FOR CLEAR, CONCISE WRITING

There's an old saying that veteran writers are fond of passing along to cub reporters. "First, get it to make sense and be sure that it's correct. Then—if you have time—make it sound pretty." Let's start with the clarity and accuracy.

Don't Make Your Writing "Academic"

There is a tendency, especially among educators, to believe that the more ponderous the language, the more impressive the message. Thus the phrase "we will meet to consider the alternatives" often mutates into something like "we will form a colloquium to interface in regards to the multifaceted ramifications we are cognizant of."

Journalists—the primary group you try to reach when you do your own public relations—are not likely to be awestruck when they see an eight-syllable word. Words are their business; precisely, accurate communications is their business. Accurate communication is not served by stilted, long, and complex sentences. If you want your public relations to be successful, decide right now to hack your way clear of the verbiage jungle.

Journalese

In most cases, the journalistic style of writing features the so-called *inverse pyramid*. Note how most newspaper stories are written. The *lead* comes first and tells the guts of the story. This is followed by information in a descending order of importance, to facilitate editing. If the story is ten paragraphs long, but there's only room for six, the editor can cut the final four paragraphs without having to worry about losing essential details. This does not apply to *feature news*, which follows a different formula. The feature news style is explained in chapter 14. The following is an example of the inverse pyramid.

The lead contains the most important details.

CENTERVILLE—A tractor-trailer—with a full load of electronic parts—overturned shortly before noon today on Route 21, demolishing the truck and causing a massive traffic jam. The driver of the truck, 29-year-old John Smith of 1211 Maple St., Nortown, suffered minor injuries.

These details are interesting, but not essential.

According to the state police, the wreck occurred one-half mile east of the Jeffersonville exit. Traffic was tied up for 7 miles along the eastbound lane.

Here are some details that easily can be cut.

Police say it took three wreckers an hour to right the vehicle owned by the

ABC Transportation Company of Centerville. The extent of the damage to the cargo and the cause of the accident have not been determined.

That is how the inverse pyramid works. The story could continue with quotes from witnesses, names of the investigating officers, and so forth.

Regardless of how much detail follows, the basic facts must be contained in the lead. The lead is usually the first sentence or two in the copy.

Note that the story—typical of thousands that appear every year in the nation's newspapers—follows the old journalism axiom of the *five W's*.

- *Who* was involved . . . a truck driver named John Smith and a lot of angry drivers who got stuck in traffic.
- *What* happened . . . a truck overturned and caused a major traffic jam.
- *Where* it happened . . . along route 21 in Centerville. Centerville is the *dateline*, the place where the story emanates. The reader can generally assume that everything in the story happens in the locale indicated by the dateline, unless stated otherwise.
- *When* it happened . . . shortly before noon.
- *Why* it happened . . . the cause has not yet been determined.

The who, what, where, when, and why formula is effective in news writing. If the story doesn't explain who, what, where, when, and why, there's something missing. Obviously, we're not trying to train you to be a newspaper reporter, but journalistic style forces you to write a complete story.

As you gain in experience, you will want to use varied styles in the leads of your releases. An example is the anecdotal lead that is explained in chapter 14. Remember that you're always safe by using the basic lead—a lead that tells the most important points of the story. (See Fig. 2-1.)

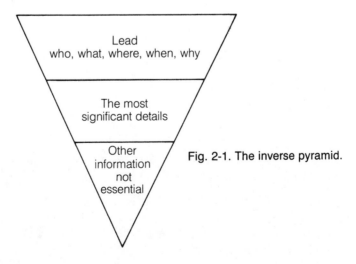

Fig. 2-1. The inverse pyramid.

Rogue Paragraphs

It seems obvious that all paragraphs should have some relationship to what the story is about, but the so-called *rogue paragraph* is a common offense among novice writers.

Research shows that when readers become confused about the meaning of what they are reading, they often stop reading and turn to something else that makes more sense. The rogue paragraph is a real obstacle. The following copy is an example of what might be found in a fund-raising brochure.

> The Catholic Community Center of Centerville serves a wide variety of needs, providing services to the poor, the emotionally ill, and those suffering from problems related to alcohol and drug abuse.
>
> Unfortunately, these services cost money—and money is in short supply these days. In order to keep giving help to those who need it, the Catholic Community Center must raise $20,000 during the current fund drive.
>
> Dr. Michael P. Waters is director of the Catholic Community Center. He has been involved in the social services field since 1956, when he received a doctorate in social work from . . .

Notice how the writing ground to a halt when the author suddenly shifted gears and brought Dr. Waters into the picture. Why did the rogue paragraph do so much damage? Because it didn't support the theme of the copy.

The theme is that the Catholic Community Center does necessary work and it needs money. Paragraphs one and two supported that theme, but paragraph three sidetracks the reader. The reader becomes unsure of what the devil this copy is about—the center's money problems or the center's director.

The PR person who wrote this (hypothetical) copy probably felt compelled to get Dr. Waters involved. Maybe Dr. Waters doesn't have a PR director and he wrote it himself, hoping to get a nice clipping for his scrapbook.

It can still be done.

> . . . is in short supply these days. In order to keep giving help to those who need it, the Catholic Community Center must raise $20,000 during the current fund drive.
>
> Dr. Michael P. Waters, director of the Catholic Community Center, says he is optimistic that the fund drive will reach its goal. Dr. Waters, who has been involved in the social services field since 1956, says that, "In my experience, the people of our city always come to the support of a worthwhile cause."

While this might not be deathless prose, it makes sense and it doesn't jar the reader. Read through your copy and make sure all the paragraphs support the theme.

Paragraph Support

Paragraphs are expressions of the individual ideas in your copy. As you surely remember from grade school, every new idea deserves a new paragraph. This also means that *ideas must not shift in mid-paragraph*. To continue the example:

> . . . always come to the support of a worthwhile cause."
>
> Without that public support, Dr. Waters said, the Catholic Community Center will be forced to abolish several of its programs, including the drug abuse hotline and the meals-on-wheels program that brings hot meals to needy city residents who are homebound. Glenn M. Davis will work to preserve these and other programs in his role as director of the Catholic Community Center fund-raising campaign.

Hold on a minute! Who is Glenn Davis and why did he suddenly materialize in that paragraph? The first sentence of the paragraph mentions that the lack of public support will cause some programs to be cut. The fact that Glenn Davis will be in charge of the campaign is a totally different idea. It belongs in a different paragraph.

> . . . hot meals to city residents who are homebound.
>
> Ensuring that these programs are maintained will be the primary responsibility of Glenn M. Davis, the center's development officer, who will serve as director of the fund-raising campaign.

Now, the introduction of Davis makes more sense. More information about Davis and his activities can be added to the paragraph, as long as the idea doesn't change. In other words, don't put any information into the paragraph if it doesn't tell more about the fact that Davis is responsible for raising money to save the programs. That is the idea expressed by the first sentence of the paragraph.

To review the information on paragraph structure, remember that:

- All the paragraphs in the copy must back up or otherwise be related to the main theme.
- All the sentences in the paragraph must support the idea expressed by the first sentence of the paragraph. If a new idea is introduced, a new paragraph must be started.
- In order for the separate paragraphs in the copy to have a logical flow, they should have some relationship to one another.

Transitions Between Paragraphs

Notice how the following example seems graceful:

> . . . hot meals to city residents who are homebound.

Ensuring that these programs are maintained will be the primary responsibility of Glenn M. Davis, the center's development officer, who will serve as director of the fund-raising campaign.

This way of phrasing it seems abrupt:

... hot meals to city residents who are homebound.
Glenn M. Davis, the center's development officer, will serve as director of the fund-raising campaign.

Even though both examples make the same point, the first sample uses a transition to ease the jump between paragraphs. Transitions are among the best-kept writing secrets. Some good writers use them unconsciously, but many professionals mechanically set up transitions to keep their copy flowing.

For some reason, transitions don't seem to be a staple of high school or college writing classes. The best way to learn about transitions is to pick up a magazine article and see how professionals do it. You're likely to observe some basic types:

- A transition that *refers* to the previous paragraph. The example given above is of this species. By adding the phrase "Ensuring that these programs . . ." makes a direct relationship—a transition—between the fact that programs will be cut and the appointment of Davis.
- Here is a transition that *shows contrast*:

    ... and they believe that it has no place in the office.
    That view is far from universal, however. The director of a group which . . .

- Here is a transition that *asks a questions*:

    ... spent almost a million dollars in a public relations campaign.
    But did it do any good? A report by . . .

Keep an eye out for the different types of transitions. As long as the result isn't outlandish, there's no reason why you can't nip and tuck your copy for the sake of creating transitions. They really do add favorably to the writing.

You don't always have to have a transition. Sometimes the paragraphs will, by the information they contain, assume a logical order.

Correct Meanings

"The answer to all your home maintenance problems," the brochure gushed, "is simplistic!" What the writer meant, of course, was that the answer is *simple*. Simplistic means simplified to the point of ignoring significant details.

Because the writer of this *copy* (copy means anything written for publication) mixed up the usage, the meaning of the text is comically distorted. In order to preserve clarity in your writing use a dictionary.

Pay special attention to not confusing similar-sounding words, such as *profound* and *prolific* or *tenuous* and *tenacious*. Never use the phrase *fulsome praise* unless, of course, you know the meaning of fulsome. What are we talking about? Look it up and you'll see how a word you are *almost* sure of can backfire.

Make Sure Pronouns are Referenced

It's easy to get careless with pronouns, and the result often is that the reader can't tell to what or to whom *he, she, it,* or *they* refers.

> Members of our firm do not generally attend sales meetings. They are generally considered too unproductive.

Fig. 2-2. This brochure was proofread by several people before final printing and yet the mistake was not detected. After it was discovered, one of the authors asked six people to look at it and find the mistake. None of the six could find it. Can you?

Ahem . . . who or what is unproductive? Is it the meetings or the members of your firm?

Always Write A Rough Draft

You won't save time by trying to turn out final copy from every sheet you roll into the typewriter. You'll spend too much time agonizing over not making a mistake. Take the time to rewrite.

Read it Out Loud

If it doesn't sound right when you read it out loud, it will be awkward to your readers. Reading copy out loud will pinpoint difficult-to-understand sentences.

Proofread the Final Copy

It sounds obvious doesn't it? Well, take a look at Fig. 2-2. This pamphlet (the names have been obliterated to protect the guilty) was handled by dozens of people before the error was noticed. By that time, thousands of the pamphlets were in the mail. Nobody bothered to proofread the final copy.

Aside from saving embarrassment, careful proofreading of the final copy aids in improving clarity. Most writers will make changes from the rough draft to the final copy. Final copy is the last place you want a mixup.

Even experienced writers have difficulty proofreading their own copy. A phrase that makes perfect sense to the writer might be hopelessly obscure to another reader. Get somebody else to check for lack of clarity. Proofing your copy for typographical errors is also difficult. If you can't get help, start at the end of the copy and read backwards, word by word.

Shorten Copy Whenever Possible

Be merciless in editing your drafts. Shortening copy will almost always make it more precise. Also, it will tend to make it more readable.

Obtain a Reference Library

The easiest way to guarantee that your grammar, spelling, and usage are correct is to maintain a reference library where you can look up items when in doubt. Here are some suggestions:

The Associated Press Guide to Good Writing
Rene J. Cappon
Published by Addison-Wesley Publishing Co.

The Elements of Style
Strunk and White
Published by Macmillan Publishing Co. Inc.

The New York Times Everyday Dictionary
Published by Times Books

The New York Times Manual of Style and Usage
Edited by Lewis Jordan
Published by Times Books

There are many fine reference books to keep at arm's reach, but the preceding books comprise a good starter collection. Other dictionaries or stylebooks might suit your individual preferences better than the ones cited. Feel free to shop around. Two other excellent stylebooks are the *Associated Press Stylebook and Libel Manual* and the University of Chicago Press *A Manual of Style*.

Fine dictionaries abound, but we don't think you could do much better than the *The New York Times Everyday Dictionary*. It is easy on your eyes, it gives up-to-date information, and it doesn't give you more information than you'll need.

LIVELY AND INTERESTING WRITING

Many editors maintain that the most readable writing is technically well constructed and conversational in tone. In addition, lively, interesting writing is loaded with "hooks" that hold the reader's attention. Here are some tips.

Use Specific Detail

If you are reading a story about a former professional football player, which line will hold your attention more closely?

- John Dawson is a big, former pro football player.
- John Dawson is a 6-foot-5-inch former linebacker for the Washington Redskins.

Likewise, a fellow shouldn't be characterized as "a good golfer." He's an "avid golfer who carries a four handicap." By the same token, a "woman who runs a great deal in her spare time" is much less interesting than "a graceful, athletic-looking woman who wears out three pairs of running shoes a year."

This technique improves writing because it creates images. Novelists use detail in much the same way to create images. A character will only "leave the room and catch a bus" in a bad novel. A respectable writer will have his character "slam the door shut, vault down the stairs two at a time, and make a running catch of the crosstown bus."

Use Quotes

People are what make stories interesting. Which would you rather read?

- When Joe Bennetti wrote up after the accident, he didn't remember who he was for two days. He says it's hard to express how it felt.
- "When I woke up the day after the accident," Joe Bennetti says, "I couldn't remember who I was for two days. Can you imagine what that's like? Unless you've experienced it, I'm not sure I can make you understand the feeling that came over me."

Using quotes also has a very specific purpose known as *attribution*. See chapter 6 for more details.

DEMONSTRATE INSTEAD OF DESCRIBE

Use examples to make your point. Notice the difference between the following:

- In his witty fashion, the recipient of the honorary degree made light of the fact that he was a college dropout.

- Receiving his honorary degree, Smith won a laugh by noting that he had entered with the class of '59 and received his degree with the class of '83, proving that there's hope for even the slowest student.

As with adding detail, using examples to show what happened—rather than telling what happened—makes the event more realistic and compelling to the reader.

Use the Active Voice

The *active voice* means that the subject of the sentence performs the action indicated by the verb.

- The elderly patient was operated on by Dr. Smith.

The preceding statement is the passive voice. This makes the sentence less powerful than the following example:

- Dr. Smith performed the operation on the elderly patient.

There's no reason why the passive voice can't be used from time to time, but as a rule your writing will be made more forceful by using the active voice.

Avoid Adverbs

An *adverb*—a word that describes an action—is usually the first word to be struck out by an editor's pencil. As demonstrated, it's much better to show the action than to describe it. Adverbs add a particularly amateurish quality to writing. They also can add a questionable editorial slant to the piece.

Writing that, "Mr. Holtz responded angrily," puts the writer in the position of being the judge of whether Mr. Holtz was angry or not. But if you accurately report that "Mr. Holtz slammed his fist on the table while responding to the charge," you are on much safer ground. You also give a better picture of what actually happened.

Use Contractions When Appropriate

Contractions might not be appropriate in some writing, such as press releases, but they certainly belong in lighter copy. They are essential in speech writing because a speech should come out sounding like conversation.

Nevertheless, be careful when using *can't* and *didn't* in anything that will be read out loud, including a press release for radio and television. These words can easily be confused with their exact opposites when not pronounced distinctly.

Using the Second Person Pronoun

Because *you* are the reader, don't *you* feel more comfortable when the writing is directed specifically toward *you*? This might not be appropriate in formal communications or a press release, but use of the second person pronoun has a definite place in informal writing such as brochures or advertising copy.

Vary Sentence Length and Style

Sentences of the same length and style can be very boring. They should be avoided if at all possible. No one likes to read dull and hypnotic copy. But it is a very easy habit to get into. Are you getting the point?

By varying the style and length of sentences, you can give your copy some punch, some drive. Why bother? Because the reader becomes bored very quickly with repetitive length and constructions. It's your job to make sure that doesn't happen.

Avoid Cliches Like the Plague

"Progressing by leaps and bounds" is a good example of an overworked cliche that marks the author as an amateur. Not much else needs to be added, except, as we've said, avoid cliches like the plague. By now, we hope you realize that we're trying to be funny, which brings us to another important point.

Use Humor, But Use It with Caution

A little bit of humor can spice up an otherwise dry topic, but remember that nothing falls as flat as a poor attempt at humor. If there is the slightest doubt in your mind as to whether or not your joke is funny, it probably isn't. You will be better off not including it in your copy.

ONE MORE NOTE

All the tips on clarity, liveliness, and readability won't help you a bit unless you put them into practice. The key word here is *practice*.

Writing is largely an acquired skill. Even the best writers in the business will blanch at the clumsiness of their high school term papers found in the attic.

The secret is to keep at it. Write hypothetical news stories, advertisements, or announcements. Use the tricks of the trade presented in this chapter. Always write with the reader in mind. Ask yourself: Will this make sense to the readers? Will it interest them? Polishing your skills will pay great dividends when you start writing press releases that must pass under the critical eyes of professional editors.

3
Newspapers

HOW DO YOU GET YOUR MESSAGE TO THE MEDIA? UNDERSTANDING HOW THE media operate is the key to doing this. There are very few "tricks" to obtaining coverage. The most important aspect of doing your own public relations is giving the media what they want, the way they want it, when they want it.

This doesn't mean that following the proper procedures will guarantee you column inches or airtime. But you can increase your chances dramatically by knowing the rules. Otherwise, you won't even be in the right ballpark.

THE WORKINGS OF A MODERN NEWSPAPER

Late on a Wednesday afternoon, the reporter took the phone call. Here's an approximate recollection of how the conversation went:

CALLER: I'm _____, public relations director for the _____ Theater Group. I want to put an article in the paper about our fund-raising dinner.

REPORTER: Excuse me, but I'm the police reporter. This is a little out of my line. Why did you call me?

CALLER: Well, I called the switchboard and asked for a reporter. Can't you write up this simple little story for us? We have to get a lot of people to come to our dinner, so that's why we want you to advertise it for us.

REPORTER: If you give me some information, I'll put you in touch with the right desk.

CALLER: I already gave you the information.

REPORTER: *Me?*

CALLER: No, you people. Don't you have it?

REPORTER: Who did you give it to?

CALLER: I don't know. I called up last week and told somebody about our dinner. You people didn't put it in the paper so I decided to call again. I figured you'd lost it.

REPORTER: Ma'am, there are about 70 reporters and editors on this paper. There's no way I could track down who you talked to. But why don't you talk to the entertainment editor? I'm sure he could mention the dinner in the calendar of events. But I'll warn you right now that he won't take listings over the phone. He requires a press release with a listing of the time, date, admission price, the purpose of the event, who to contact . . .

CALLER: Oh, I can't get that done in time. It'll take me a day to write it up and two days for the mail, and the dinner is Friday.

REPORTER: This Friday? The day after tomorrow? Ma'am, the calendar comes out on Thursday. It's in a special section that was printed last week.

CALLER: Are you kidding? Boy, that really puts us in a bad position. You know, we've always gotten lousy press from your paper, and I think . . .

You can guess the rest. This exchange has probably been repeated in so many words in every newspaper in the country, and it points out some very common mistakes beginning PR people make.

Learn the Ropes

Our caller in the above case history obviously had no idea how a newspaper functions. And the results were predictable. Although television taught us that Perry White, Lois Lane, and Clark Kent put the *Daily Planet* together all by themselves, newspapers never have and never will function that way. There is a veritable army of employees who are responsible for specific portions of the product.

Imagine how many specialists it takes to put out a daily paper—a massive document that is put out fresh each day, with entirely new material. Even a weekly paper, which will generally have less news and serve a smaller coverage area, requires a considerable amount of editorial and technical skill to construct.

The person in charge of the entire operation in a newspaper is the *president* or *publisher*; often the two positions are combined. Under the publisher are a variety of executives who control various aspects of the business. One of these executives, the *editor*, is in overall charge of the editorial staff.

In most newspapers, the *managing editor*, who reports to the editor, handles most of the day-to-day mechanics of news coverage. This person directly supervises individual *department editors* and *reporters*. In small weekly newspapers, there might be only one editorial position and a small reporting staff.

Department editors, sometimes called *subeditors*, are responsible for areas such as business, sports, entertainment, Sunday supplements, and lifestyle. They will generally have their own staff of reporters. One of the most important of the various editors is the *city editor*, who is in charge of general local news and who supervises a staff of reporters.

These reporters, often called *general assignment reporters*, will field a variety of assignments. Some specialize in areas such as courts or police. A *city room reporter* would probably not handle a story on a dinner for the theater group. This would most likely be the domain of a reporter who worked for the *entertainment editor*.

Photographers often report to either the city editor or the *photo editor*. They will be assigned to take photos for certain stories the editors feel will have an item of visual interest.

Depending on the size of the paper, there might be additional editorial staff. *Editorial* refers to any department having to do with news coverage. There are many other departments with the newspaper, including *advertising*.

Advertising, by definition, is bought and paid for; advertising is not the same thing as publicity. The two terms should never be used interchangeably, as they were by the Wednesday afternoon caller.

How News Gets Into the Paper

In the case of an afternoon daily, the staff of subeditors will generally meet with the managing editor early in the morning. Each subeditor will tell what is on tap for the day. The lifestyle editor might inform the staff that he has a piece on local day trips. The financial editor might describe a report on layoffs at a local firm. The editor who handles page one might describe the major national and international stories expected from the wire services. The city editor will outline the important local events and talk about what kind of coverage each will be given. Remember that much of the planning for these stories has been done days or weeks in advance.

Reporters will be given assignments. Sometimes those assignments will be given on the basis of a press release, and the reporter will go to an event described in the release. If the press release is intended to publicize an upcoming event, he might write a story based on the release. At the larger, better newspapers, releases will not usually be used verbatim. They will be rewritten and facts will be checked. At smaller papers, the release might be typed directly *into the system*, but some facts might still be checked. Typing into the system means that the story would be entered on a *video display terminal*. A VDT is shown in Fig. 3-1.

From a video display terminal, the story can be routed to a number of destinations. After a reporter writes the story, it generally goes to his or her editor—electronically. The editor will call it up on a VDT screen, checking for content. The story will also be seen by a *copy editor*, who will check for spelling, grammar, and *holes* in the story. Holes are gaps in information or unanswered questions. The copy editor will also write the headline, a difficult task performed under almost unbelievable technical restrictions.

At the city desk, the newsroom's headquarters for local news coverage, editors will be "making up" the pages. This process essentially involves deciding what stories go where and *what will fit*.

Fig. 3-1. A reporter works at a video display terminal, known as VDT.

News that Fits

At many newspapers, the emphasis is less on all the news that's fit to print and more on all the news that fits. Did you wonder about the purpose of the inverse pyramid style of writing? A day at the city desk will convince you of its merit. Because so many stories must be trimmed to fit—and because time is at such a premium—items are cut quickly from the bottom. Stories written in the inverse pyramid style will hold up under this type of editing.

Even at the largest paper, there's a limited amount of space for all types of news. Only a limited number of pages will be reserved for local news. If there's not enough room for all of the stories, a few might be held for the next edition or the next day, but they will most likely be discarded. It's not uncommon for staff-written, assigned stories from reporters to be scrapped because there's no room. Remember this when you are brimming with indignation because your press release didn't appear.

After all the cutting and winnowing is completed, the news pages will be laid out and proofs will be sent to the editors for checking. The presses will roll, and various editions of the paper will be produced. The first run might be a *regional edition* that will be shipped to the outlying districts of the paper's coverage area. The last run will be the *final edition* distributed in the immediate metropolitan area. A morning newspaper will probably be "put to bed" between midnight and three in the morning. An afternoon paper will generally be printed and out on the streets between noon and three.

The modern newspaper is a large machine with many different functioning parts. As shown in Figs. 3-2 and 3-3, the modern newspaper has changed signifi-

Fig. 3-2. A modern newspaper newsroom (reprinted with permission from the Worcester Telegram and Gazette).

Fig. 3-3. A newspaper newsroom of several decades ago. Instead of using wires and computer memory, stories were transmitted by pneumatic tube. (Reprinted with permission from the Worcester Telegram and Gazette).

cantly from the newspaper of decades ago. Modern technology adds to the speed with which news can be processed and the amount of news that can be handled.

WHAT DO NEWSPAPERS WANT TO PRINT?

A newspaper will print items the editors feel have the greatest impact on the interest of the public. The most common mistake among people who are doing PR for their organization is to forget this fact and consider all information from their organization as equally newsworthy.

Actually, their information might not always be newsworthy from the editor's point of view. A story about reduced bus fares for all senior citizens in the city will stand a much better chance of making the paper than a release on the latest meeting of a garden club.

This does not mean that a small organization or an organization that doesn't have a large impact on the public will be excluded from coverage in daily or weekly newspapers. If you are acting in the role of public relations representative, keep in mind the second half of the *impact and interest* equation. News of interest to the public will always be of interest to the newspaper. A good public relations person can keep an organization in the news by being aware of the kinds of things that make news. A press release or a telephone call to the right newspaper staffer can bring gratifying results.

You won't always be able to interest the media in your piece, especially if there is a lot of hard news crowding the paper. Be aware that *hard news*—reporting of a significant event—will always be given precedence over *soft features* such as human interest.

If you have legitimate hard news, such as a major staff appointment or announcement of an important public event, you'll have little difficulty making the paper. But if your organization doesn't turn out a lot of hard news, and if you feel it is in your best interests to appear in print often, keep an eye open for potential attention-grabbers. The following are some examples of stories newspapers like to run.

Local Angles on National or International Stories

The next time there's a recurring, major national or international story, look through your local paper for a *sidebar* (a small item related to the major story) with a local angle. If a space shuttle has radio transmission difficulties, there just might be an interview with a local scientist, familiar with radio transmission, who will explain the difficulty in receiving the signals. If much of the nation is in the midst of a brutal cold wave, there will undoubtedly be an interview with a local oil dealer concerning the fuel supplies and the local impact. The latest story concerning a war or massacre in an overseas nation might be covered in your local paper with a sidebar featuring a local person—a native of the country or someone who lived there for a time—commenting on "what it was really like."

There are other angles that might suit almost any organization. The spokesman for a local charity might call the editor on the day when unemployment figures come out and explain some of the programs offered for local people out of work. So when there's major news, start thinking of a legitimate local angle involving your firm.

Anything Unique or Unusual

Historically, newspapers have always been enamored of the "man bites dog" story. But you don't necessarily have to have an earthshaking event happen to make news in the unique or unusual department. Does your organization teach yoga to employees? Do you put on a Christmas program where children dress up in ethnic costumes and follow the holiday rituals of various nations? Is your hospital or rescue unit staging a mock disaster to test procedures?

Human Interest

The human interest angle covers a lot of ground. The fellow who works in your foundry and does needlepoint on his lunch hour would probably qualify. So would the political candidate you are working for who spends his spare time working on a conservation project. The office worker who saves a life because she knows cardiopulmonary resuscitation will certainly be a legitimate subject of a story.

Human interest profiles are a good avenue for profit-making organizations. The PR person for a shoe factory will have a tough time convincing the paper to carry a story about shoes, but if the corporate vice-president climbed Mount Everest, he could be the subject of a very interesting personality piece.

Striking or Unusual Photographs

Photos are the showpieces of newspaper layout. Photo editors are always on the lookout for something that will draw the eye of the reader. In most cases, newspapers will want to have their staff photographers take the photo, but some papers will use photos furnished to them.

It's difficult to describe what makes a striking photo, but you'll know it when you see it. Keep in mind that this is one of the easiest ways to get a newspaper to give you some publicity.

Pay attention to the kind of photos carried in the local papers. Perhaps the morning daily likes pictures of children. Keep an eye out for a photo opportunity, such as Fig. 3-4, that might satisfy the photo editor's eye.

Continuing Columns

A column eats up a horrifying amount of material (horrifying, at least, from the standpoint of the person who writes the column). If you or your organization have something you feel might be appropriate, get in touch with the columnist.

If you do the legwork, the columnist just might give your organization, group, or firm some terrific exposure. A packet of information about your sports club (including names and telephone numbers of people who could give interesting interviews) might prove a godsend to a sports columnist facing a tight deadline. By the way, sports writers are usually receptive to phone calls from coaches or team members reporting scores.

Seasonal Events

The ethnic Christmas party cited earlier would probably appeal to an editor because of the holiday angle. So would a charity's Thanksgiving dinner for the needy. For that matter, a grocery store's incoming shipment of a record number of turkeys might make an interesting photo and story.

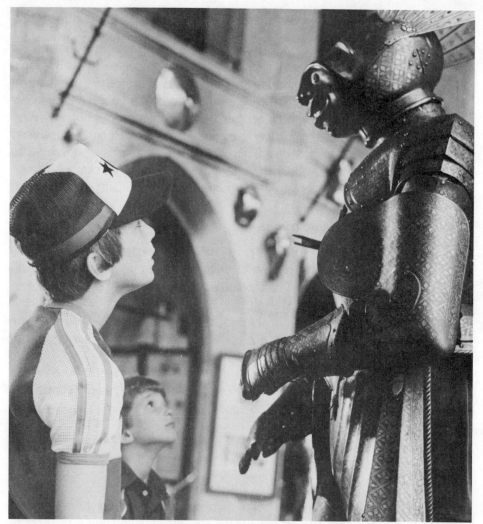
Fig. 3-4. Photos with children are always appealing (courtesy of Higgins Armory Museum).

A firm with a special program for hiring disabled veterans will have a much better chance of making news on Veterans' Day. With a little imagination you might be able to come up with Halloween, Memorial Day, or even Ground Hog Day.

In any event, do your planning early. Some of the special sections—such as holiday gift sections—might be put together months before the holiday itself.

Exclusives

Any story of reasonable interest might receive better coverage if it is offered exclusively to one newspaper. Let the editor or reporter know that you're not going to be on the phone to the competition with the same idea.

This applies only to the softer type of stories we've been discussing. In most cases, you'll be much better off not trying to give an exclusive on hard, breaking news—such as the opening of a new division of your firm. This would be considered everybody's business, and you're obligated to inform all the media.

These categories obviously don't touch all the bases, but you can learn a great deal about what the newspapers in your locality want by studying them. Look for a particular editorial slant or a type of story that keeps recurring. Once you know how papers work and what they want, the next job is to get your message to them.

GETTING YOUR STORIES IN THE NEWSPAPER

Essentially, there are two avenues to follow when you want to contact a newspaper: send a written press release or call on the phone. It is usually preferable to put your story in writing, but if you're dealing with reactions to breaking national news or offering an exclusive, a phone call might be in order.

Reaching the Right Contact

First, let's make a distinction among the newspapers that might be destinations for your press releases. Some may be in neighboring towns or states, A tourist attraction, for example, would certainly want to gain more than just local exposure.

This section deals with the local newspapers. As far as deciding whom to contact, there's a simple way to find the answer. Call the managing editor and explain who you are and what you represent. Ask the following questions:

- What editorial departments might be interested in news from our firm, group, or organization?
- What are the names of the department editors or columnists I should contact? Be sure to find out the name of the city editor.
- When is a good time for me to call so that I don't interrupt them when they are on deadline?
- Does the newspaper have preferences as to the style of press releases, mechanics of delivery, or content?
- Is there a booklet published by the newspaper for the purpose of helping PR people get news into the paper?
- What should I know about the newspaper's deadlines?

☞ How far in advance are special sections put together?

In most cases, you'll find the managing editor cooperative. After all, the paper's function is to get news to the public, and a great deal of that news is filtered through public relations specialists. In larger metropolitan papers, the managing editor will not be as accessible, and you'll wind up talking to a staffer somewhat lower in the hierarchy. But it will be a rare newspaper indeed that makes no provision for explaining the procedures for getting a story into its pages.

Now that you've determined which departments might have the greatest interest in your news and information, make some phone calls and introduce yourself. Be brief. If your organization is new or expanded, offer to send an updated packet of material. Ask about deadlines and about the kind of material used. Also, delicately inquire as to any of the paper's taboos.

The business editor, for example, might not want to photograph *ribbon cuttings* or *check passings* (staged enactments of donations). These are not uncommon taboos, by the way, as many editors consider such photos just too trite to use.

Along the same lines, there will probably be a set policy on running stories of business appointments. A photo of the appointee might be included, for example, only if the appointment is at the level of vice-president or above. Some newspapers might not be too keen on running stories on hiring of sales personnel.

The most pervasive taboo you'll find will be against *puff* pieces. These are stories lacking in substance or interest to the public. They are obviously designed to be of direct benefit to a firm or organization.

Does this mean that a commercial interest doesn't stand a chance of getting good coverage? No, of course not. What it does mean is that a profit-making organization will be able to get coverage for a particular event or aspect of the organization only if the general interest to the public supersedes the firm's commercial interest.

A real estate agent offering a seminar on new ways to obtain mortgages, for example, will probably have little difficulty getting a mention of the upcoming event. You and I and the editor know that he's not doing it completely out of the goodness of his heart. But after all, it is a subject of intense interest. If the seminar is open to the public, it is something the public will want to know about and will expect to see in the pages of their local newspaper.

Distributing Your Releases

You'll have to maintain a delicate balance between overloading the newspaper staff with releases or missing an important connection. You might have as many as six or seven destinations at a local newspaper (arts and entertainment editor, city editor, editor of the calendar listings, etc.). In some cases, a release from your organization will have no interest at all to a particular department.

On the other hand, a release might interest several departments. There's a chance that editors or reporters might get annoyed when, at the morning meeting, they discover that somebody else is working on the same thing. There are several options to solving this problem. First, find out from any of the editors how they feel about multiple releases. Second, don't send releases to departments when you know there's no way that department would be interested. Third, you can send multiple releases within the same newspaper and indicate on the release to which departments you are sending the information.

Keep in mind that this means sending multiple releases to different departments within the *same* newspaper. Unless you are offering an exclusive on a soft news story, you owe no obligation to inform a newspaper that you have or have not sent the release to its competition.

A very common mistake among novices is to assume that newspapers that share the same publisher and even the same building share their news. Few things are further from the truth.

In many cities, one company will own the morning and the evening daily. These papers are competitors despite the fact that they are under the same ownership, and perhaps the same top management. This caveat usually won't apply to different weeklies housed under one roof. In most instances, especially in the case of *shoppers*, the weekly papers serve different geographic locations. They might be edited and written by the same people.

When you first begin distributing information, take the release to the editor with whom you'll be working. An editor will feel more comfortable running your release if he or she sizes up and determines that you're a forthright person. Remember, the editor will have to place a certain amount of trust in you by assuming that your release is accurate and legitimate.

Don't rule out contacting a reporter from time to time instead of just dealing with an editor. Although most of your contact will be through an editor (who customarily assigns stories), remember that reporters often pitch their own stories to editors. This is especially true if that story is within their specialty or area of interest. It might be easier for you to place the story by first contacting an enthusiastic reporter rather than trying to convince an editor.

From the standpoint of a PR person, the local paper offers a distinct advantage over other media. You can clip and save articles for future reference or for your personal scrapbook. But don't overlook the drama and immediacy offered by the electronic media.

4
Television

HERE'S HOW A TELEVISION NEWS DIRECTOR SUMMED UP THE TIME PRESSURES he encounters: "During the 6 o'clock news, I've got a total of maybe 14 minutes of actual news. I get 10 calls a day from PR people who want me to guarantee them coverage. Know the only way to guarantee TV coverage? Burn down your headquarters."

The message is facetious, but the problem is real. There just isn't much time or content in a typical TV newscast. As print journalists are quick to point out, there are about the same number of words in a half-hour newscast as there are on the front page of *The New York Times*.

But don't get the idea that one medium is somehow superior to the other. Television, obviously, is different from print. It's not better or worse, but different.

"Television can't begin to offer the in-depth coverage a newspaper can," argues the TV hater. "No, it can't," admits the apologist, "but it can cover breaking news events. A morning newspaper is really yesterday's news . . ."

The argument will probably never be settled. However, if you're looking to gain publicity through the local or regional TV stations remember that, because TV is different from other media, its requirements are also different.

HOW A TV STATION OPERATES

When you turn on the television, be aware that—in theory, at least—you own the airwaves over which the show travels. A government agency, the Federal Communications Commission, is in charge of guiding television stations in the way they utilize the public airwaves.

Part of what the FCC mandates is that a small portion of air time be devoted to public service broadcasting, and that the public has reasonable access to the airwaves. This accounts for the continued survival of the Sunday-morning "Meet Your Community" talk shows that are of interest to few viewers and certain don't make money for the station.

Money is made on the newscasts at 6 and 10 or 11. These time blocks account for a significant portion of the station's income. For an entirely locally produced program, all the commercial spots available within the show will produce revenue directly to the station. That is not the case for network shows.

The news department in a television station is usually under the supervision of a *news director*. In the case of very large stations, the chief news executive might be a vice-president of the organization. Under supervision of the news director is an *assignment editor* who will handle the complex job of scheduling *reporters, technical crews,* and equipment.

On-the-air reporters are only the tip of the personnel iceberg. *Directors* sit before several monitors in a control room, similar to the one shown in Fig. 4-1, and decide which shot or program source will go over the air.

The director supervises a *control room crew* that controls *videotape machines* and *audio consoles*. Within the control room, technicians supervise the intricate equipment that governs the TV signal (Fig. 4-2). Outside in the *studio*, where local shows are produced, technicians control cameras, lights, and microphones.

A number of *camera operators* are assigned to the news department. They will travel with reporters to the scene of the news event to be covered. Sometimes only a camera operator will be sent to an event when only footage is required. An example is a few seconds of a concert. The camera operator will use a modern portable video camera (Fig. 4-3) hooked up to a portable videocassette recorder, referred to in the industry as a VCR.

After the tape is shot, it will be taken to the station where the reporter or a technician will edit the tape. Unlike film, the tape is not cut and spliced. Instead, various portions of the tape are *dubbed* (copied) onto another tape in the final form using equipment such as shown in Fig. 4-4. The edited tape is what will be broadcast.

Most on-the-air news people are journalists as well as announcers. Although some stations employ full-time writers, on-the-air people often write most of their own copy. National news is obtained from the *wire service teletypes* that churn away in a corner of the newsroom (Fig. 4-5).

On-the-air news people might or might not moderate the talk shows. Sometimes these shows are produced under the supervision of a specialized *public service department*. These talk shows range in approach from the deadly serious

Fig. 4-1. A television control room.

Face the Nation format to the more gossipy styles represented by *Oprah Winfrey, Sally Jessie Raphael* and *Phil Donahue*.

The public service department (in smaller stations, it will be a one-person department) is also responsible for *public service announcements*, referred to as PSAs. A PSA is an announcement made for a nonprofit, public service organization.

Let us remind you once more that television time is tight. Getting a positive news story on the air will usually be something of a coup. The breaking news—

Fig. 4-2. Television is very complex. That is something every PR person should be aware of the next time something is needed in a hurry. Here a technician prepares to adjust the quality of TV cameras.

Fig. 4-3. A cameraman covers a story using a portable video camera and a videocassette recorder.

Fig. 4-4. Videotape being edited. It's not cut and spliced like film. It is dubbed electronically from one video tape recorder to another. It's important for a PR person to be aware of the newsgathering and editing process if for no other reason than to be able to carry on a conversation intelligently with TV people about their work.

the building burning down—will take care of itself. With this in mind, try to think like a TV newsperson thinks.

Simple Stores

The typical TV news story will be over and done with in about a minute or a minute and a half. Local TV news is not the place to elaborate on the marvelous intricacies of your new pension plan. Even simple stories can become complicated if the people involved don't understand the way television must work. Many a college public relations officer has shriveled as the professor with the

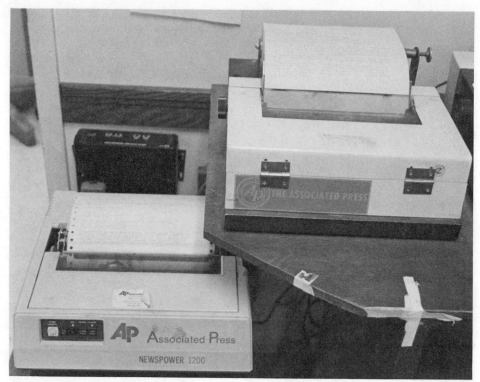

Fig. 4-5. Most TV stations get national and international news from the wire services. Modern wire service equipment has come a long way since the days of large bulky teletype machines that had to be housed in soundproof boxes to cut down on noise.

wonderful invention rebels at the reporter's request for a short answer to a direct question.

Visual Stories

A concert of medieval music where the players dress in period costume is a natural for TV coverage. So is a new medical device that does something you can demonstrate on TV. In presenting your idea to the news director or assignment editor, it will be extremely helpful if you can show that your story will have visual interest as well as news value.

The obligatory groundbreaking ceremony, for instance, will be far more appealing to the TV people if you assure them that there is a large-scale model of the building available. You will also fare better if you can assure them that the company president will be glad to answer questions about the economic impact of the expansion of the business. A related strategy is to make up slides of the important people in your organization and give them to the TV news department. If they have a slide of your company president to show in the background, they might be more inclined to read the press release about him. Some stations want *key slides* in a special format to appear behind the newscaster. Consult the news directors about this any special style or format requirements for slides.

Easy In, Easy Out

Local TV people have pressing deadlines, and they will have a number of destinations within a working day. They want to get the story and leave for their next assignment with a minimum of fuss. If you can time arrangements to make things easy on the TV news crew, you will score some valuable points. Also, don't forget that a TV news crew wants to see everything when they come. If you don't have a vital piece of information, a newspaper reporter can usually arrange to call you back when he or she's sitting down to write the story. But a TV reporter can't very well get more footage by telephone.

If you have your heart set on making the TV news, but can't seem to make any headway with your standard news releases (which face even stiffer competition for space than in newspapers) or your suggestions for soft news stories, perhaps a specially tailored TV news event might be in order.

HOW TO SET UP A TV NEWS EVENT

By an *event*, we mean something more than convincing a TV reporter to cover a human interest story. The word event signifies that something important is happening, and that there will be something for the TV people to point their cameras at once they arrive.

There's no reason why an event can't be shared by newspapers, television, and radio. Nevertheless, the physical surroundings and other factors probably will have a bigger impact on the electronic media than they will for print journalists. By planning the event with these factors in mind, you might stand a better chance of getting TV coverage.

The event might be a kickoff dinner for a fund-raising drive, the unveiling of a new piece of art at a museum, the dedication of a building or major new piece of equipment, a visiting dignitary making a speech for your cause, or a press conference.

Be extremely wary of setting up a *press conference*. The term implies that the only purpose of the event is to get the press together with your speaker. If the press doesn't show up, your event will be a failure and you, the public relations person, will look like an idiot. If nobody shows up for your groundbreaking, you can still do the business with the shovels.

If you think you can pull off an event that will attract media coverage—for television alone or for all media—the following are some pointers on how to satisfy the TV people and get your message across.

Schedule it Properly

You won't be out of line to call up the local TV news directors and ask them what is the best time to schedule an event. Because you are scheduling an event, rather than inviting a reporter to cover a soft news story, you will generally want to invite all TV stations in the area.

Television stations don't have as much flexibility in scheduling as newspapers. There is a crew and equipment to consider as well as a reporter. Although this is not a hard and fast rule, some television stations will have more crews available quite late in the afternoon after most of the roving crews' work for the 6 o'clock news is complete.

Many television stations today include a "live" segment in one or more of their newscasts. Typically a microwave or satellite truck is dispatched with a camera crew and reporter to the scene of a news event to report live on a story.

Of course, stations that do this are dependent on something newsworthy taking place at the exact time they have slotted to "go live" during that particular newscast. The "news" value of such coverage is often questionable at best. But the rationale from the station's point of view is to appear to be instantly in touch with happenings that interest its viewers. The news value is secondary to the impression created for viewers.

Public relations people can take advantage of this gimmick by scheduling events to coincide with such live breakaways. Often a participant in a conference, a visiting celebrity, or an officer of a business or organization can be offered to "go live" with an important announcement or with a celebrity interview. Stations which might be reluctant or unable to cover an event in the normal manner (tape, edited for later broadcast) might jump at the opportunity to cover it live.

Give the TV People Direction

When the crew arrives on the scene, they will want to be told what's going on, and they will appreciate being given a press release, a fact sheet on the event and organization, biographies of the VIPs involved, and any other relevant material. This is usually referred to as a *press packet*. Have the relevant information on hand and give it to the crew.

Remember, they might be on a 15-minute stopover between a fire and a circus, and they might not have much of an idea of what's taking place at your event. Don't be afraid to suggest that they interview a specific person in your organization. Make sure that you carefully choose speakers. A poor speaker can reflect badly on your entire organization.

Brief the Designated Interviewee in Advance

The PR person is expected to be the house expert on dealing with the media.

Pass along the following guidelines to anyone in your organization who is going to be interviewed on TV. Try to closely follow the guidelines if you wind up being the one on camera.

- ☞ Speak in bite-size phrases. A rambling lecture is impossible to edit down and still be coherent.
- ☞ Look at the reporter and talk naturally. Don't look into the camera.
- ☞ Avoid saying things such as "Like I told you before . . ." The viewer won't know what was said before the cameras started rolling.
- ☞ Answer the questions straightforwardly unless the reporter is way off the track or is being hostile. If that happens, figure out a way to give the answer you want regardless of the question. For example, if the event is a groundbreaking for a new building you probably want to publicize the ways in which the new business will help the local economy. If the reporter throws in a question about whether the company is taking a big gamble after such a big loss last quarter, all is not lost. Deal honestly with the issue, but get to the point the organization really wants to make. "We don't think it's that big of a gamble. There was a downturn last quarter, but our losses were among the lowest in the industry. We're confident in the rebounding economy, and also confident in the growth of Centerville. This new building will provide jobs for almost a hundred local people, and . . ."

Where to Hold the Event

Weather is particularly important for TV coverage. If it typically pours in October, have a tent nearby.

Don't position your speaker in front of a window, causing the TV and newspaper photographers to be unable to get a decent picture. Make sure that there are no loudspeakers nearby. This is a common problem in airport press conferences.

Another physical consideration concerns putting your organization's logo on the lectern or making some other arrangement to link your organization's name with the event. The news people won't always do it for you. Because the event is primarily for the purpose of publicity, you're really not out of line trying to get in your plug.

If you think setting up a TV news event is a lot of work, you're right. You're also taking a gamble that you won't get a good media turnout. If there's a fire at the same time as your groundbreaking, you know which event will get preference. Getting TV news coverage is difficult. There are options; consider using public service announcements or talk shows.

PUBLIC SERVICE ANNOUNCEMENTS

Public service announcements are usually 10, 15, 30, or 60 seconds long, and they are scheduled by the public service director. They are generally announcements of public interest on behalf of nonprofit organizations. In most cases, the shorter spots are the easiest to schedule. Check with the public service directors at your local TV stations to find out their individual requirements.

PSAs are free and they can be of enormous benefit to you. A nonprofit organization can publicize upcoming events, make a subtle pitch for membership, or pass along other relevant information. Although TV stations are more than willing to run PSAs, they are not inclined to go through a lot of production hassles to make them for you (except for having a staff announcer record your message).

One of the easiest ways to get a PSA on television is to send the station a script and a slide. Include a cover letter or give the public service director a call before you deliver the PSA. The slide should be a color transparency that is an interesting photo representative of your organization. If you have an artist on staff or know one who will work for a reasonable rate or for free, you can have a logo made up and shoot a slide of it yourself.

The script might look something like this:

The Centerville Historical Society Museum
115 Main St.
Centerville, NY 14534
(716)000-000

15-SECOND PUBLIC SERVICE ANNOUNCEMENT

Interested in finding out what life was like in your neighborhood a century ago? Visit the free exhibit, *Our Last Century*, at the Centerville Historical Society Museum, 115 Main Street.

The slide could feature a photo of the exhibit or an outdoor shot of the museum. If you have access to an artist, it would be helpful to have the museum logo incorporated into the slide. It would be even more helpful to have the television station's logo and call letters incorporated into the artwork. If you can arrange to have this done, the television station can arrange for your public service announcement to double as a station identification. You might want to include the station's call letters in the text of your announcement: "Presented as a public service by WXXX-TV, Centerville, New York." Ask the TV station for a clean copy of a piece of stationery carrying the letterhead and logo.

One of the most important factors in getting publicity through public service announcements is to get to know the public service director. At a newspaper, there can be dozens of people who will determine the fate of your publicity efforts. At a TV station, fewer people make the decisions.

No matter how good your relationship is with the public service director, you probably won't be able to sneak by a blatantly commercial announcement. There is, however, ample room for commercial enterprises as well as for nonprofit groups on TV talk shows.

TV TALK SHOWS

Most stations have a handful of talk shows. They are generally not high priority items, except for the more show-business oriented ones in larger markets; that variety will be more difficult for you to crack.

Be aware of one thing right now. You might wind up wishing you had never attempted to place a guest on a TV talk show if you pick the wrong person or the wrong topic. Television is not merciful. A bumbling, inarticulate speaker—no matter how well informed—can do more harm than good to your organization's image. Don't say you haven't been warned.

How to Get Guests on TV Talk Shows

If you decide that you do have a topic of public interest and have a competent person to talk about the topic, call the local television station and find out who should be contacted about placing someone on the show. In some cases, the show's host will be in charge of lining up guests. In larger markets, there will be a producer assigned full-time to the show.

A nonprofit organization will usually have an easier time getting a guest on a talk show, but a profit-making firm won't necessarily be excluded as long as the spokesman for that firm addresses a topic that would be of interest to the public. The initial contact made with the producer is best made with a letter. It might look something like this:

Mr. Robert Loudon
Producer
The Community Soapbox
WXXX-TV

Dear Mr. Loudon:

    I have watched The Community Soapbox for several years, and have noticed that many of your recent segments concern home security. Part of my duties as director of marketing at the Hypothetical Security Company includes public relations. I'd like to suggest an interview with our senior security consultant, Ted Lundgren.

Mr. Lundgren, a retired New York City police captain, is a specialist in spotting weaknesses in home security. He could demonstrate door and window locks and talk about home security systems.

Mr. Lundgren has been interviewed on television talk shows several times; he is a very well-spoken fellow. He is aware that I have contacted you, so feel free to call him directly. He can be reached at the same number as the one listed on my letterhead. If you prefer, call me for more information.

Sincerely,

Allen H. Winters
Director of Marketing

Follow up the letter with a phone call. Sometimes production people get so swamped that they don't follow up on even the ideas they consider to be promising.

How to Look Good on a TV Talk Show

First, don't assume that the talk show host will know much about the subject or care much about it. It might be up to the guest to steer the conversation in the right direction if the host gets off on a tangent.

Some PR counselors suggest taking along a list of sample questions. We think this might alienate some talk show hosts or producers who might think you're trying to control the show. Instead, try bringing along a *fact sheet* that outlines some of the more important points of the subject. (See Appendix A.)

Physical appearance is important. Wear subdued clothing, and especially avoid garish patterns. Women should avoid bulky necklaces because they tend to knock against the clipped-on microphone. The producer of the show might give you some guidance on dress when he or she contacts you to confirm the appointment.

When you talk about the subject you are expected to be knowledgeable, but an extended recitation of facts and figures is not an ideal way to demonstrate that knowledge. Try to keep an informative, informal tone. It should be a conversation, not a lecture.

We don't want to belabor the subject, but do remember that going on television is not always easy. As you can see from Figs. 4-6 and 4-7, there are many distractions. The studio will be full of moving cameras and people talking into their headphones. Try to pick someone who has been on television before. If you don't have access to an experienced person, consider entering the talk show market on a more modest level—radio.

TV Talk Shows 47

Fig. 4-6. A TV talk show host checks over his notes (foreground) while a large studio camera is being warmed up.

Fig. 4-7. On the set the show begins. Visible at left is the outline of the floor director who will throw cues to the host.

5
Radio

THE FIRST RADIO BROADCAST TOOK PLACE IN 1906, AND FEATURED A SCHOLARLY gentleman named Professor Fessenden singing, playing the violin, and quoting the Bible.

True to its tradition, radio is still the most diverse electronic medium. Stations today might devote the majority of the broadcast day to news, country music, or programming in a foreign language. Or perhaps to a little of all three.

Radio also offers a wide range of opportunity for anyone doing public relations. Like TV, radio stations use the public airwaves, and, even though regulations have eased, most stations broadcast a certain amount of news and public service.

HOW A RADIO STATION OPERATES

The radio stations in your locality might vary in size from one with hundreds of employees to a station where the one person on duty runs the whole show during his shift. The larger stations will be found in correspondingly large cities. Small stations (with modest facilities and fewer employees) will be found in both large and small cities and towns.

The person in charge of the radio station usually carries the title of *general manager*. Reporting to the general manager are several department heads, including the *program director* and the *news director*. In most cases, the program director is in charge of the *staff announcers* (*disk jockeys*, if you prefer) and takes a role in planning the type of music that will be broadcast by the station. The news director might have a full-time staff, might supervise a couple of part-timers, or might be the only newsperson on staff. At very small stations, the news director might also double as an on-the-air personality.

Although some stations do have a public service director, that function is often handled informally in either the programming department or the news department.

Radio is a stressful occupation. Radio news people often face a deadline every half hour. The disk jockey generally will run his own *board* (Fig. 5-1). He will handle all of the electronic controls that mix the outputs of microphones, tape recorders, turntables, and incoming transmission lines from the various radio networks to which the station subscribes.

Members of the radio news team will often run their own board from the newsroom. During a newscast, the newsperson will plug in tape recorded interviews or staff-produced news reports and play them when appropriate. The news is sometimes read from a small studio similar to the main control room. This allows the news person to play back and edit tapes and cartridges (Fig. 5-2).

Fig. 5-1. A radio announcer running a "combo" operation. He cues up his own records and operates all his equipment.

Fig. 5-2. A news program being produced (courtesy Syracuse University Public Relations Office).

Understanding the technology used in radio broadcasting shows newspeople that you have made an effort to understand how their business works. For example, *actuality* refers to a tape or live segment featuring an interview or audio of some other happening, such as a snippet from a music performance or a funeral march. The word is used so often that a radio reporter just might forget himself and ask you for an actuality. It'll help if you know what he means.

TYPES OF RADIO NEWS

Because radio news often comes on the air every hour or half hour, it can become stale over the space of a morning or afternoon. As a result, the reporter will be looking for a fresh piece to brighten up the news; you'll find that even marginal soft news stories might be welcome. Because many small and medium-sized stations rely on the newspaper for much of their copy, a lack of local stories in the morning paper will send the radio people scurrying for something to fill those five empty minutes.

Although we're not trying to imply that radio stations will be receptive to any half-baked idea (larger stations definitely won't be), we do feel that there is a great deal of opportunity to get publicity on the radio airwaves. Your story will have a better chance of being used if it gives radio people what they want.

Actuality

Radio stations will use press releases, but they will be much happier if they have an interview they can play back. The trend in radio is to get as many voices into a newscast as possible.

If you are waging a campaign against drunk driving, your group will have a much better chance of making the radio newscast if you can provide someone to be interviewed. The same theory applies to new product news or promotion of an event. You can provide an actuality by offering to bring a spokesman for your organization to the studio for an interview or you may handle the interview yourself.

Another way of providing an actuality is through a phone interview. Be aware that if you find a message on your desk from a local radio reporter and you think he is calling in response to a release, you might be interviewed over the phone and have the interview recorded for airplay. Many PR people are a bit taken aback when they return the call to the radio station and hear: "Hi, I've got your release and I'd like to get a quick interview over the phone. The tape's rolling. Now, tell me, why did . . ."

If you don't want to be interviewed or if there is someone who can do a much better job than you, speak up. But don't be surprised if the newsperson doesn't follow up on your referral. That reporter just might be following the path of least resistance. Calling another person in your organization might mean five minutes explaining what's going on and another five minutes doing the interview if he can track down that person in the first place. And the next newscast goes on in 15 minutes!

Simple Stories of Interest to the General Public

We mentioned that the newsperson might be calling in response to a release. Although press releases are covered in their entirety in the next chapter, it's worth noting here that radio stations do use releases. Most of the releases sent to newspapers don't lend themselves well to radio news. The average radio news story is well under a minute in length, and a lot of stories just can't be chopped down that far. Other stories simply aren't all that interesting when read aloud. If your release concerns something that is simple and is of interest to the general public, it just might be used by radio stations.

Reaction

Notice how many radio news stories introduce a brief interview segment by saying "so-and-so had this reaction to the event." Radio wants reactions of individuals because that's one thing radio does very well and presents very quickly. As is the case with other media, radio wants local angles on national stories. A reaction over the phone can get the story on the air very quickly. All radio stations have equipment for recording incoming phone calls or putting them on live over the air. The bank employee in charge of public relations might do very well to get on the phone to a local radio station immediately after the federal government announces a drop in the prime rate (assuming the bank will have something positive resulting from the drop).

Stories That Can Be Trusted

Your trustworthiness and your story's accuracy might be the most important factors in placing a story on radio news. Bear in mind that while a newspaper might have the wherewithall to check out the facts in each press release or probe the background of the person offering reaction to a story, a radio station generally does not.

Even a good-quality station in a medium-size city is likely to have times when only one newsperson is on duty. In small stations, the one-at-a-time newsroom shift is the rule, not the exception.

A radio reporter airing your story is placing a great deal of faith in the veracity of your facts and your motive. If the reporter doesn't know you, he might be extremely reluctant to take your story at face value. Because he probably has no way of checking it out, the story stands a good chance of being *canned*, as they say in the trade.

Get to know radio reporters and try to win their trust. And, of course, don't take advantage of your friendship by stiffing them with an inaccurate story. You might never get another chance.

Stories During Slow Periods

Blue Monday has its own special meaning in a radio newsroom. Because staffing is usually short on weekends, and not a lot happens on Sunday night, filling up the Monday morning newscasts can be a brutal experience. Your call or press release (try mailing it on Saturday) might be most welcome on a Monday morning.

Stories in the Early Morning

If you want to call the local radio station with a timely news item, such as reaction to a breaking national story or a weather-related cancellation, do it early. By early, we mean 6:30 or 7:00 A.M., if you can arrange it. For one thing, your story—if it gets used—will air during *drive time*, radio's version of prime time. Also, the bulk of the day's interviewing and editing might be finished by 9:30 A.M. (when the morning newsperson might be at lunch).

PUBLIC SERVICE ANNOUNCEMENTS

The Public Service Announcement offers another avenue for radio exposure, but it is generally limited to nonprofit organizations with information of public interest. You can occasionally hear PSAs from profit-making organizations dealing with public service issues such as traffic safety. To prepare a PSA for radio, follow the same procedure as with the TV PSA described in the preceding chapter. Of course, there is no need to send along a slide.

The 15-, 30-, and 60-second PSAs are the most popular lengths. You might want to submit a batch of PSAs to radio stations. That's all right, but it's best to put them on separate pieces of paper. If you have access to radio production equipment, you might want to produce your own PSAs. This can be expensive, and some stations won't use such PSAs.

RADIO TALK SHOWS

In the past several years there has been an explosion in the number of radio talk shows. Because FM radio has largely supplanted AM radio as the medium of choice for music programming, many AM program directors have settled on the talk format as the means to salvage lagging fortunes. Talk shows can capture a profitable market niche, and they have an amazing ability to attract a loyal listenership.

Radio talk shows typically operate by posing a topic and inviting listeners to call in and discuss the topic on the air with the show's host. Often the topic of the hour is presented by a guest expert or newsmaker who is knowledgeable about the subject being discussed. The expert/guest can be present in the studio, but more often he or she is connected to the studio by phone.

The host of the show spends a short time interviewing the guest and then the phone lines are opened to the listeners for questions. The segment usually lasts no longer than 20 minutes or so and guests need only be near a phone to participate.

With a large number of stations using the talk show format, there are numerous opportunities to place people on these programs. Some book publishers have become adept at using these programs to publicize their books. Authors have been placed on literally hundreds of these programs all over the country.

To find out which stations broadcast talk shows, you can consult the listing of radio station formats found in industry publications like the *Broadcasting/Cable Yearbook*. Once you know where talk shows exist, you can do targeted mailings that describe what you have to offer them.

In pitching your expert, list the broad issues that can be addressed by your spokesperson and describe the qualifications that make your person well-suited to the task. If your expert has not written a book, list speaking engagements or consulting activities and anything else that qualifies him or her as an expert.

Other items to include in your pitch are sample questions and a listing of any big name appearances your expert might have made.

Another way to interest talk shows in your people is to use one of the publications that are sold to talk show producers listing experts who are available as guests. *The Broadcast Interview Source*, for example, calls itself a directory of experts, authorities and spokespersons. It is published in Washington, D.C. and offers anyone the opportunity to buy ads promoting people for talk show appearances.

Competition for good talk show guests has intensified in recent years because of the large numbers of stations that have switched to the talk format. This means that there are more opportunities than ever before for public relations people to gain exposure for people in the organizations they represent.

Though talk show producers tend to look first for experts who have written books on the subject at hand, they will often be happy to have someone who can simply talk knowledgeably and succinctly about the topic. The head of a medium-size business in a small community, for example, might be prominent in a national or statewide industry organization. What better person is there, then, to talk about trends affecting the business climate, or the need for federal policies that would aid businesses in general?

A sharp public relations professional will spot opportunities like this and take the steps necessary to let the right people know about the availability of such a person for talk show appearances. If you do decide to promote someone for radio talk shows, however, be sure to secure agreement from the would-be guest that he or she can be available on short notice to pick up a phone and go on the air. Talk show topics usually arise from breaking news stories, and producers will often ask for guests on as little as an hour's notice.

For local talk show opportunities, call the program director of the station you're interested in and find out how guests are booked. Next listen to the program. Don't waste your time and the producer's time by trying to place a guest on a talk show without knowing something about it.

Send a letter similar to the sample presented in chapter 4. The range of ideas you can push are limited only in that the content must be in the public interest, and that it is a topic that people are likely to find interesting. The exact ground rules can best be explained to you by the producer of the program.

PRODUCING YOUR OWN RADIO

An investment of between $100 and $200 can equip you to gather your own actualities and furnish them to radio stations. By spending more money, you can do it on a more elaborate scale. But you'll still be far below the enormous amount of money needed to produce even the most rudimentary form of television programming.

Record Your Own Actuality

The bottom line basic radio kit includes a decent-quality cassette tape recorder and a good microphone such as the one shown in Fig. 5-3. The microphones that come with the cassette might not provide you with satisfactory quality.

Fig. 5-3. A Shure 565 SD microphone. Purchasing a good microphone such as this one will enable you to get high-quality sound recordings that can be given to radio stations.

One way to put your purchase to good use is by recording (with their permission) speakers who visit your institution and by sending the tape to a cooperative radio station. Send along a written summary of the speech and indicate what portion of the tape is, in your opinion, especially significant. If you are reasonably articulate, and the station's policy permits it, you might try recording your own report in the same style as a reporter.

The advantage for you in sending tape to a station is added coverage for your organization, and the station gets a piece of actuality without having to commit a reporter to sit through a two-hour speech.

Feed Your Actualities

If you want to send the tape to distant stations, if you don't want to bother hand-carrying the tape to a local station, or if you want to get the information out very quickly, try feeding the tape over the telephone. Radio reporters know what is required to feed the output of their tape recorder over a telephone so that it can be recorded or put live over the air. Figure 5-4 shows how to do it. Politicians often use this method to get their statements to radio stations throughout their district.

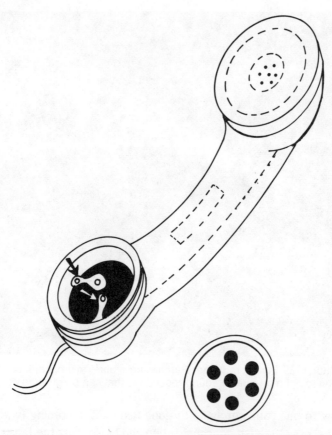

Fig. 5-4. Alligator clips attach to the prongs (shown by the arrows). You can buy alligator clips and the adapter needed to plug into your tape recorder at almost any electronics store.

If you have a lot of news you think many radio stations should be interested in, some sort of syndication service might be in order. The most common meaning for the term *radio syndication* is to mail out produced programs to various stations. This will usually involve a great deal of clerical work and expense.

There's a more modest approach. An electronic device will automatically feed out a prerecorded actuality to radio stations who call in. A sophisticated model, using a broadcast cassette machine, is shown in Fig. 5-5. A college might feed out prepared stories on research or expert opinions on news events. Pro-

Fig. 5-5. The Dickinson College News Service. This equipment feeds out stories automatically to radio stations calling in to the news service (courtesy of the Dickinson College Communications Office).

fessional, trade, or political organizations might also consider this type of approach in sending out consumer information, ski conditions, or similar information.

If you are involved in a firm or organization large enough to consider such an option, the easiest way to find out more on the subject is to call organizations that currently have a radio news service and ask some questions. We have found that they are usually quite willing to share their experiences. You can find out who has these services by calling acquaintances at local radio stations.

Radio is a very influential medium, and it is certainly worth exploring. It's important to keep in mind, however, that radio people don't ad-lib their newscasts. They write their news stories and they need written material to use as references. Don't get into the habit of trying to do all your business with radio stations via the telephone.

6
The Press Release

A COMMON MISTAKE AMONG PR PEOPLE IS TO PICK UP A GUIDEBOOK, FLIP TO the section on writing press releases, and start banging them out—without first understanding:

- ☞ The needs and requirements of the individual media.
- ☞ The proper writing style.
- ☞ What the press release might accomplish for your firm or organization.

Your release might be intended to get publicity for a new product, to announce an appointment of an executive, or to show what a great bunch of people work at your organization. Depending on your preferences, all three goals are perfectly valid. Let's find out how to put those press releases to work.

THE PURPOSE OF A PRESS RELEASE

A press release is a written message, generally copied and mailed to a variety of media, that is designed to tip-off the media to a good story or to serve as the story after being edited. Every press release should be written with the expectation that it will be reproduced verbatim. It probably won't be, however, usually as a matter of newspaper policy. Editors don't like to spend a lot of time reworking poorly written releases or checking for facts that have been omitted. Editors also won't be inclined to trust the accuracy of a sloppy or poorly constructed release.

PRESS RELEASE FORMATS

Usually, a press release will be written in the inverse pyramid style of straight news reporting. Sometimes, however, you might prefer to send out a feature story—a human interest profile, perhaps. Feature stories are more conversational—and take the form we're more used to seeing in a magazine article—rather than a straight news report. It's usually not difficult to tell the difference. While the lead in a straight news release written in the journalistic style might look like this:

> Linda Nelson of 122 Washburn St., Southville, has been appointed vice president of the Acme Computer Company. Mrs. Nelson will be responsible for . . .

A feature story could start with:

> "When I started in the computer business, computers that would fit on a desktop today filled up an entire room," says Linda Nelson, the newly appointed vice president of the Acme Computer Company. "The other difference is that the rooms that weren't filled with computers were filled with men; a woman in the computer business was a real rarity."

Feature stories are usually a bit more leisurely in their approach than a straight news item. Nevertheless, feature stories aren't necessarily longer than straight news stories. Many items sent out as news releases will probably teeter on the edge of being feature material. A straight news report can be developed into a feature story. A report of a woman being promoted is straight news. A biographical sketch that tells about her early days in the field and details her feelings about working in high technology is a feature.

CATEGORIES OF PRESS RELEASES

Feature stories are only one category of the various types of press releases you'll probably be sending out. The following are the major topics of press releases.

Hard News

Hard news is usually a timely report on something that has happened recently. A true hard-news item can also be defined as good news or bad news, but unquestionably news—without regard to the interests of the organization. Hard-news items might include layoffs, opening of a new division, death of an employee, relocating headquarters, or a hike in tuition.

Hard news is not always good news, but it's news all the same. And you have something of an obligation to present it in a straightforward manner as in Fig. 6-1.

FOR IMMEDIATE RELEASE: November 18, 1982   CONTACT: David L. Mona
                                                     (612) 831-8515

TORO REPORTS INCREASED SALES
SMALLER LOSS IN FIRST QUARTER

MINNEAPOLIS--The Toro Company today reported a net loss of $2.3 million or 48 cents per share on sales of $32.5 million for its first quarter ended October 29, 1982.

The loss compares with a net loss of $6.5 million or $1.24 per share on sales of $23.8 million in the first quarter the year before.

The size of the loss was reduced by a non-recurring net gain of $466,000 after tax resulting from the retirement of industrial revenue bonds in Mason City, Iowa.

Toro President Kendrick B. Melrose said he was pleased with the results from the first quarter which is historically the company's weakest. "Our turnaround continues on schedule, and I would expect the company to show a quarterly profit in the very near future," Melrose said. "Our goal of breaking even for the year continues to be a reasonable prospect in light of the first-quarter results.

"However, we remain concerned about the softness of the consumer economy in all of the markets we sell."

Stephen F. Keating, chairman of Toro's Executive Committee, said the biggest factor in the 37 percent increase in sales was the increase in snowthrower business where sales improved from $2.8 million in fiscal 1982 to $11.4 million this year.

(more)

Fig. 6-1. A press release from the Toro Company.

-2-

"We have had reasonably good retail movement of snowthrowers this fall," Keating said, "especially in areas that experienced heavy snowfall late last winter. Our distributor inventories are being worked down, and we are sold out of the new gas power shovel and several other snowthrower models at the factory level."

The company's international business showed an improvement during the quarter and its irrigation business was off slightly.

"Both our operating expenses and our finance charges were down considerably from last year," Keating said, "and we see these trends continuing throughout the year."

He said the company is optimistic about the second quarter because of expectations for "reasonably strong" lawn mower orders based upon heavy initial demand for the company's new line of 2-cycle engine walk mowers which will appear at retail after the first of the year.

"Second quarter sales should be up over both the first-quarter levels and the second quarter of last year," Keating said.

Toro is the nation's largest independent manufacturer and marketer of lawn care and outdoor maintenance products.

(tables attached)

Fig. 6-1. Continued.

Soft News

New products, new production methods, or the achievements of workers are examples of items that will reflect favorably on your organization, but usually aren't really hard or breaking news. Feature items such as human interest stories and biographical sketches are definitely in the soft news category.

Local comment on national or international affairs usually falls somewhere between hard and soft news, having characteristics of both categories. For example, note how the release from the Stanford University News Service (Fig. 6-2) combines reaction on a timely news item, the death of Soviet President Leonid Brezhnev, with a soft news item about the erosion of Soviet studies in

STANFORD UNIVERSITY NEWS SERVICE

STANFORD, CALIFORNIA 94305
(415) 497-2558

FOR INFORMATION CONTACT: Millicent Dillon
FOR IMMEDIATE RELEASE

SOVIET STUDIES HAVE DECLINED SHARPLY IN U.S., STANFORD EXPERTS SAY

STANFORD—

The death of Brezhnev with its attendant speculation has dramatized the extent to which Americans are not ready to answer serious questions about the Soviet Union, according to two Stanford Soviet experts.

A lack of support in the last 15 years by the government and private foundations for research in Soviet policy has been accompanied by a serious erosion of programs of Soviet studies within universities nationwide.

"Since the late 1960s many aspects of Soviet and East European studies have been deteriorating and are approaching a state of crisis," says history Prof. Alexander Dallin, chairman of the international relations program.

"There has been a major decline in support on the part of the foundations (notably Ford, Rockefeller, and Carnegie) which had previously contributed generously to the development of the field, and in some instances also on the part of the private universities and state legislatures supporting public universities."

As a consequence, adds Dallin, we probably now have fewer experts in the field than at any time since 1945. Further, of the top specialists in this field, more than one half will retire within the next five to ten years and there will not be highly experienced people to replace them.

The most exact indicator of the decline in Soviet studies is the decrease in language enrollments in Russian and East European languages, says Dorothy Atkinson, executive director of the American Association for the Advancement of Slavic Studies, currently based at Stanford.

Enrollments in Russian peaked in 1968 and have steadily declined since that time. By the fall of 1980 Russian enrollments in over 2,000 institutions of higher learning surveyed by the Modern Language Association had dropped 40 percent as compared to 1968. Enrollments in secondary schools declined by over 70 percent in the same period, according to Atkinson.

The report of the Presidential Commission on Foreign Language and International Studies in 1979 stated that the situation was critical. "Since that time, over 50 institutions of higher education in the U.S. have completely shut down their Russian programs of instruction in the Russian language," says Atkinson.

She notes that there are currently more teachers of English in the Soviet Union than students of Russian in the U.S.

A bill is currently before Congress, which attempts in part to remedy the situation. Introduced by Senators Richard Lugar (R-Ind.) and Joseph Biden (D-Del.), the bill asks for a government endowment to aid certain institutions in need of support of their programs in Russian and Soviet studies.

If approved, the bill would allocate $50 million to be invested in government bonds, the interest from which would be dedicated to enhancing programs at centers such as the Kennan Institute for Advanced Russian Studies.

The recent Harriman grant to the Soviet Studies program at Columbia University may also indicate a turnaround in private support, says Atkinson.

Both scholars admit, however, that serious damage has already taken place, which will take years to remedy. As an example of our current unpreparedness in this field, Dallin noted that two years ago a Soviet soldier defected from the Russian troops in Kabul and sought asylum in the American embassy. "There was no one there who could talk to him," because no one knew Russian.

11/16/82   —30—

EDITORS: Dallin's office phone is (415) 497-4514 or 4547, Atkinson at 497-0428.

Fig. 6-2. A release involving commentary on international issues from the Stanford News Service.

the United States. However, if a feature story is keyed to a particular event, it can be prone to go stale.

Announcement of a Coming Event

Announcement releases often don't run as an entire story. They can be condensed into the calendar events listings found in almost every newspaper or the bulletin board type of announcement made on radio. Television does not typically do as much as newspapers or radio in the way of promoting events.

Personnel Changes

Promotions, reassignments, and hiring of employees are commonly sent out in press release form. Information from these type of releases will usually wind up in the business section of local newspapers. Only major personnel changes will make radio or TV news.

Statements of Position

If your organization goes on record as opposing a certain piece of legislation, it's a *statement of position* and it stands a good chance of making the news. Other examples include statements from politicians or consumer information groups.

The releases you send out will be judged on the amount of interest they will hold for the public. A story that has little public interest probably won't stand a chance no matter how brilliantly it's written.

On the other hand, a poorly written release can kill a good story. The most important part of learning to do your own public relations is to write releases properly.

HOW TO WRITE A PRESS RELEASE

First, organize your press release correctly. On a plain, white sheet of good-quality paper, type your release double-spaced. Use only one side of the paper.

Include the name of the person to contact for more information (usually you), the telephone number, and—if the telephone is not manned at certain hours—times when you or the contact person can be reached.

You also must include the release day. In most cases, your releases will be intended for use as soon as they are received. In that case, mark the release "For Immediate Release." If you are giving advance information (the text of a speech to be given next week, for example), you will want to *embargo* the story until after the speech is made. It would certainly steal your speaker's thunder to have his remarks printed a week before he shows up on the podium.

To embargo a story, write "For Release 10 A.M., October 21" prominently on the release. If you're really concerned about bringing it to the editor's attention, circle the release date in red ink. The reason for giving advance information is to make things easier for the reporter. This often will result in better coverage.

Write "Press Release" or "News Release" on the top of the page (the terms are synonymous). "News Release" seem to be the more commonly used phrase today. This separates the release from the mountains of other correspondence that reach a news organization daily.

Now comes the *headline*. Some PR people don't use headlines, but we do recommend that you use them. The headline should always summarize the story. Don't try to come up with catchy phrases that don't give the editor a hint as to the content of the release. Also, don't expect the headline to be the same as the one that will appear in a newspaper. Newspaper headlines are written to fit within a prescribed width and height as determined by the page layout.

For a straight, no-nonsense announcement of an upcoming event, you definitely will want to use the inverse pyramid format for the text of the story. Give the facts in descending order of importance. The story should appear in much the same fashion as the truck accident report in the sample article in chapter 2. Give the five Ws—who, what, where, when and why—early in the story.

NEWS RELEASE
FOR IMMEDIATE RELEASE
FOR MORE INFORMATION, CONTACT: Tom Griffin,
Phone (213) 555-0000

HISTORICAL SOCIETY TO
    HOLD TOUR OF CAPTAIN'S HOUSE

The Southtown Historical Society will hold a tour of the 18th-century building known as Captain's House on Thursday, Sept. 11 from 10 A.M. until noon. Captain's House, located at 12 Commercial Street, is an 18th-century structure that was the home of Captain Robert Wiley, a seafarer and industrialist who figured prominently in the development of Southtown's commercial district.

Captain's House features period furnishings and historical artifacts of Southtown's maritime era.

Historical Society President Harriet T. Miller will conduct the tour, which is free and open to the public.

—END—

It's important to indicate where the release ends. Otherwise, a busy editor might wonder whether there was a second page to the release and if it was lost in the shuffle. That's why reporters and writers—at least the ones still writing with typewriters and paper—always indicate the ending of their story with END, ###, or —30—. Using —30— is a very old-fashioned way to indicate the end of a story, and is considered somewhat passé, but it will still do the job. If your release will run more than one page, type —more— on the bottom of the first page(s).

An optional addition to your press releases is a *pronouncer* for difficult names; this is very helpful for TV and radio people. If your release concerns a man named Keough, for example, it would be helpful to write on the release: EDITORS PLEASE NOTE: Keough is pronounced KEE-oh.

Because radio and TV newspeople read releases aloud, they will generally rewrite the releases to make them sound more natural. Television and radio newspeople expect to do this. It really isn't incumbent upon you to write separate releases in broadcast style. You will, however, want to use broadcast style when writing scripts or broadcast public service announcements. See Appendix B for instructions.

It's acceptable to put a release on plain paper, but if your organization has letterhead stationery you should use it. Be sure to list the contact person, the release date, and include the words "news release." Some organizations have special stationery for their releases. This isn't necessary, but if you have the inclination you can have a printer modify your letterhead to read: News From ——————.

To save money, a PR person with an artistic bent can use *press-type* to make up a news release form. Press-type, available in many print styles from art supply and stationery stores, allows you to transfer letters from the plastic backing onto paper by rubbing the plastic with a pencil or burnisher. See Figs. 6-3 and 6-4.

Use specially designed layout paper with blue grids that won't reproduce when the paper is copied. This will allow you to keep the printing level without having to draw pencil lines with a ruler. It will be much easier to cut out the individual words after you've transferred them to paper and cement them to another piece of layout paper (Fig. 6-5). Use rubber cement. Doing this will save you the trouble of trying to do everything right the first time.

Unless you're really good at using press-type, the results might not look very professional when prints are made from the pasted-up piece. The finished letterhead (Fig. 6-6) is acceptable, but not exceptional. Press-type is inexpensive so you don't risk much by experimentation.

If you are lucky enough to have desktop publishing technology (see chapter 9), producing a professional-looking news release form is a relatively simple operation. Once a master of the form is produced, all that is needed is a copy machine to generate as many copies as needed.

Fig. 6-3. Using press-type, the letter is first rubbed.

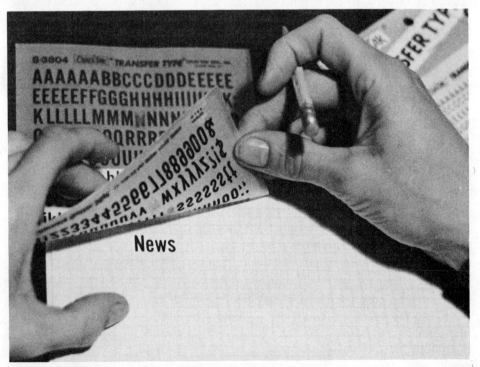

Fig. 6-4. With press-type, the image is transferred to the paper.

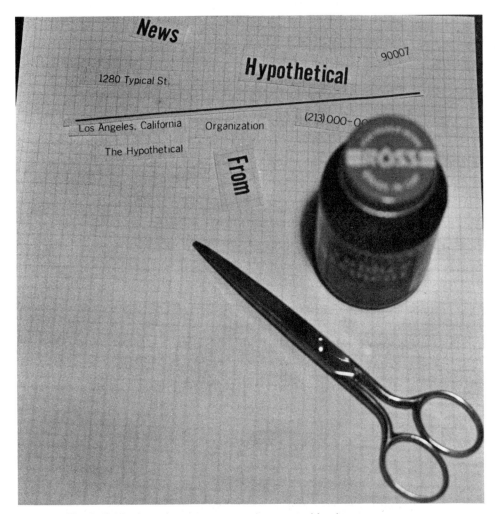

Fig. 6-5. The individual words are cut out and cemented in place.

Desktop publishing capability, in this application, allows you to tailor your release form to the specific needs of the moment. You may, for example, wish to incorporate a special designation into your heading such as "Science News" or "Business News." With desktop publishing you can design as many variations of your basic release form as you wish. Be careful, though, not to lose sight of the need for a consistent overall visual identity.

So far we've covered the basics of writing a release. Type it double-spaced on plain white paper or put it on your letterhead or news release form. Always include the name and phone number of a person who can be contacted for more information, and always give the date of release. It will also be useful to include the date mailed somewhere on the release for the information of the editor and

68 CHAPTER 6 THE PRESS RELEASE

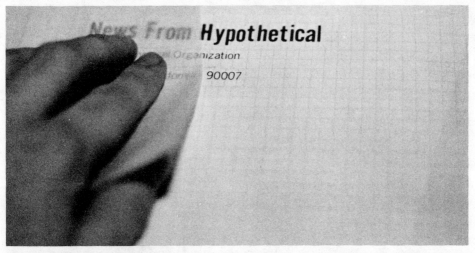

Fig. 6-6. The finished letterhead is pressed flat with a piece of tissue paper. It is now ready to be reproduced on printed forms. See Appendix A for examples.

to help you keep your own records. Your release should be in the inverse pyramid format unless you're writing a feature story. These guidelines are just the basics. There are a few other pointers that must be followed to make sure that your release stands a chance of making the newspaper or the airwaves.

Use Attribution

If you were the editor of a newspaper, would you run the following item?

> An exhibit of prehistoric art will be on display at the Jenkins Museum in October. On loan from the Royal Museum in London, this is the best exhibit of its kind in the world.

No, you wouldn't run it. For one thing, you don't know that it is the best exhibit of its kind. If you ran the release verbatim, it would put the newspaper in the position of saying the exhibit is, indeed, the best in the world. As a humble newspaper editor, you have no way of knowing that.

But how about this?

> An exhibit of prehistoric art will be on display at the Jenkins Museum in October.
>
> The display is on loan from the royal Museum in London. Professor Marcus Q. Galt, director of the Jenkins Museum, says the display is recognized as being the finest of its kind in the world.

If the release is phrased this way it gets the editor off the hook. *Professor Galt* says the exhibit is the best in the world, and Professor Galt presumably is an authority on such matters. Also, by reporting that Professor Galt says the exhibit is "recognized as being the finest in the world," Galt implies that other experts—a consensus—agree with him. Another way to handle this would be to use a direct quote from Professor Galt.

Do not interpret use of attribution as an excuse for using any statement, no matter how outrageous, and expect it to pass the editor unchallenged. More cautious editors might even balk at the revised version of the museum story. The second version might survive intact, while version one won't stand a chance. Not including attribution in a press release is one of the most common mistakes made by people doing their own press releases.

Public Understanding

This might sound obvious, but people involved in a particular field forget that others will not be so well-informed. We've seen releases from hospitals, for example, that glowingly praised the new, expensive, CAT scanner—without once explaining what it is. Although some readers, listeners, or viewers will know what a CAT scanner does, many will have no idea. A definition is needed.

Use Your Stylebook

The style manuals listed in chapter 2 will help you pick up on the conventions used by journalists. For example, did you notice the difference between Historical Society President Harriet T. Miller and Marcus Q. Galt, director of the Jenkins Museum? One title is capitalized and one is not. The reason is that, by convention, a title is capitalized when it comes before a name, but it is not capitalized when it follows a name. Your stylebook will answer this and many other questions, and help you to make your releases accurate and credible.

Give Complete Information

Read your release over and ask yourself if there are any questions left unanswered. Are the Five Ws all stated clearly?

Give complete names. Some newspapers are insistent on using middle initials; save a reporter the effort of calling to find out this detail. It's usually preferable to give complete information in the release instead of giving a phone number to call for additional information. Some newspapers are reluctant to run phone numbers because of the possibility of misprinting the number and exposing some unknowing citizen to a deluge of phone calls.

Triple Check All Important Information

The need for checking information has been repeated so often that it gets ignored about as often as safe driving messages. But there are very few public relations people who haven't, at one point in their career, gotten a little careless and let a mistake slip by.

There are few things more mortifying than to have a group of people arrive for a lecture that won't be given until tomorrow. A close second on the mortification scale is the humiliating experience of calling five newspapers, three television stations, and 10 radio stations and asking for them to run a correction. Enough said.

KEEPING YOUR PRESS RELEASES OUT OF THE WASTEBASKET

Well, your releases are all going to be discarded eventually, of course, but it would be best if they didn't take a direct path to the wastebasket from the envelope. Certain stories have a higher chance of never being printed or used on the air than others. Journalists have been known to refer to these as *nonstories*. They just don't have an intrinsic news value or interest to the public.

Yes, an interesting angle can sometimes get a nonstory into print. "Acme Firm Says No Price Hikes This Year" might make the business section. So might "Acme Shoe Store Celebrates 25th Anniversary." "Price of Gas Causes Steep Rise in Acme Company's Mail-Order Business," has enough of a softnews feature slant that it might be used. Many feature stories are manufactured in this way.

Don't expect all of your soft news to be used, and don't subscribe to the school of thought that purports a variety of gimmicks to somehow fool editors into using all your material. An interesting slant can move an editor to use a marginal piece. The editor will certainly be aware of your motivations in sending the release, and will also be aware that the interesting slant or angle was the deciding factor in using the marginal story.

All this is fine until you start thinking your talent for inventing angles is infallible. If you start sending out bushels of nonstories, more and more are going to wind up in the trash. In fact, editors might start identifying your logo with a puff piece not worth reading. The most obvious route to keeping your releases out of the wastebasket is not to send out reams of marginal material.

Secondly, don't violate any journalistic taboos such as failing to use attribution. Poor spelling and grammar will put you in the editorial doghouse. Misspelling a proper name is unforgivable among journalists; at some publications, such as *Newsweek*, it is considered a firing offense.

HOW TO DISTRIBUTE PRESS RELEASES

Even the best press release won't do much good if it doesn't get into the hands of people who will use it. Identifying where you would like your releases to go is fairly obvious. It is certainly an easier task than getting them used. Don't overlook national publications that are specifically geared to your interests such as specialty magazines or the so-called trade press. There might be specialized publications in your local or regional area interested in your releases. This is why media directories are useful. A few hours studying them can pay off handsomely.

Mailing Press Releases

In any event, most of your releases will be going out by mail. If you've never done it, be forewarned that mailing releases can be time-consuming beyond your wildest dreams if you individually address each envelope. If your public relations needs involve more than an occasional release to the local paper and a handful of broadcast outlets, set up your mailing list for use with reproducing labels (Fig. 6-7).

Your mailing list will be typed in such a way that the individual addresses will be reproduced onto individual peel-off labels that are run through a photocopy machine. There will be instructions with the labels.

The most obvious consideration at this point is that you will want different coverage for different types of releases. A theater group's appointment of a marketing director probably will be of only local interest. Nevertheless, a release to the new employee's hometown paper might be useful if he's an out-of-towner. The announcement of the plays scheduled for the new season will merit wider coverage. This is true especially if the theater is located in a resort area that attracts tourists from surrounding localities.

You can deal with most contingencies by use of a road map and a media directory. Using the map's scale of miles as a guide, draw circles in a 5-mile, 10-mile, 25-mile, 50-mile, and 100-mile radius of your locality. This is only a guide. Depending on your location, a much better way of doing this might occur to you.

Next, identify the media to which you'll probably want to send releases. Locally, you'll probably want to send releases to most or all of the media. In more outlying areas, you may want to send releases only to the larger media or to media with which you have developed contacts.

Make up separate lists of the media; you'll have a 5-mile list, a 10-mile list, a 25-mile list, and so on. Each list will be all-inclusive. In other words, the 10-mile list will include the 5-mile list and the 25-mile list will include the 10-mile list. This will be a lot of work at first, but it will more than make up for itself in the long run.

Will you need a list of specialized publications? Hospitals might want to send news of appointments to magazines and newsletters that specialize in health care. Colleges will want to send certain releases to educational publications.

Don't forget to send releases to departments in your local paper that specialize in areas pertinent to your organization or firm. A restauranteur will certainly want to send releases to the entertainment editor. Even if the releases are

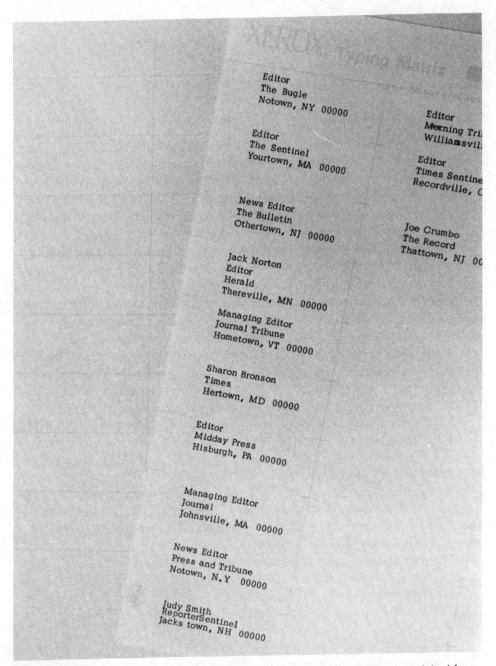

Fig. 6-7. A matrix is used to locate addresses on a paper that is used as the original form from which to copy on peel-off labels that can be fed through the photocopy machine. This saves a tremendous amount of work.

not run (and there's a good chance they won't), the releases will probably be filed for future reference. In the event a survey article of local restaurants is written, the release could be resurrected. Keep these addresses handy and include them in your mailing list if you think it is advisable. By having all the combinations at your fingertips, the release can be sent out quickly and with a minimum of clerical fuss.

Using Personal Computers with Press Releases

Personal computers have made it possible to keep an up-to-date file of names and addresses of a large number of media contracts. Sophisticated software programs that can be run on personal computers make it easy to produce mailing labels that fit the exact needs of the job at hand.

Even the smallest operation can use a personal computer to select only business editors, for example, and then to generate mailing labels ready to affix to envelopes containing your release. By sending to only those outlets who might actually use your release, you reduce the irritation experienced by harried reporters and editors whose daily mail is laden with dozens of releases that have no relation whatsoever to anything that most reporters would be likely to use.

A company called Cetex Corporation, located in Philadelphia, has developed software called "PR Manager" that allows you to generate lists of newspapers with circulations of 50,000, for example, or radio stations with listenership with an average age of 30. Using this software, you can also request a listing of all the newspapers covering a particular zip code. These and other features of the software allow you to target the specific media outlets that will be most interested in your release.

"PR Manager" is updated regularly to ensure that the information is fresh. The expense involved in purchasing the software and paying for updates makes this a tool that small operations may not be able to afford, but it can be of great assistance to organizations that generate a high number of releases.

Addressing Press Releases

One other point relating to distributing releases involves mailing to a person versus mailing to a position. In other words, do you address the envelope to Perry White, Editor, *Daily Planet* or simply to Editor, *Daily Planet*?

This is the subject of much debate. One side holds that it makes more sense to address the envelope to the position because the person might be on vacation and the release will go unopened. The journalism field is also very fluid and employees change frequently. The other school of thought contends that a release directed by name is more personal and therefore promotes better relations.

There are a couple of good compromises. One is to send local releases by name; you'll be able to keep track of personnel changes in local editorial staff. Be certain to change names on your master mailing list when local personnel change. A release addressed to the news director who quit three years ago will create a very unfavorable impression. If you are worried that releases addressed by name won't be opened if the recipient is on vacation (which is, in our experience, not a big concern), you can eliminate any doubt by printing or rubber-stamping "News Release" on the envelope.

Regardless of whether or not names are used on the press release envelopes, it is incumbent upon you to know the names of local editors. You should make every effort to meet them in person and develop a good working relationship. An editor who knows and trusts you will probably be more receptive to your press release or phone call.

Many people who are new to PR are unsure as to whether editorial contact should be made in writing or by phone. We feel that writing is usually more appropriate. A phone call is intrusive and can come at a time when other duties are pressing. This, indeed, can result in your item getting short shrift.

Use a phone call when you have timely news or to follow up on an important press release. Try asking the editor if he has any questions about the release you mailed earlier in the week. Don't come on strong and ask where and when it will be used.

MODELS FOR PRESS RELEASES

Some public relations books offer a "fill-in-the-blanks" menu of sample press releases. We think this is a bit too mechanical to be productive. You will be much better off learning how to write a good release than trying to jam the material into a prepackaged form.

Appendix A gives examples of a variety of releases. Use them as guides to content, not as blueprints. Another excellent source of press release models is your local paper. This source has the advantage of highlighting the releases that made it into print. You probably won't have much trouble identifying which stories stemmed from press releases.

Your chances of placing a release in the print medium will often be enhanced by including a photo along with the release. Photography is a major consideration in public relations, but beginning PR people often think that photography is too expensive and too complex. However, it doesn't have to be expensive.

7
Photography

THE OLD SAW ABOUT A PICTURE SAYING A THOUSAND WORDS MIGHT OR MIGHT not be true, but there's no question that thousands of words have never made the printed page because there wasn't a decent picture to accompany them.

Photography is usually the weakest link in the PR chain. Someone doing public relations might eventually feel right at home calling an editor, writing a press release, or setting up a media event. Yet somehow the use of a camera just seems intimidating, and photos either aren't taken or are relegated to a professional photographer.

We're not taking a swipe at pro photographers. Both of us have put food on the table at one point or another by taking photos. What we do want to point out is that photography can be an expensive business to operate and a pro will have to charge a large enough fee to pay the rent and the receptionist.

There will be times when you'll want to call a pro, but there's no reason why you can't take and develop some of the photos that will accompany releases to be used in newsletters and brochures. You should keep copies of the photos for display or archival purposes.

Photography, on its basic level, just isn't that complex. Producing top-quality photos will take more training and experience or the services of a pro. But we are confident that your needs will be served by this chapter.

THE CAMERA

The variety of cameras—and the collection of knobs, dials and meters on each—is probably the most intimidating hurdle to overcome for the novice photographer. At the risk of offending some hobbyists and professionals who are devoted to various camera styles, we recommend that you limit your choice to a *35mm single-lens reflex camera*, often called an *SLR*. It is by far the most versatile camera for public relations use.

There are less expensive cameras, such as the kind you take along to family picnics, but they won't give you the necessary quality. There are far more expensive cameras, but they have features you won't need and are more difficult to use. What, exactly, is a 35mm single lens reflex? Let's take some of the mystery out of the jargon and define each term.

35mm

The term *35mm* relates to the size of the film that's used in the camera. You'll seldom have trouble finding a store that sells 35mm film. Assuming that you use a decent camera and a lens, this format will provide more than adequate quality.

Single Lens

The operator of a *single-lens* camera focuses and aims by looking through the same lens that will take the photo. Some cameras have two lenses, one to focus and one to put the image on film. The SLR uses only one lens because of the next reflex feature.

Reflex

The word reflex stems from the same root as *reflection*, which is exactly what happens in the camera mechanism. There's a mirror that reflects the image through the eyepiece. This allows the photographer to see the same image as the one which the lens will place on the film. The camera mechanism flips the mirror up when the picture is taken. To give you an idea of where the mirror is and how it moves, Fig. 7-1 shows we've lifted it slightly with a pencil. We strongly suggest that you do not try this with your camera.

So what's so special about a camera with a single lens and a mirror that swings out of the way? It allows you to see exactly what will go on the film, and it also allows the use of interchangeable lenses.

THE LENS

A lens gathers light and focuses an image on the film. There are different types of lenses that alter the image in various ways and are interchangeable, snapping

Fig. 7-1. The pencil lifts the hinged mirror of a single-lens 35mm reflex camera. Don't try this with your camera.

or screwing on and off the camera body (Fig. 7-2). If you couldn't see the image given by the lens, you would have to guess at what would be in the shot. This will be a bit more clear to you after we describe the three basic lens types.

The Standard 50mm Lens

The normal or *standard 50mm lens* gets its name from the fact that it closely approximates the field of vision of human eyes. A normal lens usually has a *focal length* of 50mm.

Fig. 7-2. Interchangeable lenses are a big plus of the 35mm SLR.

A *what?* Here's where the confusion usually begins. How can a 35mm camera have a 50mm lens? Remember that the 35mm camera is so called because of the width of the film. The focal length of the interchangeable lenses are a separate issue. The only thing you need to know about focal length is that it's a measurement of the properties of the lens, and not a measurement of the lens itself. To reiterate, a 50mm lens gives an approximation of normal human eyesight. Note how the photo taken with a 35mm lens (Fig. 7-3) gives the same sort of perspective you would have upon walking into the gentleman's office.

The Telephoto Lens

As the name implies, the *telephoto lens* is something of a small telescope, bringing the image closer. The focal length of a telephoto lens is usually in the 85mm to 300mm range. There are a few gigantic lenses in the 1000mm range (actually

Fig. 7-3. A photo taken with a standard 50mm lens.

Fig. 7-4. A photo taken from the exact same position, but this time using a 100mm telephoto lens.

a true telescope). A 300mm telephoto might be useful for wildlife photography, but a PR person will probably have more use for 100mm telephoto.

Notice how the telephoto brings the image closer in Fig. 7-4. The man was photographed from the same location as the photo (Fig. 7-3) with the standard lens.

There is another interesting property of the telephoto lens: it blurs the background. A lens with a longer focal length will have a more crucial focus. It will focus on a smaller range of distances from the photographer. The lens is focused by turning a ring on the lens.

A 100mm telephoto lens is a good choice for taking portraits. You can get a close-up shot without sticking the camera right in your subject's face and making him uneasy.

The Wide-Angle Lens

Suppose you really weren't all that interested in the man in the photo, but instead wanted to show how interestingly his office was decorated. A telephoto lens wouldn't do any good unless you wanted to take individual photos of wall hangings. Even the standard lens doesn't give a wide enough field of vision. The answer is a wide angle lens as shown in Fig. 7-5.

Figure 7-5 was taken from the exact position as the previous photos, but notice the difference. The room has "opened up." The *wide-angle lens* (usually in the 24mm to 35mm range) has this property. Extreme wide-angle lenses give the *fish-eye* property most closely associated with door peepholes. They don't have that much use in PR applications. Figure 7-5 was taken with a 24mm lens. This is about the shortest (in local length) you can use without significant distor-

Fig. 7-5. Another photo taken from the same position, this time with a 24mm wide angle lens.

tion. If you can afford a 24mm lens, it's a good choice; it will be more expensive than the more commonly used 28mm lens.

The wide-angle lens is useful for taking shots of interiors, arrangements of objects rather than the objects themselves, or any instance where you simply can't back up far enough to get everything in the picture. A shot of a board meeting, for example, would almost certainly have to be taken with a wide-angle lens.

The Zoom Lens

A *zoom lens* will allow you to change the focal length, usually by pulling or pushing part of the lens. A typical zoom lens might vary in focal length from 75mm to 205mm. The value of a zoom lens is that it saves you from having to change lenses when shooting a variety of shots; it is a virtual necessity for sporting events.

Why not just buy a zoom instead of interchangeable lenses? For one thing, a zoom lens needs more light to operate. In photographers' terms, it is *slower* than the usual interchangeable lenses. Primarily, this is because there is more glass in the complex zoom lens and light loses some intensity every time it passes through glass. As you'll notice in Fig. 7-6, the zoom lens is large and it can be somewhat ponderous.

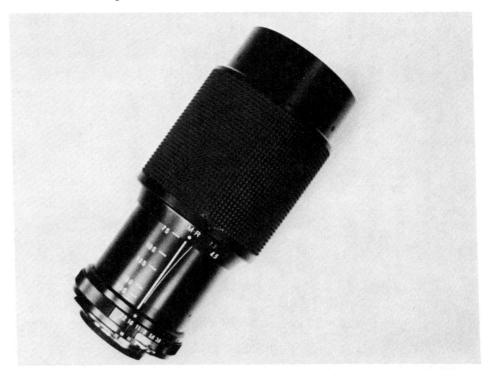

Fig. 7-6. A zoom lens.

Actually, there are a number of different lenses within a standard camera lens. All the options built into a zoom lens require more individual lenses within the lens mechanism to produce various effects. Except for the preceding explanation, every time we use the word lens in the chapter it will refer to the entire lens mechanism (the whole business that attaches to the camera).

THE F-STOP

How can you tell how much light a lens will pass? By looking on the lens and observing the lowest *f-stop*. All right, here's where things get a little complicated. The concept of fiddling with f-stops and *shutter speed* has brought about legions of photography dropouts. Keep in mind that f-stop and shutter speed are the final concepts you'll have to understand before you are all set to start taking photos.

The f-stop is a "stop" on the ring (Fig. 7-7) that is usually located near the end of the lens. The f-stop setting controls how wide the lens will open and, therefore, the amount of light it can pass. The camera needs quite a bit of it to take a photo. Most film is much less sensitive to light than our eyes.

Fig. 7-7. The f-stop setting on a camera lens.

The f-stop indicates the ratio of the focal length to the diameter of the lens system. What's really important to know is that the f-stop indicates the width of the opening of the lens, and the *smaller* the number, the *wider* the opening. Figures 7-8, 7-9, and 7-10 will show you what we mean.

In a low-light situation, you obviously will want a wide lens opening to admit more light. For an outdoor shot, a smaller lens opening will be needed. In sunshine, you'll dial the ring to a higher f-stop. Remember, the *lower* the f-stop, the *wider* the lens opening. The *higher* the f-stop, the *smaller* the lens opening. For reasons that will soon become clear, you can't use the f-stop alone in determining exposure. You'll also have to set the shutter speed.

Fig. 7-8. Here's the size of the lens opening when the f-stop is set to f-2.8.

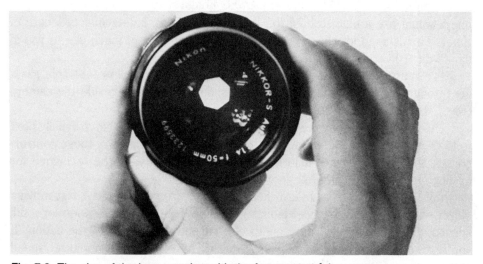

Fig. 7-9. The size of the lens opening with the f-stop set at f-4.

Fig. 7-10. The size of the lens opening with the f-stop set at f-11.

SHUTTER SPEED

The shutter speed is the length of time the film is exposed. It is controlled by a setting on your 35mm camera body. Shutter speeds on a typical 35mm SLR range from 1 second to $1/2000$ of a second. The speeds are indicated on the dial in the lower portion of the fraction; 25 indicates a 25th of a second. There's usually a "B" on the setting. This refers to *bulb* (a holdover from days when photographers would use a bulb to hold the lens open from an indeterminate length of time). This is used for timed exposures. They won't be of much use to you in day-to-day PR work.

The shutter speed will determine how long the camera allows the light passing through the lens to strike the film. A sliding mechanism inside the camera (Fig. 7-11) actually lets the light in for the specified period.

The shutter is triggered by a button on top of the camera that is usually next to the lever that winds the film. For the location and operation of these controls consult the operator's manual of your camera. Also review the technique for loading film into your camera.

Shutter speeds play a role in keeping action from blurring. A fast-moving object will blur as to be almost indistinguishable if the shutter is open for a full second. But shooting at a thousandth of a second will "freeze" the action. If you're taking photos of a football game, you will have to use a fast shutter speed unless you are intentionally trying to get the motion to blur.

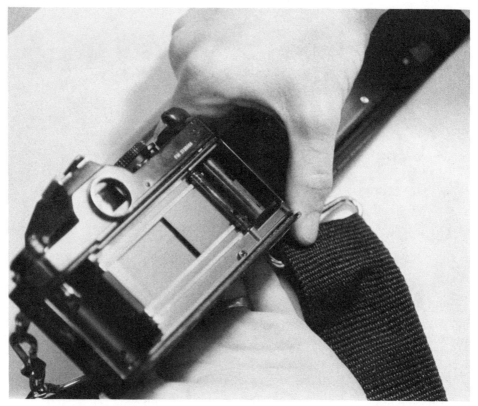

Fig. 7-11. The shutter mechanism. The rectangular windows slides across the film. The film is loaded on the left-hand side of the camera (as it's viewed in this photograph) and wound onto the sprocket on the right.

So why not just set the shutter speed at $1/1000$ or $1/2000$ and forget about it? Because you would have to open the lens up as wide as possible and, even then, you might not have an f-stop low enough to let in the proper amount of light.

DEPTH OF FIELD

Opening the f-stop as wide as possible reduces the *depth of field*. Here's a case where a picture is indeed worth a thousand words. That's about how much explanation would be needed to define this concept. Notice the difference between Figs. 7-12 and 7-13.

This is a case that is particularly relevant to public relations work. Many of the photos you'll be taking will be of people in their offices or work environment. In Fig. 7-12, notice how the background clutter is distracting? In order to eliminate this problem, the photographer repositioned the subject and changed the depth of field. The *perspective* of the photo was also changed to somewhat more vertical instead of horizontal.

Fig. 7-12. This photo has too much clutter around this woman's head. To make matters worse, it's all in clear focus. Figure 7-13 shows how selective focus and a change in composition can clear up the problem illustrated here (courtesy Hartwick College Public Relations Office).

Changing the depth of field was accomplished by opening the lens up wider (turning to a lower f-stop). To compensate for the greater amount of light coming in through the wide-open lens, the photographer used a faster shutter speed. This combination of settings results in proper exposure.

The important thing to note from this example is that the *wider* the lens opening, the *lower* the f-stop and the *smaller* the depth of field. Depth of field is the distance from the photographer in which things will be in acceptable focus. Stated another way, the depth of field is the depth of the field in which the focus will be sharp. The depth of field in Fig. 7-13, in which things would be in sharp focus, might have been something like 6 feet to 8 feet away from the lens. But with a smaller lens opening, the depth of field might have been 5 feet to 12 feet for Fig. 7-12.

Remember that a telephoto lens also creates a narrow depth of field. That property of the telephoto lens will also be affected by depth of field as a result of the lens opening. The effects will just be more exaggerated.

There will be many cases where you want to blur the background. Remember that you can use depth of field or a telephoto lens to do it. On the other hand, you will also take photos where it's important that everything be in focus over a certain distance (a construction site, perhaps). Use depth of field to achieve these effects.

Fig. 7-13. This photo is a distinct improvement over the one in Fig. 7-12.

Some camera lenses have a "depth of field preview" setting that allows you to see the scene in your viewfinder with the lens *stopped* (set to the f-stop) you have selected. This will show you what will and won't be in focus. When you normally look through a viewfinder, you are looking through the lens—via the mirror—with the lens opening as wide as possible. The lens opening, called the *aperture*, is set in the wide-open position until the instant you click the shutter.

Why is the lens open during aiming and focusing? Because you need enough light coming in through the lens to make the image visible on the ground-glass screen that forms the image that is seen through the eyepiece. Thus, the depth of field preview button is only useful in high-light situations. In low light, you won't be able to see much of anything.

Depth of field is really not as complex a topic as it seems. You might be able to shoot acceptable photos without even knowing what depth of field is or noticing its effect. Nevertheless, there will come a time when a shot could be improved by changing depth of field.

EXPOSURE METERS

So now that you understand the relationship between f-stop and shutter speed, how do you determine the proper balance? Let's say you're shooting an outdoor sports event. You'll need a fast shutter speed so you dial 1000 on the selector knob located on the camera body. With that in mind, you'll have to set the f-stop to determine the proper exposure.

You can determine the proper exposure by looking through the camera's viewfinder. Most modern 35mm SLRs have built-in exposure meters. The method of metering will vary from camera to camera, but what you'll see might look like Fig. 7-14.

Balancing between shutter speed and f-stop will give you the right exposure. Many modern 35mm SLRs have automatic exposure settings (meaning that you can pretty much point and shoot). We think these are fine, but be sure that there's a setting to override the automatic exposure. There might be cases

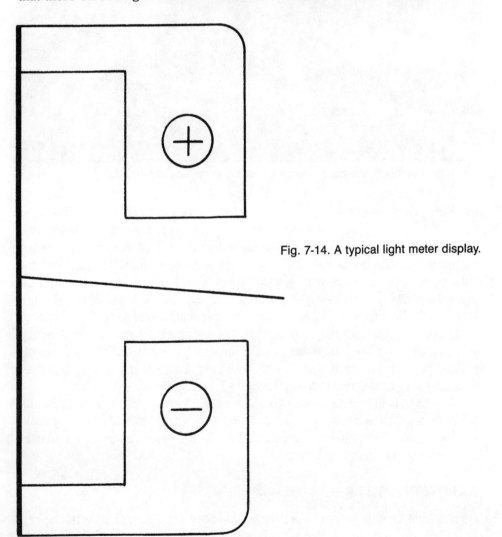

Fig. 7-14. A typical light meter display.

where you'll want to fool the camera into taking an exposure in a way other than its microelectronics select.

Sometimes a camera will read exposure from the wrong part of the scene. The photo you take of someone standing against a bright summer sky, for instance, might be incorrectly exposed because the camera took the reading on the sky instead of the person.

Experience will help you determine which exposures might be tricky. One way to be sure that you get a decent shot is by *bracketing* exposures. Take one shot with the exposure meter reader at what should be the correct level. Then take another shot with a high reading, and another with a low reading. It is always a good idea to take many more photos than you'll really need, because unseen mistakes might (and often do) make some of the photos useless.

FILM SPEED

We promised that f-stop and shutter speed were the last concepts you would have to understand before taking pictures, but we stretched the truth a bit. The *speed* of the film also plays a role. You can set the speed setting and forget about it.

In the United States, film speed is expressed as *ISO*. Film speed is also expressed in *ASA* (an older term that has recently fallen out of fashion), and *DIN*, but for the time being ISO is all you'll need to know. The ISO is given right on the package of any roll of film you buy (Fig. 7-15).

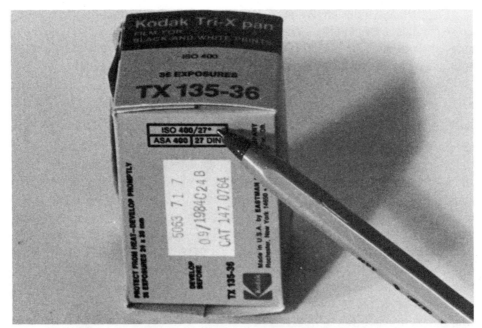

Fig. 7-15. This film package shows ASA, ISO, and DIN. Newer packages list only ISO.

There's also a setting on the camera to accommodate the speed of the film used. It is usually expressed in ASA. The manual of any camera you might purchase will explain how to set the ASA control (which tells all the other controls how to function).

So what is film speed? Speed is the sensitivity to light. A film that is not very sensitive to light will need longer exposures, hence it is a *slow film*. A *fast film* doesn't need as long an exposure.

The obvious advantage of using a fast film is that you can take photos in less light than with slower film. Most film is much less sensitive to light than human eyes. What would appear to be a normally lighted room will appear as a black abyss on your photo if you use a slow film.

There's a practical limit to how slow a shutter speed you can use to accommodate for the lack of light. In most hand-held application you can't use a speed of much less than a 60th of a second simply because the movement of your hands will cause the image to blur. Some people are steady enough to shoot at a 30th or 15th, but even then a good photo is not guaranteed. The only way around that is to use a *tripod* (Fig. 7-16). This device will hold the camera much more steadily than your hands.

A tripod won't help if your subject is moving. In that case, the only option is to use a faster shutter speed.

A fast film will allow you to use a higher shutter speed than a slower film because the film is more sensitive to light. But speed has its price because fast films are *grainier* than slow films.

Film is made up of tiny crystals of a silver compound. Light effects each of these crystals, changing them chemically. In order for a film to be faster, it has to have larger crystal clumps. This results in a grainier or lower-resolution photo. Your choice of film might be affected by this and other considerations.

SELECTING FILM FOR PR WORK

With few exceptions, you will use film for black-and-white prints and color slides. You very rarely will use color prints except for displays or similar uses. Color prints are *not* used by publications. Newspapers and magazines use black and white prints or color slides. However, it is an all-too-common occurrence for someone to send in a color print, thinking it is what the editors will want.

A great deal of effort and money is wasted by people who take color prints and expect them to be used by publications. This can't be stressed enough. Color prints will have very little value to a PR person.

Black-and-white prints will probably comprise the overwhelming majority of your photo work. Film for making black-and-white prints is called *negative* film because it produces a negative image (white will be black and black will be white). You probably know what negatives look like. They are nothing more than

Selecting Film for PR Work 91

Fig. 7-16. A tripod.

the film after it has been developed. The negative becomes a *positive* when it is projected onto photographic paper (a kind of film). This time the dark areas on the negative (which were, in real life, the light areas) will be made into light areas on the light sensitive paper and everything will be back to normal on the print.

The standard black-and-white film in use today is Kodak T-MAX. T-MAX has largely replaced the once popular Kodak Tri-X which was the most widely used black-and-white film a few years ago. Kodak states that T-MAX is less grainy than Tri-X (grain refers to the degree to which you can see evidence of the individual granules that coat the negative and combine to reproduce the image that the camera lens focused on the film.) T-MAX has an ISO of 400 for general purposes but can be "pushed" for a higher ISO rating when special developing procedures are used.

Many professionals still prefer to use Tri-X, stating that T-MAX seems to require greater precision in development. Both T-MAX and Tri-X can be developed using the standard black-and-white processing chemicals, but there is also a T-MAX developer designed specifically for that film. Tri-X is somewhat less widely available than T-MAX and some photo supply stores are under the impression that Tri-X is no longer manufactured.

Either T-MAX or Tri-X will serve your black-and-white film needs well. Given a choice, you would probably do well to use Tri-X. It allows more margin for error in both shooting and processing and most photographers say that T-MAX's alleged finer grain is not noticeable under normal circumstances. However, either film offers versatility and they both produce good results for the pros and the inexperienced alike.

Kodak also makes a version of T-MAX with the designation P3200 that produces good results at ISO ratings of 3200 and 6400. Kodak says this film can be pushed to as high as ISO 12,500! In earlier films, shooting at ISO ratings of 3200 and 6400 was only possible using special developers, and the severe graininess that resulted limited the usefulness of photos shot and processed in that way. T-MAX P3200, however, has remarkably fine grain at 3200, and it produces very useable photos at 6400. Pushed to its highest ISO ratings, though, the film tends to develop noticeable grain. Needless to say, this film has been received with great excitement by photographers who do a lot of low-light shooting.

You might be wondering why we haven't brought up the seemingly simple solution of using a flash attachment instead of using fast film in extreme low-light situations. A flash attachment is often more trouble than it's worth. It also lulls a novice photographer into a false sense of security. More than one newcomer to photography has been known to point his camera at an enormous building during dusk and expect the tiny point of light produced by the flashbulb to light up the building. In reality, a truckload of searchlights might be needed.

The same situation occurs in banquet halls. A flash also distorts the natural lighting, casting a harsh glow on the features of people in the photo. We're digressing a bit from our discussion on film, but it is worth pointing out that—for PR work at least—fast film will serve your purpose better than a flash attachment.

An alternate way of dealing with low-light situations is to carry your own portable lamp (Fig. 7-17). A lamp will give you much better lighting than a flash gun.

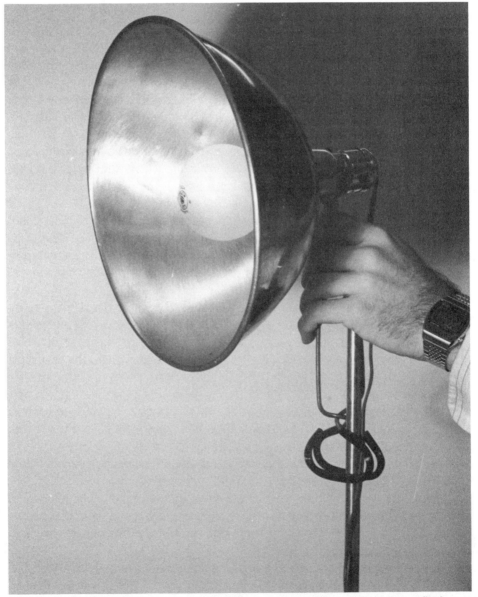

Fig. 7-17. Portable lamps are very useful, and they give more natural light than a flashgun.

Film for producing color slides (usually called *transparencies*) is known as *color positive* film. It produces a positive image when light strikes it. The transparency actually is the film itself, cut up and mounted after development.

Popular types of color transparency film include Kodachrome, which is available with ISO ratings of 25 and 64. This is a bit slow for many of the situations you'll encounter in PR work, but it will provide outstanding resolution and color saturation. A faster film, Kodak Ektachrome, comes in an ISO of 400, making it as fast as Tri-X. Fujichrome, which comes in several ISO ratings, is an increasingly popular film among professionals.

Because color transparencies will generally be used for items where you want high quality resolution—such as brochures or magazine articles—it is often worth the trouble of tinkering with extra lights or waiting for a sunny day rather than using the high-speed color positive films. There will be a noticeable difference in quality. Some editors will request that you do not use Ektachrome.

Color transparencies, many of which were once developed at Eastman Kodak in Rochester, New York, are now processed by various photo labs in many locations. If you request Kodak processing, your film will be sent to laboratories operated by a company called Kodalux, which bought the processing operations once run by Kodak.

Kodachrome requires special development techniques and is routinely sent to Kodalux for processing. Other color transparency film can be processed by virtually any reputable color lab, but many photographers using Kodak film prefer to specify Kodak processing, which processing centers will now interpret as Kodalux.

Black-and-white negatives and prints can be developed at virtually any photo lab. Don't bother having your black-and-white film developed at the ubiquitous drive-up photo stands. These places do the bulk of their business on color prints, and they take longer to process black-and-white film. Also, the snapshot-style black-and-white prints you'll typically get back won't be the right size for PR work.

You won't want to develop every print. You will want a *contact sheet* such as the one shown in Fig. 7-18. A contact sheet is a positive print of your negatives.

The contact sheet, also called a *proof sheet*, will enable you to order prints of only the photos that turned out the way you wanted. The prints you will use in PR work, by the way, will be larger than the typical snapshot.

In order to get these prints, you will have to go to the photo lab, have them develop your film and print a contact sheet (often done routinely in one or two days), and then order the prints you want. You can specify the size; this will usually be 8 × 10 inches or 5 × 7 inches.

If you need photos only on occasion, and don't need a large quantity of individual prints, a good photo lab can handle all your needs. Check you local phone directory to find out what photo labs do business in your area. Better yet, call acquaintances who use black-and-white photos and ask for a recommendation. Consider that large photographic orders quite quickly surpass the cost of a darkroom to do the work yourself.

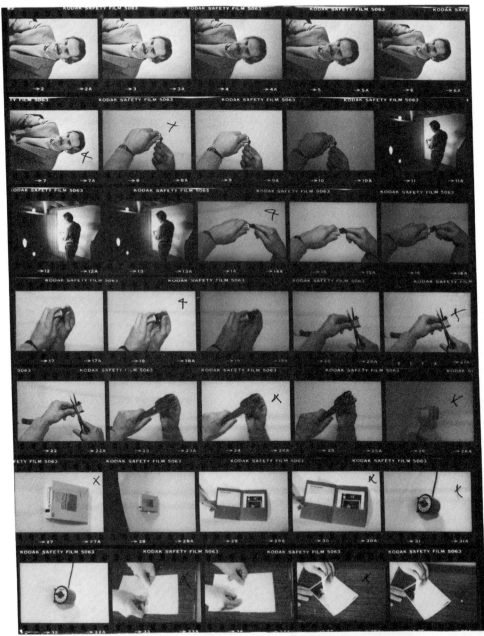

Fig. 7-18. A contact sheet. The markings indicate which photos were chosen for printing.

EQUIPPING AND USING A DARKROOM

Developing your own black-and-white photos is nowhere near as complex as you might imagine. In addition, it is not particularly expensive. All you'll need for a setting is a private area that can be made totally dark and has a reasonable amount of ventilation. Running water is a great convenience, but not an absolute necessity.

Fig. 7-19. An enlarger is used to blow the negatives up to full-size prints.

Even though there's no mystery to the process of developing your own photos, a complete course in darkroom technique is beyond the scope of this book. We will, however, give you a complete introduction to the equipment needed and the methods of development. For more detailed instructions, refer to the various darkroom guides in libraries and bookstores. Don't forget the instruction manuals that come with the equipment and the leaflets that are packed with the film and paper. These leaflets contain a surprising amount of information.

The heart of the darkroom is the *enlarger*. This is a projecting lamp (Fig. 7-19) that focuses the image of your negatives onto the large sheet of photographic paper. The negatives are held in place by a *negative carrier* (Fig. 7-20) that is

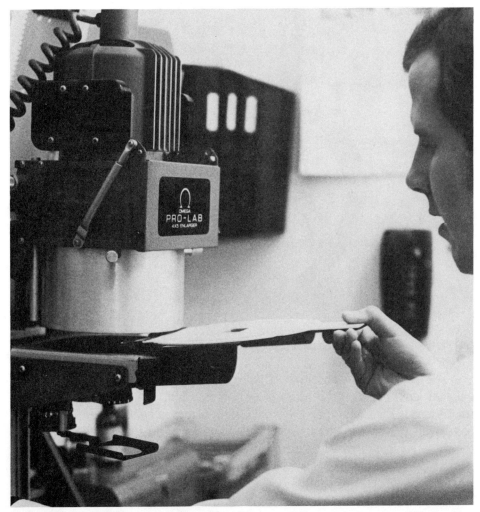

Fig. 7-20. A negative carrier holds the negatives within it, and it is inserted into the enlarger.

inserted into the enlarger near the bulb. Controls on the enlarger and the enlarger lens enable you to adjust the size of the image and to adjust the exposure. The photographic paper must be exposed for the correct amount of time.

Exposure is determined by the opening of the lens mounted on the bottom of the enlarger (the lens that actually projects the image onto the paper). There is an f-stop ring on the lens similar to the one on the lens of your camera.

Exposure is also determined by a *timer* (Fig. 7-21) that controls how long the enlarger projects the image onto the paper. The paper is held in place by a special easel (Fig. 7-22).

Fig. 7-21. An enlarger is turned on and off by the timer that sets the length of the exposure.

The paper is light sensitive; it will retain the image focused on it by the enlarger lens. For most PR applications, an excellent choice is Kodak Polycontrast Rapid II RC paper, type F (Fig. 7-23). It comes in light-tight envelopes and boxes, and it is sold in various sizes and quantities. The *RC* label indicates that the paper is *resin coated*. This means that it dries quickly and is less delicate than some other papers. The *F* is an indicator that the paper gives a *glossy finish* which most publications want.

Polycontrast paper can be exposed with different filters to affect the contrast. This is an option that will prove handy to you in more advanced darkroom work. There are a myriad of papers on the market, and the options can be quite

Equipping and Using a Darkroom 99

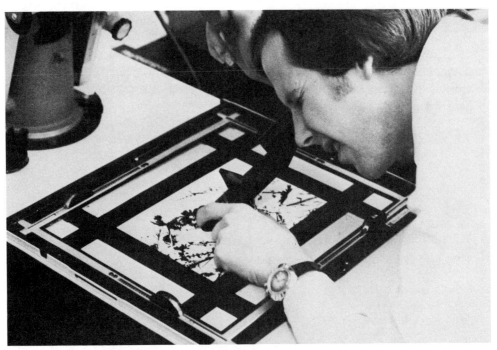

Fig. 7-22. The easel holds the photographic paper. A special magnifying device is used to check that the image projected is in sharp focus.

Fig. 7-23. Kodak Polycontrast Rapid RC F paper is an excellent choice for all public relations work.

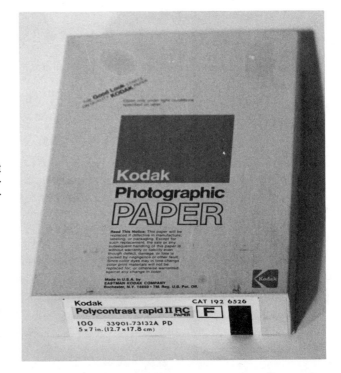

confusing, but keep in mind that you can never go wrong in PR work using Kodak Polycontrast Rapid II RC paper.

How do you use light-sensitive paper in such a way as to see what you're doing, but not expose the paper? A special light called a *safelight* (Fig. 7-24) provides a special frequency of light to which the paper is not sensitive. This type of light will provide enough illumination for you to see.

Fig. 7-24. A safelight allows you to see in the darkroom, but it won't expose your paper.

The photo paper, once exposed by the enlarger, is developed in three separate trays (Fig. 7-25) that contain these chemicals:

- A *developer* to start the chemical changes in the silver crystals that will produce the print.
- A *stop bath* that interrupts the chemical reaction.
- A *fixer* that ends the whole process and makes the paper no longer light-sensitive.

The chemicals are bought in packages or jugs (Fig. 7-26) and are mixed with water to obtain proper strength. The directions are on the packages.

The chemicals are inexpensive and they can be discarded after use. The developer and the fixer can be retained until they lose potency. This will be apparent by the results of the photos you develop or from special test chemicals.

The final step in developing the print is washing it. This is where running water and a sink come in handy. Nevertheless, you can mix your chemicals near

Equipping and Using a Darkroom   101

Fig. 7-25. Developing trays hold various chemicals.

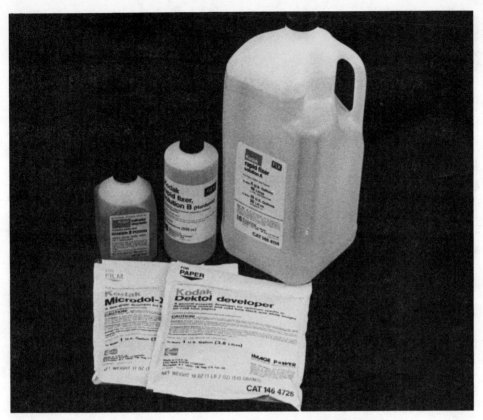

Fig. 7-26. The chemicals you'll need to start work in your own darkroom.

a sink, carry the mixtures to the darkroom, and cart the fixed prints to the running water to be washed in the sink. Prints are hung until dry. You'll also need some incidentals such as a thermometer to measure water temperatures, a graduated cylinder to measure chemicals, a funnel, some jugs to hold the chemicals, tongs to handle the prints when they're in the trays, and clothespins to hang the prints from a string while they dry. And, of course, you'll need a room that can be darkened. The room must have good ventilation and it should have running water.

Your darkroom need not be expensive. Inexpensive equipment can be used to completely furnish your "black-and-white" darkroom for under $700 (Table 7-1). A "color" darkroom will cost more.

You can also develop black-and-white film. This can be done inexpensively with a *developing tank* similar to the one shown in Fig. 7-27. In total darkness, the film is loaded onto the spindle, which is placed in the light-tight tank. Chemicals are then poured in the top of the tank. (There are baffles to keep the light out.)

Table 7-1. A Guide to Pricing a Darkroom.

Basic Black and White Darkroom	Approximate Prices for Equipment		
Enlarger	150.00		
Lens set for enlarger	400.00		
3 trays	15.00	to	20.00
3 print tongs	6.00		
Plastic developing tanks	18.00		
Stirring rod	1.80		
Film clips	1.70		
Sponge	2.00		
Thermometer	3.80		
2 graduates	3.10		
Filter funnel	2.65		
4 in 1	20.00	to	30.00
5 bottles	8.50	to	30.00
Print squeegee	4.50		
Safelight	3.25	to	17.25
Large tub print washer	8.00		
Tray siphon	20.50		
Paper	6.50	to	46.50
Dektol	2.10	to	3.50
Stop bath	3.20		
Fixer	1.40	to	2.85
Photo flo	2.30		
Hypoclearing agent	8.00		
Anti-static cloth	3.50		
	695.80	to	772.15

You'll need a special developer for the film (a different developer than you used with the paper), but otherwise the same chemicals are used for film development as were used for paper development. The flyer inside the film package explains the whole process. A popular type of film developing chemical, Kodak Microdol, is shown in Fig. 7-28.

Developing your own film can be something of a hassle. For one thing, the film must be removed from the cartridge and rolled onto the spindle in total darkness; you can't use a safelight. We've illustrated the process (in light, of course, which you can't do because it will fog your film) in Figs. 7-29, 7-30, and 7-31.

Bear in mind that ruining your negatives is much more serious than destroying a print. If the print turns out badly, you can try again. If the negatives are ruined, you have to go out and shoot the photos all over. A photo lab will usually develop a roll of film for under $5. Keep that in mind when you are establishing priorities.

Fig. 7-27. This tank is designed to develop film. Film is loaded onto the spindle.

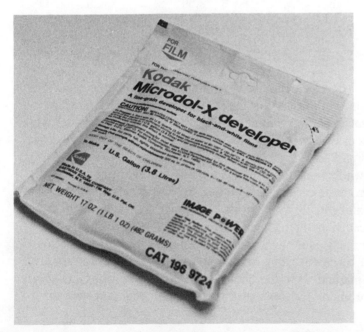

Fig. 7-28. A close-up of the chemical you'll need to develop film. Mix this powder with water according to directions on the package.

Equipping and Using a Darkroom 105

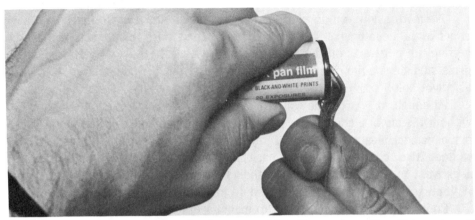

Fig. 7-29. To develop film, it must first be removed from the carriage. Step #1 is prying off the top with a bottle opener (in total darkness).

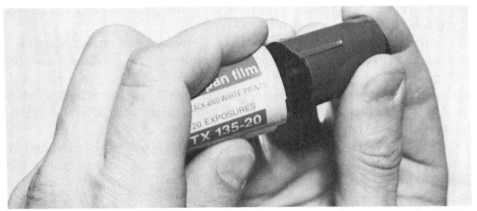

Fig. 7-30. The film is then removed from the container. You'll have to snip the end off the spool with a pair of scissors.

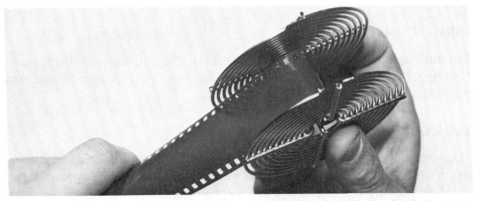

Fig. 7-31. Wind the film onto the spindle. The spindle is then placed in the developing tank, and chemicals are poured in through the light-tight opening on top of the tank.

No matter how you develop the film, you might still want to make a contact sheet of the negatives. A contact sheet is nothing more than a picture made by setting the negatives on the photo paper, pressing them down with a sheet of glass, and shining the enlarger light on them. In a pinch, you can even use a regular light bulb.

Although you can decide which negatives to print by looking at them directly, without the aid of a contact sheet, contacts make judging the quality of a photo much easier because you're not trying to mentally reverse the blacks and whites. Also, contact sheets are easier to keep track of and refer to than the negatives. You can put your contact sheets in a notebook and flip through them. With negatives, you have to hold them up to the light.

Photography is very important to many facets of PR. Knowing how to take photos saves money involved in hiring a photographer to come to your place of business or to cover your event. Also, photographers usually can't come on a moment's notice. If something unusual happens, the moment will be lost forever if you don't know how to work a camera.

Setting up and using a darkroom will save a tremendous amount of money if you have large photo demands. Inexpensive equipment can produce reasonably high-quality results. You won't get the same quality black-and-white photos as from a pro lab, where the enlarger might have cost thousands of dollars, but if most of your photos are going to be printed in newspapers that difference probably won't be all that noticeable.

Another advantage to having your own darkroom is that you can develop any part of your photo. If the subject isn't prominent enough, you can enlarge the image so that the subject takes up more of the frame. This is known as *cropping* the photo.

But there's one consideration that transcends technical familiarity with a camera and knowing your way around a darkroom. The photos you take have to be good if anyone is going to use them.

PHOTO COMPOSITION

You don't need to be a professional or a great artist to compose a photo properly. Learning the key points that photo editors use to judge a photograph can help you obtain excellent results.

Think In Terms of Thirds

The human eye doesn't find a photo very pleasing when the subject is stuck smack in the middle of a photo. If you were taking a photo of a farmhouse, it would appear very dull indeed to take the photo so that sky and ground cut the photo in half horizontally, with the farmhouse directly in the center.

The eye wants to find things on the thirds of a photo. Draw imaginary lines on a scene, cutting it into three equal sections, and try to place your main items—such as the horizon—on those thirds. Note how pleasing the photo in Fig. 7-32 appears. It is nicely balanced and it actually has three horizons, each of which occupies a third of the photo.

Fig. 7-32. Divide the scene into thirds to produce an attractive scene (courtesy Hartwick College Public Relations Office).

If you are taking a close-up photo of an object, you won't want to stick the object in one-third of the photo. Do look for a way it can fit the *thirds rule*. Perhaps a significant part of the object can fall along the upper third of the photo.

Always use the thirds rule when taking portraits of people; the eyes should be on the same level as the top horizontal line that divides the photo vertically into thirds (Fig. 7-33).

Give Looking Space

If the subject is facing in any direction except straight forward toward the camera, there should be some *looking space* provided. Notice how much more natural the subject in Fig. 7-34 appears in contrast to Fig. 7-35.

Fig. 7-33. Here's how the rule of thirds applies to portraits.

Direct Attention into the Photo

Use devices to direct attention to things in the focal point of the photo. A path winding toward the center of the photo, such as the one shown in Fig. 7-36, is a handy technique. Another way to do this is to have a person on the outer portion of the photo looking in toward the center.

Include People in Photos of Objects

Public relations photography involves a lot of pictures of objects. Examples are a manufacturer's product or a piece of equipment in a hospital, laboratory, or

Photo Composition 109

Fig. 7-34. The proper amount of "looking space."

Fig. 7-35. Not enough "looking space."

Fig. 7-36. Note how the winding path draws your eye into the photo (courtesy Hartwick College Public Relations Office).

school. Some editors express a preference for people in the photos to show scale or to demonstrate the use of a device. See Figs. 7-37 and 7-38. For commercial purposes, such as advertising, it's important to have a signed release from the person pictured in the photo. See Appendix C for details.

Photo Composition 111

Fig. 7-37. People are included to show scale.

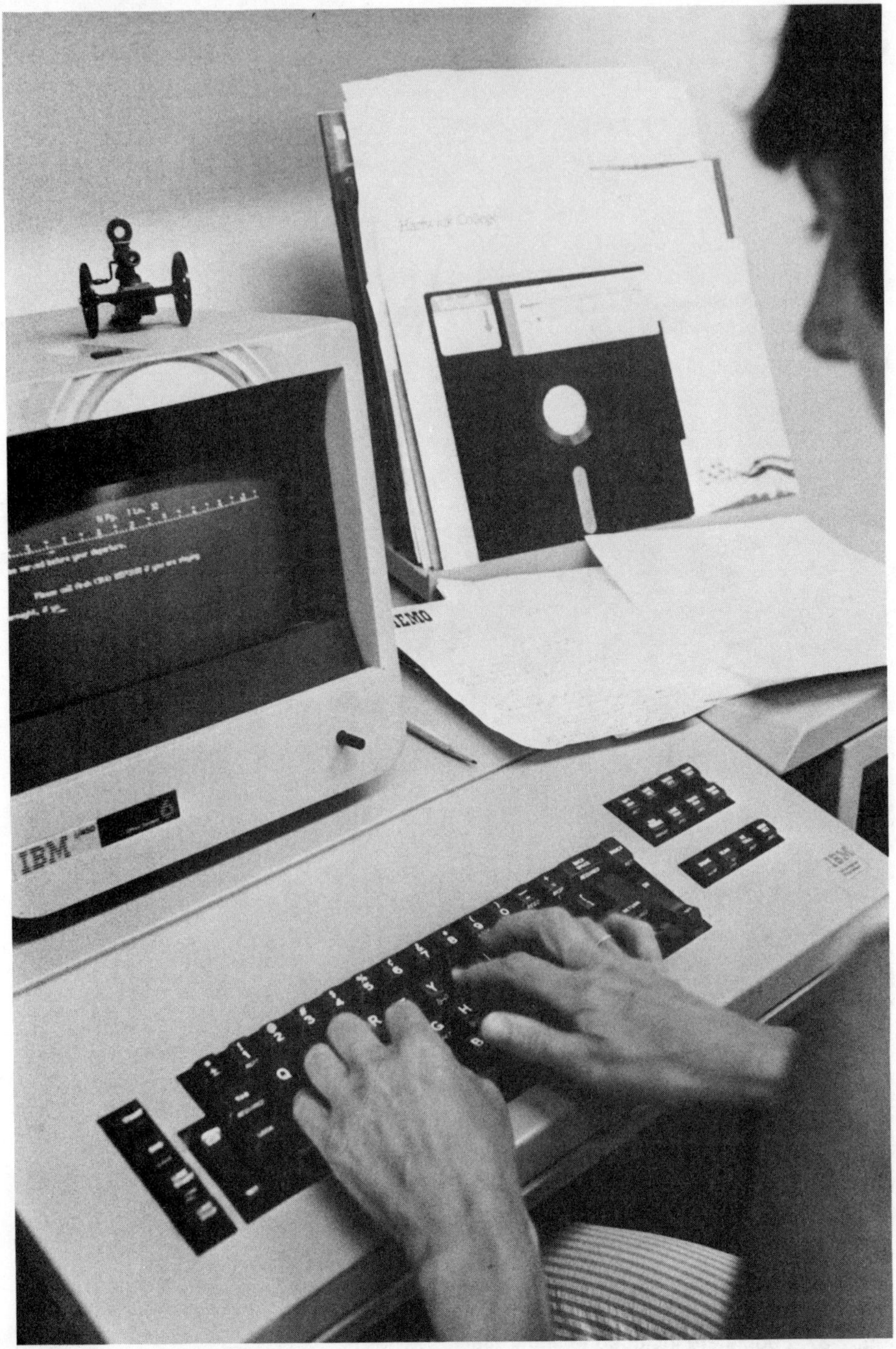

Fig. 7-38. The person demonstrates the intended use of the object (courtesy Hartwick College Public Relations Office).

Look For Striking Patterns

Daily newspapers sometimes run photos that exhibit a striking pattern even if the nature of the object is not readily apparent. Can you guess what's shown in Fig. 7-39?

Fig. 7-39. Pipes in a pipe organ. Didn't it catch your eye? Photo courtesy Hartwick College Public Relations Office.

An unusual photo of your building or an object that belongs to your organization might not really say much of anything, but it still keeps your organization's name before the public. If you think that's of any value, submit an occasional photo that is purely of visual interest. If you notice any sort of opportunity for a striking photo, you can also try the idea out on the photo editor of the newspaper. The editor might be interested enough to dispatch a photographer if you can give a clear and concise sales pitch.

Use Framing

Something in the foreground, a tree or doorway, will often add interest to a photo. Tree branches, like the ones shown in Fig. 7-40, are almost always useful for outdoor shots.

Fig. 7-40. The use of framing (courtesy Hartwick College Public Relations Office).

Use Selective Focus

Review the section of f-stops and depth of field. Notice how much better the photo (Fig. 7-13) of the woman is when the background clutter is out of focus.

Tell A Story

The secret of an excellent photo is for it to be expressive. Keep an eye out for any photo opportunity that won't need much of an explanation. Is there any doubt as to what just happened in Fig. 7-41?

Fig. 7-41. This photo tells a story (courtesy Hartwick College Public Relations Office).

Use Vertical Formats

The two ways to hold a camera are shown in Figs. 7-42 and 7-43. You should learn how to use both methods comfortably.

By holding the camera on end, you get a photo with a vertical format (taller than it is wide). Most publications are geared toward vertical-format photos. Some photo subjects will fit better into a vertical format. The series of photos taken to demonstrate different lenses shows how awkward a closeup photo of a person can be if it is taken in a horizontal format. Note the difference between Figs. 7-4 and 7-44.

Many newcomers to photography are reluctant to hold the camera vertically because they're not used to doing it that way in snapshot photography. Simply turning the camera 90 degrees can, in many cases, dramatically increase the usability of your photos.

Fig. 7-42. Holding the camera this way produces photos that are taller than they are wide (vertical photos).

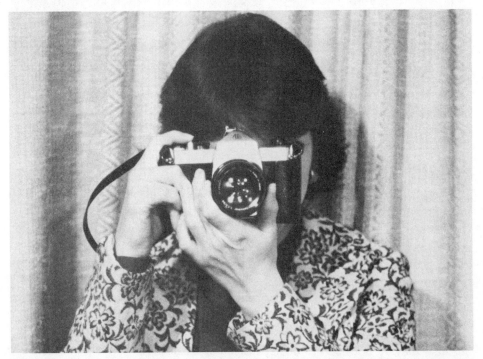

Fig. 7-43. Holding the camera this way produces photos that are wider than they are tall (horizontal photos).

Fig. 7-44. A vertical format works much better for portraits. Vertical photos are usually preferred by most publications. Compare this to the horizontal format of Fig. 7-4.

HOW TO USE YOUR PHOTOS

The most obvious use for your photos is to send them along with your press releases. By including a photo, you increase the chances that the story will be used in some form. Even if the entire story doesn't run, the photo might run with a condensed version of the story as a *caption* or, as it's sometimes called in the trade, a *cutline*. The availability of a photo gives editors more options. This assumes that the publication uses photographs (almost all do). It also assumes that the publication will use photos sent to it (most will, under varying conditions).

Most papers and magazines prefer an 8- × -10-inch glossy print. Kodak Polycontrast Rapid II RC F will give glossy prints. If you have a photo printed by a photo lab, make sure to specify a glossy. More and more publications are becoming willing to accept 5- × -7 prints. This can result in greater economy.

There's another reason for including photos with your press releases. A photo will increase the likelihood of your message getting across when and if the photo and release are printed. Research shows that more people read photo captions than actually read the stories in a newspaper.

You should always caption or identify any photo you send out. If it's a photo of a person, the name and title of that person should be attached to the photo. The same holds true for a building or an outdoor scene—any photo you mail out.

Don't write the caption on the back of the photo. If you want the caption on the back, type it on a label first and then stick the label on the photo. Typing or writing on the back of a photo can ruin it. You're better off by not writing on the back except in the margin areas of the photos. Another way to caption a photo is to rubber cement a typed piece of paper on the back or tape a piece of paper to the back and fold the paper—with the caption written on it—over the front of the photo. See Figs. 7-45 and 7-46.

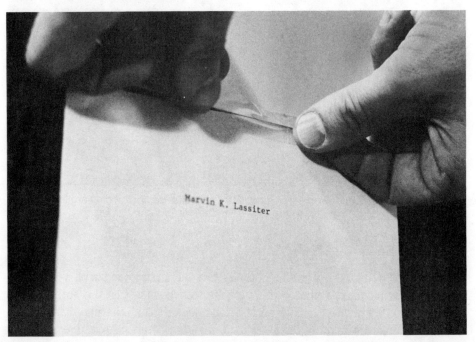

Fig. 7-45. A good way to attach a caption. Tape it to the back of the photo.

How to Use Your Photos 119

Fig. 7-46. Fold the caption sheet over the front.

When you mail a photo, put a piece of cardboard backing in along with it. The type of cardboard left over after you've used up a writing tablet is fine. Write or rubber-stamp PHOTO—DO NOT BEND on the envelope, but don't write on the envelope after you've inserted the photo.

Sending out 8 × 10 photos can be expensive. The most logical thing to consider first is whether or not the photo really adds to the story, and whether the subject is important enough to you to go to the trouble and expense of sending along a photo.

Many of the photos a PR person sends out in the mail are photos of a VIP, perhaps the director of an organization. In some cases, such as colleges, there will be an eventual need for photos of many people. If this is the case—if you feel that you have a wide number of photos that will be useful—it would be worthwhile to have a file of the negatives. Punch holes in the contact sheets and insert them in a three-ring notebook. A *negative holder*, available in almost all camera stores, will allow you to store your negatives in the same notebook right next to the contact sheet (Fig. 7-47). Transparencies can also be kept in a special plastic holder designed to fit into a three-ring notebook.

Use some sort of cross-referencing method to keep track of the photos. An alphabetically filed box of 3 × 5 cards, for example, could carry a listing like this:

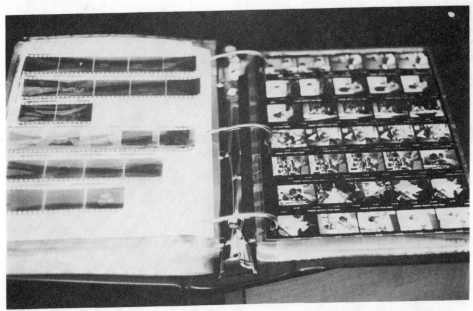

Fig. 7-47. Negative holders, available at any camera store, are essential for any PR person who wants to start a photo file. A three-ring notebook is ideal.

Johnson, Carl P./Contact sheet #52, frame 12. If you need a photo of Mr. Johnson to send out with a release concerning his promotion, it's a simple matter to find the negative, print up the photo yourself, or take the negative to a nearby photo lab.

It is always advisable to keep prints on hand of your organization's VIPs. A local paper might want one in a hurry if the VIP makes news. In any event, you should always have some sort of photographic likeness of your organization's VIPs because VIPs have a habit of being on intercontinental jetliners when you need a picture of them.

There are other uses for photos besides sending them along with press releases or giving them to the press in response to an inquiry. They can be printed in brochures, annual reports, or for displays.

Another important use of photo prints is in *press packets*. A press packet is a collection of releases, fact sheets, and other material that usually relates to a particular event. The familiar double-pocket folders, such as the one shown in Fig. 7-48, make excellent press packet holders. You might want to have a printer emblazon your organization's logo on the press packet.

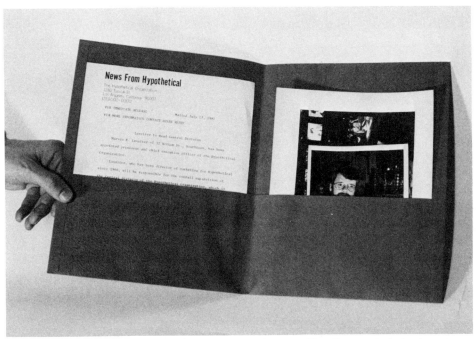

Fig. 7-48. Double-pocket folders are good for use in press kits. If you put photos in a press kit, it helps to put written copy in one pocket and photos in the other.

8

Producing Publications

AS A PR PERSON, YOU MIGHT BE CALLED ON TO PRODUCE A VARIETY OF PRINTED matter. In order to do this, you'll need a certain knowledge of aspects of the printing industry. Unfortunately, the whole business of printing is so full of jargon that a lot of us are intimidated by the whole process.

"Let's see the body copy in 9 point Bodoni," the printer says, "and do the piece in four colors."

"Sure," you mutter. "Sounds good to me."

Perhaps you haven't understood half of what's going on, but you don't want to admit that you don't know something you really should know. Yes, it's difficult to pick up the basic information by osmosis. This chapter gives you a firm foundation to use in putting together your printed material. First, we'll examine the basic principles that apply to all publications, and then look at some specific kinds of publications.

TYPE

Many people think of type as a routine part of a publication that doesn't require any decision. But selecting the proper *typeface* will be an important consideration in the *design*, the overall "look" of the piece. *Type style* and *type size* will also play a part in the length of the publication and fitting the copy into the *layout*.

The Major Breakdowns

Traditionally, scholars have divided type varieties into *races* and "ethnic" subdivisions. Lately, however, graphic artists have come to view type in only two categories. If this seems complex—well, it is. We'll explain both methods so you won't be snowed the next time you talk to a printer.

The traditional races of type are Roman, monotone, square serif, written and ornamental. The most common races, the only ones you'll probably need to know, are Roman, monotone, and square serif. Samples are illustrated in Fig. 8-1.

ROMAN

monotone

SQUARE SERIF

Fig. 8-1. Some races of type.

The *Roman race* is so named because it evolved from the alphabet of the ancient Romans. The distinguishing features of Roman type are the *serifs*: the feet or finishing strokes at the end of the large strokes. Roman type also has a difference in width of the main strokes of the letters. The horizontal strokes are usually slimmer than the vertical strokes.

The *monotone race* is so named because the strokes are all the same width. There are slight variations in width of some monotone typefaces to accommodate the technical requirements of the printing process. Monotone type does not have serifs.

For most normal printing operations, all you'll need to understand is the basic difference between the Roman and the monotone. The *square serif race* might be encountered from time to time and especially in newspaper headlines. The *text race*, which includes the typeface sometimes known as *old English*, might be used on occasion. The *written race* and *ornamental race* will be used rarely and only for special effects.

Races are divided into ethnic subcategories and then into families. Ethnic subcategories of the Roman race include *old style* and *modern*. Ethnic subcategories of the monotone race include *gothic* and *sans serif*.

The ethnic subcategories are further divided into families. A family of the subdivision might actually assume a family name such as *Bodoni*. This typeface was named after an eighteenth-century typographer who designed type in the modern Roman style. Another popular Roman type family is known as *Bookman*.

A popular family of type in the sans serif ethnic subdivision of the monotone race is *Helvetica*. This clean-lined variety of type is popular when a streamlined, modern look is preferred.

Confused? We don't blame you a bit. It is rather complex. We felt an obligation to explain it in what many experts consider the academically correct format. Most people nowadays take some liberties and divide typefaces simply into serif and sans serif. Sans serif means without serifs.

Serif

Most graphic experts agree that the serifs make type easier to read. Type with serifs is very common in newspapers. Bookman, a popular variety of type with serifs (it's really a family of Roman), is illustrated in Fig. 8-2.

BOOKMAN 6 POINT MEDIUM
ABCDEFGHIJKLMNOPQRSTUVWXYZ
abcdefghijklmnopqrstuvwxyz
1234567890

BOOKMAN 8 POINT MEDIUM
ABCDEFGHIJKLMNOPQRSTUVWXYZ
abcdefghijklmnopqrstuvwxyz
1234567890

BOOKMAN 10 POINT MEDUIM
ABCDEFGHIJKLMNOPQRSTUVWXYZ
abcdefghijklmnopqrstuvwxyz
12345678909

BOOKMAN 12 POINT MEDIUM
ABCDEFGHIJKLMNOPQRSTUVWXYZ
abcdefghijklmnopqrstuvwxyz
1234567890

BOOKMAN 14 POINT MEDIUM
ABCDEFGHIJKLMNOPQRSTUVWXYZ
abcdefghijklmnopqrstuvwxyz
1234567890

Fig. 8-2. Sizes of Bookman type.

Sans Serif

The development of Helvetica type (Fig. 8-3) went a long way toward making sans serif type more readable and attractive. It is interesting to note that one subdivision of the monotone race is called gothic. The word gothic, in this case, has nothing to do with gothic churches. It translates, roughly, to "ugly."

Some of the old gothic typefaces certainly are on the stark and ugly side, but modern sans serif type can be quite attractive. Sans serif is often used for headlines. It's become popular to use sans serif for headlines and serif for the body of the copy. Helvetica is a popular sans serif type.

Other Classifications

Just to confuse matters a bit, there are some other classifications to typeface that come into play. As you can see in Figs. 8-2 and 8-3, a type family can come in a bold variety. Most typefaces come in *italics* where characters are slanted to the right. **Boldface** is often used for captioning in publications. Italics are used for emphasis or to highlight unfamiliar words.

BOOKMAN 6 POINT BOLD
ABCDEFGHIJKLMNOPQRSTUVWXYZ
abcdefghijklmnopqrstuvwxyz
1234567890

BOOKMAN 8 POINT BOLD
ABCDEFGHIJKLMNOPQRSTUVWXYZ
abcdefghijklmnopqrstuvwxyz
1234567890

BOOKMAN 10 POINT BOLD
ABCDEFGHIJKLMNOPQRSTUVWXYZ
abcdefghijklmnopqrstuvwxyz
1234567890

BOOKMAN 12 POINT BOLD
ABCDEFGHIJKLMNOPQRSTUVWXYZ
abcdefghijklmnopqrstuvwxyz
1234567890

BOOKMAN 14 POINT BOLD
ABCDEFGHIJKLMNOPQRSTUVWXYZ
abcdefghijklmnopqrstuvwxyz
1234567890

Fig. 8-2. Continued.

HELVETICA 6 POINT MEDIUM
ABCDEFGHIJKLMNOPQRSTUVWXYZ
abcdefghijklmnopqrstuvwxyz
1234567890

HELVETICA 8 POINT MEDIUM
ABCDEFGHIJKLMNOPQRSTUVWXYZ
abcdefghijklmnopqrstuvwxyz
1234567890

HELVETICA 10 POINT MEDIUM
ABCDEFGHIJKLMNOPQRSTUVWXYZ
abcdefghijklmnopqrstuvwxyz
1234567890

HELVETICA 12 POINT MEDIUM
ABCDEFGHIJKLMNOPQRSTUVWXYZ
abcdefghijklmnopqrstuvwxyz
1234567890

HELVETICA 14 POINT MEDIUM
ABCDEFGHIJKLMNOPQRSTUVWXYZ
abcdefghijklmnopqrstuvwxyz
1234567890

Fig. 8-3. Sizes of Helvetica type.

Measuring Type

Each style of type comes in different sizes. In the typical printer's book, the type is broken down into point sizes. A *point* is roughly $1/72$ of an inch.

Another printer's term is *pica*. A pica equals 12 points, and there are approximately 6 picas to an inch. A point is used to express a measurement of height. A pica is used to express width. There is a proportional relationship between the height of the letters and the width of the line they will occupy. The size of the print is identified by the point measurement. Therefore, "8 point Helvetica" will always be the same size, no matter what printer you visit.

Printers think in terms of points and picas. You'll have an easier time communicating if you have a general idea of the definition of points and picas.

LAYOUT

Layout is the eventual appearance of the printed page—the combined effect of the print, photos, and design. A good layout person is half technician and half

HELVETICA 6 POINT BOLD
ABCDEFGHIJKLMNOPQRSTUVWXYZ
abcdefghijklmnopqrstuvwxyz
1234567890

HELVETICA 8 POINT BOLD
ABCDEFGHIJKLMNOPQRSTUVWXYZ
abcdefghijklmnopqrstuvwxyz
1234567890

HELVETICA 10 POINT BOLD
ABCDEFGHIJKLMNOPQRSTUVWXYZ
abcdefghijklmnopqrstuvwxyz
1234567890

HELVETICA 12 POINT BOLD
ABCDEFGHIJKLMNOPQRSTUVWXYZ
abcdefghijklmnopqrstuvwxyz
1234567890

HELVETICA 14 POINT BOLD
ABCDEFGHIJKLMNOPQRSTUVWXYZ
abcdefghijklmnopqrstuvwxyz
1234567890

Fig. 8-3. Continued.

artist. The artistic side of a layout is partially dependent on a talented eye, but there are some basic principles that can dramatically improve the layout abilities of any PR person.

There's no reason why you have to understand all the technical jargon or artistic principles that govern laying out a publication. You can simply hand over the copy and the photos to a good printer or graphic artist and say, "Do it." Some people like to exercise greater creative control over the process. Others just don't have the money to turn over the entire project.

We recommend that you take the middle road. Rely on the expertise of a professional whenever possible. Professionals generally make a living at what they do because they are good at it. On the other hand, relying on a pro to do the basic tasks that you could and should do will cost money. And things could wind up with the project slipping out of your control or getting off on a tangent.

It's advisable to do your own basic layout, but don't hesitate to ask for expert guidance if it's available. A good layout will be visually attractive and it will subtly help the reader get through the copy.

Emphasize Important Things Visually

Your most important story should have the largest headline. Your most important picture should be larger than the less significant photos.

Use Columns to Make Reading Easy

The eye gets tired traveling across the entire page. Columns will make the product more readable. In addition, it would be extremely difficult to lay out various items in a newspaper if each item ran the full width of the page.

Research shows that the most readable size for columns is from 35 to 45 characters wide. Publications such as newsletters are usually printed on $8^{1}/_{2}$-×-11-inch pages. This means that three columns will usually be ideal. Note the layout of the publication shown in Fig. 8-4.

Make an Easy Path for the Eye

Note how the headline PARENTS AND STUDENTS URGED TO WRITE CONGRESS only stretches across two columns. The eye only has to back up one column to begin reading the body of the story. So-called *banner headlines*, which stretch across the page, have fallen into some disfavor in modern newspaper design. Research indicates that the reader is distracted by having to back up a number of columns.

The reader expects to find the most important story at the top of the page. This is a convention adopted by newspapers. Most newspapers place the major headline in the upper right-hand corner. Some papers, however, use the upper left, the same effect used in Fig. 8-4.

The term *justified* is often used. Figure 8-5 shows an example of justified lines of type.

Create Contrast

With a screen, the box with the Globetrotters story (Fig. 8-4) was shaded. That creates *contrast* for the reader and breaks up the tiring design of the layout. Contrast is also created by using a variety of headline type sizes and different-size photos. Contrast also applies to the shapes of the blocks of text. The box (shaded or unshaded) is a popular way to break up the pattern of blocks of copy. The boxed-in story is one case where it's standard procedure to use a headline across all columns. The copy is contained and the reader has no doubt about where to return to start reading. Be careful not to overuse this device when striving for contrast.

Did you notice that the *Parent* newsletter's headlines are printed in sans serif type, while the copy typeface has serifs?

PARENT

A NEWSLETTER FOR HARTWICK FAMILIES - MEG CONWAY '82, EDITOR - MAY 1982

PARENTS AND STUDENTS URGED TO WRITE CONGRESS by Jason Moses

The Hartwick College Chapter of the Independent Student Coalition, a New York State based student organization representing the interests of over a quarter of a million students enrolled in New York's independent colleges and universities, has begun a massive letter-writing drive to Congress and the President.

The purpose of the drive is two-fold: 1) To raise student awareness on the relevant public policy issues which affect them and their families, and 2) To articulate to Washington student concern and opposition to the latest proposed cuts in federal student financial aid.

During last year's budgetary process several cuts were made in student financial aid, which effectively halted a 20 year progressive trend in federal support for higher education. On February 8 of this year the President released his proposed budget for next year. Included in it were reductions which represented a single year move to cutback overall appropriations for student financial aid by 50%, most importantly, a 40% cut in the Pell Grant program, a 27% cut in the College Work-Study program, total elimination of further funds for Supplemental Educational Opportunity Grants, State Student Incentive Grants, and National Direct Student Loans. For the Guaranteed Student Loan program, proposals would raise the interest rate on loans during repayment, increase the origination fee from 5% to 10%, and eliminate all graduate and professional students from the program.

Although students and parents alike recognize the necessity to control governmental spending, cuts in student financial aid which would restrict access, choice, and quality of higher education can only be deleterious to the nation in the long-run. Especially when education is viewed as a basic investment in human resources, which once made, helps to maintain and strengthen a more productive, high technology-based, economy.

For this reason Hartwick's Independent Student Coalition is urging all parents, and others concerned, to join students in writing to Congress and the President. Let your elected officials in Washington know about your concern. Write today!

Jason Moses ('83), is the Director of the Hartwick College Chapter of the Independent Student Coalition.

HARLEM GLOBETROTTERS PERFORM AT WICK

The Harlem Globetrotters entertained a sellout crowd of 2,000 on Tuesday, March 30 with their world-travelled performance of basketball expertise and entertainment. "General Lee" Holman performs the well-known waterbucket prank which sent a bucket of confetti into a crowd expecting a bucket of water.

Fig. 8-4. A well-laid-out front page.

Anchor the Corners

The eye just doesn't like to look at a page that fizzles out at the corners, drifting off into nothingness. For this reason, designers recommend that visually interesting elements be placed in the corners. Note how the page shown in Fig. 8-6 has headlines or important visual elements anchoring all four corners.

```
          This is an example of the flush-left,  flush-
     right style of printing.   The right-hand  column
     is justified;  that is, the edge of the right-hand
     column  lines up as straight as a ruler.  This is
     the type of printing you will most commonly use in
     a typeset document.



          This is an example of the flush-left, ragged-
     right style of printing.  The left-hand column is
     lined up, but the right-hand column is not.
     Flush-left ragged-right is the way copy will come
     out of a typewriter.  Sometimes, though, a printer
     will typeset it this way on purpose to give the
     copy a more informal look.
```

Fig. 8-5. Justified versus ragged-right type.

Balance the Page

Draw an imaginary vertical line down the center of the page pictured in Fig. 8-7. Notice how it seems balanced? Note how the same effect is achieved, in a different fashion, in Fig. 8-8.

Don't Crowd the Page

Novices to layout sometimes have the tendency to cram as much material onto the page as it will possibly hold. Resist this temptation. *White space* can be an attractive design element. In effect, it gives the eye a break.

Fitting in Copy and Pictures

One of the trickier tasks in putting together a publication involves deciding what material will fit where. The first thing you'll need to do is set up a dummy to show the printer the size and position of articles and photos. The dummy shown in Fig. 8-9 was used to lay out the page shown in Fig. 8-4.

The editor of the publication submitted copy along with the dummy. The copy, shown in Fig. 8-10, was marked to fit into the appropriate slot.

How did the editor know the amount of copy that would fit? Basically, she knew from experience. The printer will also give you guidance. A couple of basic principles printers work with will help you understand how your copy and photos will be inserted into the space you have available.

Let's say you have all the copy for your publication typed and you've completed the dummy. Now, you'll want to do some checking to make sure the copy will fit properly. If it will not fit, you will either have to change the length of the copy or make alterations in the layout.

PARENT

DEWAR HALL DURING AND AFTER RENOVATION

The student mailbox area in Dewar Hall during reconstruction.

Hartwick student Doug Weaver '84 enjoys the comforts of the Dewar Hall Lounge after its renovation.

A WONDERFUL MEETING PLACE

The long-awaited Campus Center, located in Dewar Hall, opened its doors for operation on September 1, 1981. The center provides a variety of services to the campus and is a comfortable place for students, faculty and administration to gather.

The renovation of Dewar Hall has been in the planning stage for the past seven years. This summer the construction and improvements were completed and the Center opened in time for the increased level of activity that fall always brings.

The Campus Center offers many facilities devoted to various functions including two new student lounges, a snack bar, student activities offices, the book store, a new central mailroom, the college switchboard and student mailboxes. The two story addition also provides a student information office and dining facilities for small gatherings.

The coffeehouse, which includes the campus pub and entertainment center, has been enlarged and the adjoining Student Union area has been remodelled and equipped with a large television viewing screen.

College administration hopes the new Dewar Center will become a crossroads of the campus which will attract students, faculty and staff, on and off campus, to a central facility.

APPLAUSE FOR HARTWICK THEATRE

Hartwick is now able to maximize its operations of Slade Auditorium in Yager Hall due to the renovation of its theatrical facilities.

The additions include new theatrical lighting, a larger theatrical space and an annex of dressing rooms. These theatre improvements will make it possible for programs such as dance recitals and plays to be held in Slade.

By the way, the outstanding theatre programs Hartwick provides are not news to the theatrical community. Recently, Hartwick College was featured in a special picture display of **PLAYBILL** magazine which gave tribute to selected theatre programs. **PLAYBILL** is one of the oldest and largest theatre honorary publications in the United States, and Hartwick is proud to be honored by this well-respected organization.

The improvements and additions to Slade Auditorium, along with the growing reputation of the theatre program at Hartwick, will provide for theatre productions of increasingly high quality and will broaden Hartwick's many entertainment operations.

ASIAN STUDIES AT HARTWICK

The annual New York Conference on Asian Studies was held at Hartwick College on October 9 and 10, 1981. The conference was chaired by political science professor, Dr. John Lindell.

The conference consisted primarily of concurrent panel sessions addressing social, economic, political, and historical issues in Asia. These sessions were presented by prominent scholars from 45 major colleges and universities. The panelists delivered papers on various topics of current interest to Asian scholars around the world.

Fig. 8-6. A page with all four corners anchored.

The printer will mathematically calculate the size of the copy blocks as they will appear when the type has been set. This is done by estimating the number of characters (typewritten strokes, including spaces) in the copy. The printer can then calculate how many lines of copy will appear in the typeset piece.

PARENT

ALUMNI CAREER DAY

On February 23, the Alumni Office in conjunction with the Career Planning and Placement Office, hosted a Career Day for Hartwick students. The main objective was for Hartwick students to have the opportunity to meet and talk with alumni in various professions.

Twenty alumni were selected, with expertise in their specific field. The alumni were chosen on the basis of a student survey from tne alumni office, which gave students a chance to select the different types of occupations that were of interest to them.

Alumni participants talked with students individually, and many gave lectures to classes throughout the day.

Donald Laidlaw, Director for Executive Resources at IBM, spoke at a dinner following the day's activities. He based his remarks on the value of a liberal arts education in today's job market. Noting the importance of liberal arts in finding a job and in advancing a career, he also stated that communication skills and the broad range of knowledge acquired from a liberal arts education, help people to be more effective, efficient and better all-around managers.

Andrea Connolly (left, '82), at Alumni Career Day. Connolly talks with Frank K. Facey ('72), who is currently involved in sales and marketing for American Can Company.

CAREER PLANNING

The Career Planning and Placement Office offers the opportunity to Hartwick students to identify and develop career objectives and potentials. Director Bob Casper states that one of the main functions of the office is, "helping students to gain a better understanding of their interests and the availability of jobs in different fields."

The Career Planning Office also provides students with background information about specific employers and potential job opportunities, and arranges for campus recruiters in corporate and government agencies to visit the college. Some of the companies which have recruited at Hartwick recently are: Marine Midland, IBM, Procter & Gamble, Key Bank, K-Mart and Riegel Textile Corporation.

Other programs and services include: a career resource center which is constantly updated, individual counseling, workshops and instructions on job hunting procedures (the letter, the resume, the interview), a student employment program for parttime and summer job opportunities, and reference credentials, sent on request to graduate schools and potential employers.

A program just getting underway, called the Career Exploration Program (CEP), is designed to establish a link between certain alumni and selected students. The objective of the program is to allow students to spend time with an alumni sponsor during a 1-3 day period while the sponsor goes through his or her normal job activities.

Director of Career Planning and Placement, Bob Casper, instructs students in a resume writing workshop.

Fig. 8-7. A balanced page.

Calculating the Space for Copy. After choosing the type (both style and size) the printer uses pica measurements to obtain the estimation of length. Let's say your copy has a total of 1000 characters and each column in the printed piece will be 18 picas wide. Assume we're using 9 point Helvetica type; it measures 2.7 characters per pica. A line of 18 picas would have 49 characters. By

PARENT

Eddie Hawkins '84 (right) expresses his excitement after scoring against Princeton University in front of a cheering crowd at the Homecoming game.

MEN'S SOCCER

The men's varsity soccer team has played a very tough schedule this season, involving many challenging, fast moving and exciting games. The Warriors opened the season on September 11, by winning the Oneonta Mayor's Cup Tournament, and then continued to follow a very rugged game pattern against several top ranked opponents.

The team is composed of many strong and talented athletes, many of whom are returning players who were part of last year's team which finished fourth in the nation.

The varsity squad's record is 8-4-4 with three more games (as of this writing) to complete before the end of the regular season's competition.

OUTSTANDING WOMEN'S SOCCER

The women's varsity soccer team had a very successful fall season with an outstanding record of 12-3. They then traveled to William Smith College the weekend of October 30 to participate in the NYSAIAW Championships, where they finished third in the state and ninth in the region. In addition, central midfielder Lisa Sposato '84 and sweeper Karen Berkel '85 were named to the All-Tournament team.

Dave Robinson, head coach of the women's soccer team, is very pleased with the amazing progress and strength of his team. This fall marks the second season ever that Hartwick women have played soccer on a competitive intercollegiate level.

Sweeper (left) Karen Berkel '85 and No. 10 Sue Fisher '85 assist in defensive play while goalie Laura Bartlett '85 captures the ball.

Freshman Mary Searles (right) attacks the ball while teammates No. 11 Jan Barnard '82 and No. 5 Ginger Hansen '83 support the play.

WOMEN'S FIELD HOCKEY

The 1981 varsity field hockey team finished the season with a 9-6 record. The "Wick" women dominated play in many of the games this year, exhibiting strong stickhandling and supportive passing.

In post-season play, they took second place in the NYSAIAW tournament on October 29-31, falling to Brockport State 1-0 after having defeated Manhattanville 2-0 and Oswego State 4-1.

The team then traveled to New England College November 3 for the Eastern Regional tournament, where they lost in overtime in the first round to New England College.

Fig. 8-8. Balance on a page achieved another way.

dividing 49 characters into 1000 (the total number of characters in the copy) we find that there will be about 21 lines of copy in the final, typeset product.

Calculating Space for Photos. Photos can be reduced to fit into various spaces. The printer will, in most cases, have to reduce them to fit into the publi-

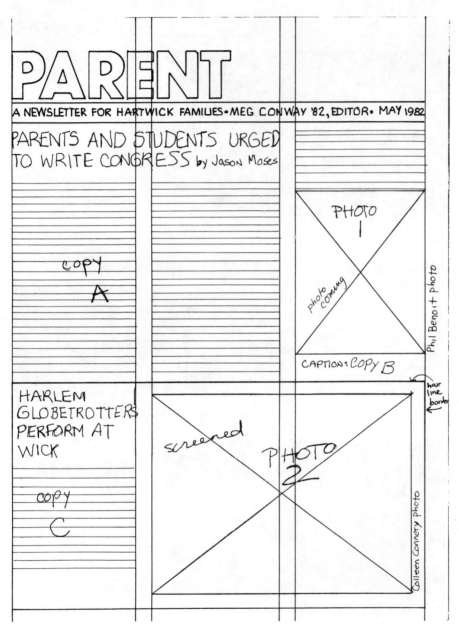

Fig. 8-9. A dummy layout for a newsletter.

cation. The printer will use a *proportional scale* (Fig. 8-11) to determine the amount of reduction that will be needed to fit the photo into the desired space.

The printer will mark the approximate size of the reduced photo on an overleaf and will note the amount of reduction. We've placed the markings directly on the photo (Fig. 8-12) for the purpose of illustration.

PARENTS AND STUDENTS URGED TO WRITE CONGRESS

by Jason Moses

The Hartwick College Chapter of the Independent Student Coalition, a New York State based student organization representing the interests os over a quarter of a million students enrolled in New York's independent colleges and universities, has begun a massive letter-writing drive to Congress and the President.

The purpose of the drive is two-fold: 1) To raise student awareness on the relevant public policy issues which affect them and their families, and 2) To articulate to Washington student concern and opposition to the latest proposed cuts in federal student financial aid.

During last year's budgetary process several cuts were made in student financial aid, which effectively halted a 20 year progressive trend in federal support for higher education. On February 8 of this year the President released his proposed budget for next year. Included in it were reductions which represented a single year move to cutback overall appropriations for student financial aid by 50%. Most importantly: a 40% cut in the Pell Grant program; a 27% cut in the College Work-Study program; total elimination of further funds for Supplemental Educational Opportunity Grants, State Student Incentive Grants, and National Direct Student Loans. For the Guaranteed Student Loan program, proposals would raise the interest rate on loans during repayment, increase the origination fee from 5% to 10%, and eliminate all graduate and professional students from the program.

Although students and parents alike recognize the necessity to control governmental spending, cuts in student financial aid which would restrict access, choice, and quality of higher education can only be deleterious to the nation in the long-run. Especially when education is viewed as a basic investment in human resources, which once made, helps to maintain and strengthen a more productive, high technology based, economy.

Photos: Jason Moses

Fig. 8-10. Articles are written double-spaced and marked to show where they fit into the dummy.

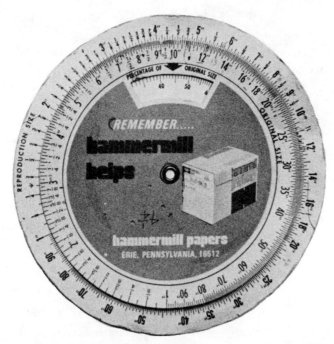

Fig. 8-11. A proportional scale that uses a slide rule type of operation to tell the printer how much room illustrations will take up in a printed piece.

Cropping a Photo. *Cropping* can change the proportion of the photo, and it can also change the content. Suppose, for example, we had wanted to show only the tape machines in the photo (Fig. 5-2) in Chapter 5 that shows the woman sitting at a microphone.

We originally considered isolating various pieces of equipment, and obtained a photo of the news production studio without the woman sitting at the microphone. Because we wanted to feature only the equipment on the left of the photo, we drew crop marks to show the area of the photo we wanted to use. The perspective of the photo was changed from horizontal to vertical.

Figure 8-13 shows the concept. Don't draw directly on a photo; that was done in this case only for illustration purposes. The best way to instruct the printer on how to crop a photo is to draw the crop lines on a photocopy of the original photo.

We eventually decided that the chair intruding into the photo was too distracting, and that the photo wasn't all that necessary.

Cropping the photo isn't the same as reducing it. The printer might still have to alter the size of the cropped area to make it fit into the layout.

Fig. 8-12. When your photos come back from the printer's, they often will carry notations like this. "Bottom page 13" tells the printer where to insert the photo in the final copy and "68%" indicates the amount of reduction needed. The brackets on the outer portions of the photo indicate the crop marks. This device is used to obtain proper proportions for the reduction and cropping.

Fig. 8-13. You can indicate cropping by drawing lines around the approximate area you would like to use. Do this on a piece of tissue paper that lays over the photo. We've drawn directly on the photo for the purpose of illustration.

NEWSLETTERS

There's no exact definition of a newsletter. It can be anything from a single sheet to a small newspaper. It is usually distributed by mail or handed out to a specified audience: members of an organization, employees, or other constituents. All kinds of institutions—colleges, museums, hospitals, charity organizations, government agencies, large manufacturing firms, unions, hospitals—have newsletters.

The purpose of a newsletter is to communicate regularly with members of a group or people otherwise sharing a common interest. One goal is to get across the idea that the organization or firm is a good group of which to be a part. Museums often place great importance in membership and they will use a newsletter as a benefit to members. Companies might talk about accomplishments of employees to install a feeling of goodwill and enthusiasm.

Advantages of Newsletters

In addition to promoting an image, a newsletter is a good vehicle for internal communications. It is especially useful for getting information from the top levels to the bottom levels. This is particularly important in combating rumors about, for instance, impending layoffs.

A newsletter can serve in lieu of a press release in notifying members and other interested people about your events. It can also lend a measure of respectability to your organization. A regular publication implies some importance and stability on the part of your organization.

Newsletters can be quite useful for membership drives or for inclusion in press kits. They often provide a feel for your organization to people who are not familiar with it. They help reflect your organizational identity.

Disadvantages of a Newsletter

Remember that a regular publication locks you into regular deadlines. You will have to rely extensively on other people—printers, other writers, and often volunteers—to help produce a newsletter.

Digging up enough material can be difficult. If the well goes dry, you'll be forced to pad with dull or uninteresting stuff. This can reflect very badly on your organization.

Remember that you will be putting yourself in the position of editor—which often translates to a hot seat. Now you are the one who has to tell associates that their article idea isn't . . . well, just doesn't have enough . . . really can't fit into . . .

Distributing Newsletters

Many newsletters are sent through the mail. A popular design is an $8^{1}/_{2}$-×-11-inch format that folds into thirds. A mailer is located on the back, as shown in Fig. 8-14, and the newsletter will appear just like a regular letter when it is folded and stapled.

Your mailing labels must be attached to the appropriate spot on the mailer. Alternately, you can choose to have a *mailing service* print the addresses for you. Mailing services, also known as *direct mail services*, will have all the equipment to maintain your mailing list and address your pieces. They are definitely an option worth considering.

Be aware that you might qualify for a bulk mailing rate if you mail a certain amount of pieces sorted in zip code order. The pieces must conform to certain size ratios. Check with your local post office before setting up the format for any publication that will go through the mail. The bulk rate can result in substantial savings if you play by the rules.

Typeset Versus Camera-Ready Newsletter

You can save the cost of typesetting and other layout fees by putting the entire newsletter together yourself. The copy can be typed into columns on a typewriter, cut out, and pasted up onto a standard form (which you'll probably want

PARENT

PARENT SPEAKS TO MANAGEMENT STUDENTS

David Depperman, father of freshman Eric Depperman of New Hartford, New York, recently gave a lecture to Hartwick's management and economics students and faculty about his career in the petfood industry.

Mr. Depperman is president of Chenango Valley Petfoods located in Sherburne, New York. He was asked by the Hartwick College Management Association to share some of his knowledge and experience concerning the petfood business.

Russell Kaufman '83, co-president of the Management Association, noted the management and economics departments would welcome other parents to talk to Hartwick students about their careers in business.

McNAMEE IS NEW DIRECTOR OF DEVELOPMENT

Thomas McNamee of New Rochelle, New York has been appointed Director of Development at Hartwick College. McNamee succeeds Jane Nile who is currently the Director of Medical Center Development at the University of Rochester Medical Center.

McNamee's job includes a variety of fundraising responsibilities, one of which is to coordinate the programs of the Parents' Executive Committee.

The function of the Parents' Executive Committee is to explore ways for Hartwick parents to become involved in supporting various activities of the college. Parents' efforts, in recent years, have been vital in meeting fundraising goals which help meet annual expenses. According to McNamee, very few colleges or universities rival Hartwick when it comes to the support received from parents.

In addition to academic use, Hartwick students enjoy a variety of recreational activities at Pine Lake.

John McKeith photo

Senator Cook

SENATOR CHARLES COOK '56

Charles Cook, New York State Senator from the 48th Senatorial District and a 1956 graduate of Hartwick College, is this year's recipient of the distinguished alumnus award.

Cook has been a member of the Senate since 1979. His devotion to the public service, however, did not begin in the Senate. He has been actively involved in community efforts for many years. He currently chairs the Senate Agricultural Committee, is Secretary to the Commission on Critical Transportation Choices and serves on the Joint Legislative Commission on Administrative Regulations Review.

PARENT
Hartwick College
Oneonta, New York 13820

```
BULK RATE
Non-Profit Organization
U.S. Postage Paid
Hartwick College
```

Fig. 8-14. The bottom third of the newsletter contains the mailing area to affix the label.

to have printed in quantity). The form will contain the *heading* on the front and the *mailer* on the back. Headlines can be made using press-type.

The newsletter dummy will then be *camera-ready*. That means it can be photographed by the printer's special equipment and reproduced. Figure 8-15 shows a newsletter made in this fashion. Later issues were revamped and typeset (Fig. 8-16). The price differential for the six-page newsletter was about $200. That was a good price for the amount of typesetting involved.

BROCHURES

Some PR specialists have separate definitions for brochures, flyers, leaflets, and pamphlets. For the sake of simplicity, let's use the word *brochure* to refer to any sort of hand-out material.

THE JOHN WOODMAN HIGGINS ARMORY
A Museum of Arms and Armor

Ventail Voice

Members Bulletin, Vol. 5, No. 4   September, 1981
Editor: Carl Hausman   Director: Warren M. Little

Goody, Clancy to Study Museum Renovations

The architectural firm of Goody, Clancy and Associates, Inc. of Boston has been retained to conduct a preliminary study of renovations at the Higgins Armory Museum. The museum's board of trustees approved selection of the firm during its September 14 regular meeting.

The study will determine basic problems with the museum's structure, recommend methods to alleviate those problems, and estimate the cost of renovation, according to museum director Warren M. Little. "We're primarily interested in two things," said Little. "We want to button up the building from an energy conservation point of view, and we want to turn the structure into a modern museum."

Physical changes to be considered include additional exhibit space on the second floor, a first floor food preparation area, a new auditorium, and revamping the main entrance. Energy-related improvements will probably involve reglazing windows and some method of internal climate control. "Climate control is important both in terms of cutting our energy bills and preserving our collection," said museum administrator John Guilfoyle. "We need to think about things like controlling humidity and preventing damage to the collection from sunlight streaming in the windows."

Although a variety of changes will be made, director Little pointed out that the basic character of the museum will not be altered. "We don't intend to change the configuration of the third and fourth floors, although there will
(please turn to page 6)

Message From the Director

This summer has been a busy one for our staff here at the museum. In June, Carl Hausman joined our staff part time as Public Information Coordinator. He immediately started work on updating the media mailing lists and developing new brochures to brighten up our image. Carl is also writing a weekly column titled "Your Home is Your Castle," which has been appearing as a regular feature in the North and East editions of the Worcester County Newspapers. It is most fitting, in keeping with our overall theme of protection. An accomplished freelance article and book writer, Carl is also experienced in photography and television, two areas we hope to take advantage of in the near future.

It has been a summer of meetings. When the staff was not assisting visitors from all over the country, there were many meetings to attend with trustees and incorporators. A subcommittee on buildings and grounds, chaired by trustee Richard West, interviewed a number of architects. The education/exhibits committee, chaired by trustee Malcolm Parkinson, met with an exhibits designer. Trustee Roma Josephs formed her collections committee and welcomed back Messers Ford and Gage--former directors of the museum--as members of the committee which will determine how
(please turn to page 5)

Fig. 8-15. A newsletter produced with press-type and a typewriter.

The important thing about putting together a brochure is to remember that it must compete visually with many other printed materials. If the brochure is going to be displayed in a rack, keep in mind that only the top third might show. Design the brochure accordingly.

It Must Have Focus

Because the brochure will generally be a short piece, it should stick to one topic. This might sound obvious, but poorly designed brochures often result from the

142 CHAPTER 8 PRODUCING PUBLICATIONS

The Ventail Voice

Spring, 1982

Ventail Voice is the quarterly newsletter of the Higgins Armory Museum, a museum of arms and armor.
Museum Director: Warren M. Little Editor: Carl Hausman.

Evelyn F. Karet   Paul S. Morgan

Six Elected to Board of Trustees at Higgins Armory Museum

Paul S. Morgan, president of Morgan Construction Co., and Evelyn F. Karet, a doctoral candidate at Columbia University, have been elected to new three year terms on the Higgins Armory Museum Board of Trustees. Four current trustees were reelected. The elections were held April 14, at the museum's annual meeting of incorporators. (please turn to page 6)

From the Director

Spring is a busy time at museums and ours is no exception. The museum's staff, accustomed to the quiet winter months, is suddenly aware that the influx of school students is upon us, with as many as 800 visitors in a day! Evening events also increase, and the first of a number of wedding receptions was held recently in the Great Hall. The museum also hosted the New England Museum Association's annual workshop and dinner for trustees, directors and administrators. Also of interest was our first evening for new members. An orientation slide program was followed by a tour of the galleries and "behind the scenes," with refreshments served by the hospitality committee.

Spring also signals the annual meeting of the incorporators, and with it some changes in the guard. After a number of years of tireless efforts, trustees Alfred Cotton Jr. and Jean Farrell resigned, with the thanks for their efforts by all who have worked with them. New trustees girded themselves for future action (see above).

Changes, too, are occurring among the staff. After sixteen years of dedicated service, our librarian Erveen Lundberg retired to be with her husband and travel more to their property on the Cape. Always cheerful and ready to help wherever needed, her workshops with primary school students were well-received and well-appreciated by children and parents. Vicki Reikes Fox, our coordinator of education, is moving to the Boston area. We will miss her southern drawl and imaginative educational handouts and workshops which she set up for the P.E.A.K. program and vacation visitors. Also leaving is our coordinator of public information and editor of the Ventail Voice, Carl Hausman. He will continue to pursue his career in freelance writing. Carl's articles in "Your Home is Your Castle" are widely read in Worcester County Newspapers North and East and the Blackstone Valley Trubune, and his press releases helped to put us "on the map."

Dr. Warren M. Little

Joining the museum staff is Chris Seivard, who will serve as gallery guide and in other areas as needed, as he did for us last summer. Chris' presence will allow other members of the staff to work with our new, part-time associate conservator, Tom Ryder, to prepare for a number of loans going out to museums this summer. Tom, an active member of our museum for over a year, is a blacksmith at Old Sturbridge Village. Recently he repaired and cleaned up a suit of armor, on his own time, for the Traveller's Insurance Company of Hartford, which had requested our help to do the job. We were happy to turn it over to Tom, who did a fine job. (please turn to page 4)

Fig. 8-16. A later edition of the newsletter using typesetting and photos.

fact that there are two programs or ideas that someone wants highlighted. When they both wind up in the same brochure the reader has a tough time deciding what the brochure is about.

Use Catchy Headlines and Other Designs

Remember that the brochure has to be an attention grabber. Use of headlines is important. Just make sure that the headline is directly related to the copy and that it is convincing.

Keep the Copy to a Minimum

Use short blocks of copy broken up by headlines and subheadlines. The best way to keep copy down is to allot a certain amount of space in the design and then tailor the copy to fit. Figure 8-17 shows a dummy for a brochure. Note how the lines representing copy to come are visually appropriate. Copy overflowing the page would detract from the design.

Fig. 8-17. A dummy for a brochure.

Keep the Size in Mind

Will the brochure be mailed out? Then be positive—before you print—that it fits into a #10 envelope. You might want to make the brochure a self-mailer, in much the same form as a newsletter's mailer.

Use a Variety of Action Photos

Vary the size as well as the content and approach of photos. Try to have people in the photos whenever possible.

OTHER PUBLICATIONS

From time to time, you might become involved in producing posters, bumper stickers, or display items. The same principles of design and simplicity apply here. In the case of a poster or other display, remember that words must be kept to an absolute minimum.

Magazine-type publications (thicker than newsletters and printed on better-quality paper) might be an option for your organization. They are expensive to produce, but they can bring excellent results.

Annual reports usually include a statement on the finances of the group or firm, a list of members if it's a nonprofit organization, and a statement from the person in charge.

A full-blown magazine about your organization might not be feasible, but keep the idea on the horizon. Perhaps your newsletter might evolve someday to a magazine format. The *Quarterly* from the University of Massachusetts Medical Center (Fig. 8-18) is an excellent example of what an institutional magazine can do. *Quarterly* Editor Sara Patten reports that the copies sent to the media often generate excellent stories about the medical center.

THE PRINTING PROCESS

You'll want to know something about the various methods used to put an image on paper. It's not necessary to become an expert on the various types of machinery and processes, but you should be familiar with the basics if for no other reason than being able to work with the printer.

Offset Printing

The *offset press* (Fig. 8-19) uses a photographic plate to impress an image on paper. It can achieve sharp reproductions and it has come into increasing use in high-quality printing. Other kinds of printing, such as *letterpress* (raised letters) and *rotogravure* (ink trapped in grooves on a plate) are less popular for the jobs you're likely to encounter in public relations.

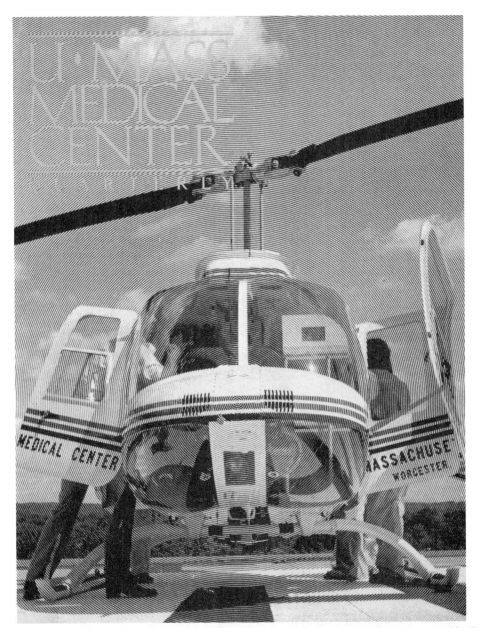

Fig. 8-18. A full-scale institutional magazine (courtesy University of Massachusetts Medical Center Public Affairs Office).

New England Life Flight/UMass:
When minutes count...

The difference between life and death may not rest with the swiftness of a surgeon's scalpel, the split-second decision of an anesthesiologist, the responsiveness of a nurse or the flawless execution of that symphony that is a trauma team in action. It may depend on time. For time dictates above all else the efficacy of the most advanced trauma care available anywhere.

Experience has shown that the victim of a very serious injury must receive definitive medical care quickly in order to have a good chance of survival: the faster the care, the better the chances—up to one hour. After an hour, the survival rate drops dramatically. Those sixty minutes are known in emergency medicine as the Golden Hour.

On September 15 a new era in emergency medical care for the region was launched with the arrival of New England Life Flight/UMass, the first complete air ambulance system in New England. Based at the Medical Center, Life Flight will serve as an essential adjunct to ground ambulance systems, to be used when time, speed and location are critical factors in getting a patient to the proper medical care. Skilled physicians, experienced critical care flight nurses, pilots, mechanics and dispatchers are on call 24 hours a day, 365 days a year, working as a team to insure precise coordination and delivery of medical care on each Life Flight mission.

Life Flight's jet turbine-powered helicopter is a "flying intensive care unit" equipped with an advanced life support system that includes ventilators, oxygen, suction, intravenous fluids, trauma, fracture and obstetric kits, burn pack and complete emergency medications. The Bell Long Ranger aircraft is capable of transporting two stretcher patients, a physician, flight nurse, and pilot. With a cruising speed of two miles per minute and the aid of an on-board computer for programming multiple locations, the Life Flight helicopter is an indispensable health care tool designed to provide the fastest, most sophisticated transport possible when a life is in the balance.

Life Flight serves nearly all of New England and the easternmost portion of New York State. Patients are transported to the closest appropriate facility within the designated service area—a 130 mile radius of UMass. Multiple trauma cases are brought to the nearest trauma facility, such as the UMass Trauma Center.

"Figures from the American Medical Association show that the combination of helicopter ambulance service and regional trauma centers can decrease a region's cardiac and trauma mortality rate significantly," says Morris Ostroff, M.D., Assistant Professor of Medicine and director of Emergency Transport Services at UMMC. Based on an estimated 500-700 Life Flight missions during its first year of operation, Dr. Ostroff expects Life Flight will save 70 lives that otherwise might have been lost. "A critical patient in a previously inaccessible area of the Berkshires, for example, can be transported to UMass Medical Center in just over thirty minutes," he points out, "whereas a ground ambulance takes two to two and a half hours."

Life Flight is activated through its sophisticated communications net-

Fig. 8-18. Continued.

Color Versus Black and White

Offset printing is commonly used for both black-and-white and color. The most common method of printing is black ink on white paper. Other options for a one-color job can involve using a colored ink instead of black ink for variety. Colored paper can also be used.

A slightly more expensive option is to use two colors of ink. This can significantly liven up the design. You'll be limited to options that can be accomplished

Dr. Morris Ostroff explains Life Flight's capabilities to Governor King

work located at the Medical Center and staffed around the clock by highly trained, experienced, EMT-qualified dispatchers, who process the telephone or radio request immediately. Within five minutes of receiving the call for assistance, the Life Flight team will be airborne and on the way to the scene of an accident or medical emergency.

"Life Flight can provide certain areas of New England with accessibility to tertiary care hospitals that wasn't available to them before," says Dr. Ostroff. "Some of the smaller hospitals that might have difficulty providing transport services to patients have been very enthusiastic about the service." The Life Flight team will also be working with MAST (military assistance to safety in traffic) and the Coast Guard, Dr. Ostroff reports, in augmenting their medical helicopter services.

New England Life Flight represents more than two years of planning and the hard work and dedication of dozens of medical professionals. Dr. Ostroff expresses the feelings of many when he says, "Emergency medicine has come of age in New England with Life Flight."

Governor Edward King cuts the ribbon at Life Flight's August 31 dedication ceremonies with the help of —left to right) Morris Ostroff, M.D., Sen. Daniel Foley and Rep. Robert Bohigian

Fig. 8-18. Continued.

in separate press runs, such as printing the name of the newsletter and box borders in red ink, and the rest of the copy in black ink.

Full-color reproduction is done with the four primary colors, and is often called *four-color printing*. The four primary colors are mixed and blended to recreate the original colors.

Part of the four-color printing process is the making of *separations* of the photos into the four primary colors. Layers of color are laid down on transparencies used later in the printing process. This process is expensive. Depending on the size of the photo, it can cost about $300 per shot.

Fig. 8-19. An offset press.

Paper

The printer will have a book of paper samples to help you choose the stock for your newsletter, brochure, or other publication. The important thing to remember is to choose the correct *opacity*. Don't use paper that will show through. Ask for a sample of something printed on the stock you're considering and hold it up to the light.

Typesetting

The printer will have a selection of typefaces from which you can choose. Most modern typesetting is done with the aid of a computerized machine (Fig. 8-20) that will produce the letters on a kind of film. The film is then pasted up (Fig. 8-21). The paste-up piece is photographed by the plate-making device, and then reproduced on the offset press.

Dealing with a Printer

The most important thing to do at the very beginning of the project is to get a price quote. It's highly advisable to get quotes from several printers. Ask the printers to break the quote down in terms of quantities, such as 5000, 10,000, and 15,000.

Fig. 8-20. Modern electronic typesetting equipment.

150 CHAPTER 8 PRODUCING PUBLICATIONS

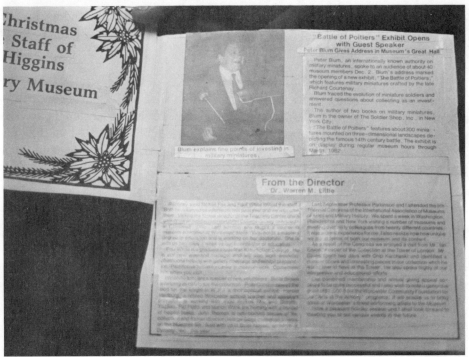

Fig. 8-21. Typeset material is pasted up to be used for reproduction.

Some printers might give you a better break than others on large-quantity orders. The prices per copy (the unit price) will decrease dramatically as the quantity of the order increases. Much of the printing bill will reflect initial layout and setup charges.

The printer will want to work with you to establish a timetable for preparing the publication. Steps in the process take a considerable amount of time. Many printers will send your color transparencies (you'll use transparencies, remember, not prints) to a separation lab hundreds of miles away. Artwork might also take quite a bit of time.

Setting the timetable will involve working backwards from the date when you want the publication delivered. The printer will tell you when he needs the materials from you and inform you when you will be able to check the various proof copies that will be made during the printing process.

As you gain in experience, it will become easier for you to specify papers, typefaces, and other technical details. But for your first few efforts, the best approach might be to find a publication you would like yours to look like and show it to the printer.

9
Desktop Publishing

THERE'S A QUIET REVOLUTION TAKING PLACE IN THE PUBLISHING WORLD: THE introduction of personal computer-based programs that can produce type and graphics closely resembling professional typeset quality.

Before detailing what a public relations practitioner needs to know about desktop publishing, let's first clear up some myths and misconceptions about the field. Here are some points worth considering before you get into the fine points of desktop publishing:

- Desktop publishing equipment and software have not yet been refined to the point where you can unpack the crates, plug in the gear, and start printing. Even people with solid computer and/or graphics experience sometimes need months to master the intricacies of the hardware and software.
- Desktop publishing gear does not produce the same quality of graphics as does a professional typesetting setup. Some desktop publishing equipment produces a decidedly inferior product. Higher-end hardware and software can produce near-typeset quality, but usually cannot meet certain demands, such as extremely high-quality graphics for magazine advertising layouts. (However, that gap is being closed, and as will be explained shortly, desktop-produced page layouts can be printed on professional-quality typesetting equipment.)
- Most importantly, possessing software with a page-layout capability does

not transform the user into a graphic designer. A software package cannot ensure good-quality work or good taste. Horrible layouts can be and are produced by desktop publishing equipment.

Having duly noted those caveats, let's explore some of the very real benefits of this advancing technology.

WHAT IS DESKTOP PUBLISHING?

Essentially, desktop publishing produces type and graphics similar to those seen in books, magazines, newspapers, and advertising. The tools of the desktop publishing trade are the computer, page layout software, and the printer, usually a laser printer.

The Computer

Desktop publishing is typically done on a personal computer. Today, personal computers capable of desktop publishing usually fall into two categories: Apple and IBM compatible. The popular Apple Macintosh (Fig. 9-1) is probably the

Fig. 9-1. This desktop publishing system consists of a MacIntosh SE and an additional screen to allow a full page to be viewed.

premier machine for desktop publishing, although IBM compatibles are catching up quickly. IBM compatibles are what the name implies: machines that mimic the hardware and operating system of IBM personal computers. The term *PC* (for *personal computer*) has generally come to mean an IBM or compatible.

Computers for desktop publishing usually need a great deal of memory, because graphics gobble up huge chunks of computer storage space. Most desktop publishers find a hard disk drive, with its concomitant large storage space, to be essential.

As a general rule, anyone contemplating using a computer for desktop publishing will want a high-level Macintosh, such as the SE or Macintosh II, or a PC with at least an 80286 processor. The designation "286" refers to the computer's central processing unit; the number is sort of a model number and has no particular meaning in and of itself. A PC with an 80386 processor is even better, but it will be more expensive.

Desktop publishers favor high-quality computers because of the speed with which those units process information. In addition to requiring a large amount of space in memory, graphics take a while for the computer to construct and reconstruct on the screen as you make changes. (In desktop publishing parlance, this is referred to as the time it takes for the screen to "refresh" itself.) A computer without a powerful processing unit takes an agonizingly long time to process graphics.

There is no shortage of PCs capable of desktop publishing. IBM Model 50 and all higher-numbered IBMs are well suited to the task, as are many so-called clones (clones of the IBM, which means the same thing as IBM compatible) with 286 or 386 processors and hard drives. Twenty-megabyte drives are about as small as you would want for most applications.

A device known as a *mouse* (Fig. 9-2) allows you to draw on the page, breaking the operator's bond with the keyboard. Utilizing a mouse, the desktop publisher can draw lines, drag images across the page, and reproportion the layout.

Desktop Publishing Software

Software is the term used to describe the computer programs that actually do the task at hand. There are many applications of software. Among the most familiar are *word processing* programs, which allow you to write and edit on the computer, and *spreadsheet* programs, which make complex multifactor calculations.

The types of programs most commonly associated with word processing are *page layout* software, sometimes simply referred to as *desktop publishing* software, and *paint programs*, which produce graphics. A paint program allows you to draw on screen. In addition, many graphics programs provide images ready-made to import into your desktop publishing program.

Fig. 9-2. The "mouse" is connected by a cord to the computer. When it is moved on a flat surface, it moves the cursor on the screen. A pad on the mouse can be pressed to call for a given function on the screen.

You'll also use word processing programs for desktop publishing. The text produced by the word processor can be edited, rewritten and then "dumped" into the laid-out page produced by the desktop publishing software. Charts and spreadsheets can also be imported into your final product.

Although there are many desktop publishing programs, two of the most common are Aldus PageMaker (Fig. 9-3) and Ventura Publisher. Each allows you to lay out columns, position graphics, produce various fonts, headlines, other design elements. The programs typically function by providing the user with a grid. The grid can be adjusted to accommodate columns and photos, and the text can then be integrated into the grid. Most desktop publishing programs allow you to produce several typefaces; vary the size of the type; kern type, that is, adjust the spaces between letters to improve appearance; and wrap the text around graphics and photos.

Fig. 9-3. Aldus PageMaker software and its user manual.

The most influential change in desktop publishing software has been the development of the capability of producing an image on screen that is identical to what will be printed. This is known as "what you see is what you get" software, abbreviated WYSIWYG and pronounced "wizzywig."

WYSIWYG software allows the user to play with the layout, rearrange elements, and experiment until the presentation is exactly right. Thus, you can electronically accomplish what formerly had to be done by manually cutting and pasting. Incidentally, optical scanners can take the process one step further; they electronically reproduce an image from a printed page and translate it into the digital format used by the computer. Thus, you can transfer many images, including your company letterhead and logo, directly into the computer's desktop publishing program.

Much of the new generation of word processing software has some desktop publishing capabilities, but do not have the degree of WYSIWYG interactivity as true page layout programs. On the other hand, page layout software, although it allows for some adjustments and corrections, does not have the editing capabilities of word processing software.

Printers

One key to the production of a desktop-published piece is the printer; usually, a *laser printer* (Fig. 9-4) is utilized. A laser printer uses a highly amplified and tightly focused beam of laser light to produce an image which has very high resolution. High resolution means that the dots that make up the image are so close together as to be virtually undetectable.

To make this a bit more understandable, consider the stippled look produced by the early generation of dot-matrix printers; they produced that stippling effect

156 Chapter 9 Desktop Publishing

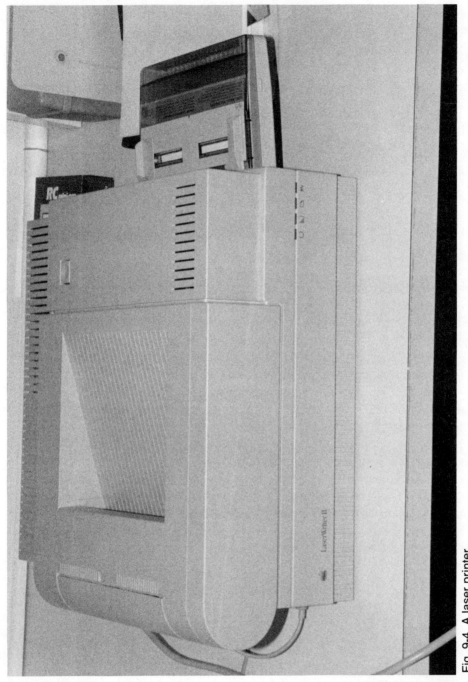

Fig. 9-4. A laser printer.

because resolution was low, usually on the order of 60 dots per inch or so. But laser printers produce images with resolutions upwards of 300 dots per inch. While not identical to a professional-quality phototypesetter, which has a typical resolution of 1000 to 5000 dots per inch, the image can be comparable.

In addition to resolution, laser printers are very fast. However, a complex graphic can still take several minutes to reproduce.

One particular strength of a laser printer is its ability to create various fonts. Some printers store font information internally, and much of the information is translated to the printed page by a special type of page processing software stored in the printer; an example of printed processing software is called *PostScript*. Another popular type of printer-based software is known as *Bitstream Fontware*. You'll need such printer-based page processing capabilities to produce highly complex publications utilizing a wide variety of fonts and graphics.

However, some relatively inexpensive printers, without PostScript capability, can produce good results. The Hewlett-Packard DeskJet, which does not use a laser but instead produces an image by spraying a jet of ink onto the page, sells for under a thousand dollars and produces a very crisp image. At the time of this writing, PostScript compatible printers generally cost upwards of $3,000 (sometimes significantly upwards).

You do have an alternative: Your discs can be sent to a print shop. Many printers now can convert the page-making output on a personal computer disc into true phototypesetting. Some services even operate by phone: you sent your material by *modem*—a modulator-demodulator, which translates computer code into a form which can be transmitted over phone lines—and the typesetting shop mails you back the printed page.

GRAPHIC DESIGN WITH DESKTOP PUBLISHING

As mentioned in the introduction to this chapter, desktop publishing hardware and software do not automatically produce a well-designed publication. In fact, the availability of so many options often results in a more poorly-designed piece than would have been produced by hand layouts sent to a regular print shop.

Good design is still in the eye, and the principles of graphic design detailed in chapter 8 will hold true for desktop publishing. For example, computer-generated publications still usually look best with sans-serif headlines and serif type. And regardless of the technical method of layout, readers still like to see the page "anchored" at the corners.

However, there are some special design points which relate generally to desktop publishing, and specifically the type of publishing you might be doing in a public relations capacity. Among those recommendations:

- Do not mix too many typefaces. The availability of many fonts prompts

some users to produce work that looks like a ransom note. Avoid this temptation.
- Allow enough white space. The convenience of being able to "pour" text into columns sometimes results in a jam-packed layout which is forbidding to the eye. Leave generous space between columns.
- Utilize the capabilities of desktop publishing to visually break up the text. Frequently, inexperienced users of page layout software do not completely understand the difference between a typed page and a typeset page. A typeset page, in addition to having proportionally spaced type, uses visual cues such as headlines and subheads to draw the reader into the text. These make a document much more inviting to the reader. Desktop publishers also use what are called pull-quotes in the publishing trade; a pull-quote is an excerpt from the text reprinted as a headline within the text, often bordered by graphic lines.
- Introduce contrast into the page. Bold lines and boxes are good ways to invoke visual contrast.
- When laying out your document, utilize the capabilities of your pagemaking software to view facing pages side-by-side. A page which looks good on its own can "fight" a facing page—and you have no other way to judge this other than viewing the facing pages on your monitor and making whatever adjustments are needed.

USING DESKTOP PUBLISHING IN PUBLIC RELATIONS

You'll find many applications for desktop publishing in fulfilling the goals of public relations, but remember that publishing is generally not a goal in itself. In other words, don't invest $10,000—a typical investment for equipment for reasonable capabilities—just for the sake of putting out a newsletter. First, honestly assess whether you need a newsletter, whether a newsletter will accomplish your public relations goals. If so, then consider whether desktop publishing is the best option.

Secondly, do not assume that desktop publishing is always a cheaper alternative than standard printing. For one thing, desktop publishing only produces the layouts, the eventual publication will still have to be printed, that is, reproduced in quantity, by traditional means.

Occasional production of a newsletter will usually not justify the cost of a desktop system. Also, don't forget that the time needed to master the system must be computed as a cost outlay, too. For example, a secretary in your organization may be able to organize an envelop full of articles and photos for the company newsletter and ship them to the printer in an afternoon; the printer might charge about two hundred dollars for the layout and mechanicals.

However, should you elect to use a desktop system, that secretary might need a full three weeks of training to master even the basics of the system. At $300 a week, that's a substantial investment. Then, the secretary will have to devote an increased amount of hours per week to the layout of the newsletter—if, indeed, he or she is capable of doing the work in the first place.

With this initial note of caution in mind, it should be stressed that there are some excellent uses for desktop publishing in PR. Here are some options presented from the standpoint of their worth and efficiency for an organization's PR.

Newsletters

If your organization regularly publishes a newsletter, and if there is a compelling reason that the newsletter look highly polished, then desktop publishing might be an excellent option—and a highly cost-efficient option over the long run. Figure 9-5 shows a simple newsletter produced by desktop publishing equipment.

Should you elect to go desktop, be sure to keep a consistent style throughout the newsletter. Make sure facing pages don't fight each other.

Desktop publishing is particularly valuable for newsletter publication because changes can be made right up to the final deadline.

Advertising

You can save quite a bit on advertising layout if you can use your pagemaking software and paint software to create your own ads. This is not a particularly viable option for those who need to design complex or highly artistic graphic presentations, but for small, simple ads, desktop publishing can work out quite well.

Flyers and Brochures

Desktop publishing is an excellent option if your PR efforts require composition of one-page flyers (Fig. 9-6). Varying type sizes and some simple graphics can accomplish striking effects.

Brochures can present problems. Desktop publishing equipment does not produce full-color graphics, at least not graphics of high quality, so you'll be limited as to what you can produce. But if your brochure needs are primarily black and white, the desktop option works well (Fig. 9-7).

Catalogs

Desktop publishing really shines in this application. If you produce listings and/or product information that needs to be regularly updated, you can save a great deal of money by going desktop. Investing in a scanner can be a cost-effective option if you need to insert many pictures into the brochure.

The Trout Gallery Newsletter

Editor, Carolyn Ruff   December 1988, Vol. 1, No. 1

From the director's chair

Now in its sixth year, the Trout Gallery has become a close link between Dickinson College and the Carlisle/Harrisburg community. As the fine arts museum for the area, the gallery sponsors exhibitions and public programs to enhance understanding and appreciation of the arts in our community. To underscore this, we note that as many area residents visit the gallery as Dickinson students, faculty, and staff. Last year's visits totaled over 6,800.

Since 1986, gallery/community activities have been supported by the Institute of Museum Services, a federal agency supporting the nation's museums, and private donations from individuals and area organizations. We are truly gratified by the response of the community to the gallery and look forward to our continued work together to make Carlisle and greater Harrisburg a richer place to live.

This inaugural newsletter is being distributed to area school teachers, senior citizen homes' social directors, scout leaders, after-school program directors, and home study supervisors. We hope this will be a valuable way to keep all of you informed about our offerings and activities in the months ahead.

Dr. David Robertson

Posed Unspoken tour

Tour groups scheduled during the month of December have the opportunity to meet the artist, Jeremy Jernegan, if we can capture him from his busy schedule.

Jeremy is teaching ceramics, photography, and sculpture this year at Dickinson College. He is replacing Barbara Diduk who is on sabbatical leave.

The gallery has prepared a worksheet for each student to use to compare sculpture, paintings, portraits, and lettering used in Jeremy Jernegan's art works with art works from Dickinson's permanent collection in the lower gallery. The Jernegan works also are compared with other examples of abstract art. A discussion of architectural form follows completion of the worksheet.

With tour groups of younger children, we select one child to pose while the class sketches that child's pose on paper.

Terms studied: Pose, sculpture, abstract, carving, modeling, constructive, form, shape, architecture, medium.

Fig. 9-5. A newsletter produced on desktop publishing equipment. In this case the desktop system was used to design and lay out the newsletter. Then the disk was sent to a typesetter where the type was set into a page layout for printing.

Stationery and Forms

Desktop publishing equipment can easily produce a variety of forms, letterheads, and even envelope designs. A good application for a public relations function might be the production of a special news release letterhead, or the distribution of an attractively laid-out calendar of events.

<u>**NEWS ADVISORY**</u>

THE DICKINSON COLLEGE NEWS NETWORK

will present a special four-part series on

"Labor Racketeering and Other Organized Crime"
Interviews with investigative experts who lectured at the
Pennsylvania Crime Commission's annual seminar
held at Dickinson College earlier this month

June 27-30

Monday, June 27
G. Alan Bailey
Deputy Executive Director of the Pennsylvania Crime Commission

Tuesday, June 28
Ronald Goldstock
Director of the New York State Organized Crime Task Force

Wednesday, June 29
Edwin Stier
First court-appointed trustee to oversee a union local

Thursday, June 30
Michael Goldsmith
Professor of law at Brigham Young Law School

To record stories and actualities for on-air use
call toll free in Pennsylvania
1-800-422-7279

For more information contact Nancy Freiberg at 717-245-1289

Fig. 9-6. A flyer produced on a desktop publishing system.

One warning: Don't attempt to typeset press releases. Print them in standard, unjustified type, double-spaced. Editors will react negatively to a news release format which they have difficulty editing.

But you can make your press release stationery distinctive. Try, for example, a reversed line at the top—a black line with the words PRESS RELEASE spelled out in white.

DICKINSON
Men's Basketball

Fig. 9-7. This brochure was assembled using desktop publishing equipment.

Business Correspondence

In combination with your word processing software, you can generate striking direct mail pieces and other business correspondence. Most high-quality word processing software packages have a *merge* feature, which allows you to print out a standard letter while automatically inserting selected information (name, address, and other personalized information) into the text of the letter.

This capability, combined with a fast automatic-feed printer, can produce a sizable mailing in short time.

A final note: Desktop publishing equipment and software is a sizable investment. To complicate matters, the technology is also in constant transition, so today's prices may be substantially reduced in the near future and the equipment you buy next week could be rather old-fashioned by next year.

However, people experienced with computers know that the "wait and see" attitude can sometimes be counterproductive. Many individuals and organizations have fallen behind the times and the competition because they continually waited "for the technology to sort itself out," or for "the prices to bottom out."

Whether you wish to invest now or wait for the inevitable improvements and price reductions is, of course, a personal choice. But even if the equipment you buy today is obsolete in five years—a very real possibility—don't forget that you'll get five years' use out of it. And if you do wait for five years, the equipment you buy then will probably be outmoded in another five years.

Such is the problem—and the promise—of computer technology.

10

Fund Raising

MONEY DOESN'T MAKE YOU HAPPY, AS PLAYWRIGHT SEAN O'CASEY NOTED, BUT it quiets the nerves. There's simply no way to get along without at least some money, and the responsibility for raising it might someday fall to you.

The public relations person is sometimes called upon to be in charge of fund raising. More often, a *development officer* will have the fund-raising responsibility. In some organizations, the development officer is in charge of PR. Even if the PR person is not directly responsible for the fund-raising operation, he or she will be in charge of communicating a positive enough image of an organization to convince people that they should support it by contributions.

The fund-raising function is almost always limited to nonprofit institutions. At a commercial enterprise, generating income is not the specialized area, but rather the primary goal of the entire organization. It's done through sales of products and services. Public Relations play a role by publicizing products and services.

A non profit organization might not be able to support itself from direct revenue. This is when fund raising plays an important role. The PR person will support the effort by generating publicity and goodwill, and might also be expected to help with the fund-raising effort. Regardless of which function you're called upon to fulfill, you'll need to know the nuts and bolts of the fund-raising operation.

GETTING STARTED

Many people who have little or no experience in fund raising find that the thought of going out and asking for money brings on a fair degree of anxiety. But successful fund raisers will quickly point out that fund raising can be exciting and rewarding.

Experts recommend a method of getting started that is somewhat akin to starting a session of swimming in cool waters: Force yourself into it. Have your boss come up with a dollar figure and a deadline when he expects to see real dollars in hand. Now, you'll have a real incentive to get moving.

ORGANIZING

Large charitable organizations have developed complex organizational structures for fund raising. This kind of effort involves promotion and publicity, setting goals, giving staff assignments, and recruiting volunteers. Following the initial rudiments of organization, leading donors are sought out. On a more modest level, your planning needs to include many of the above considerations.

Goals

At the outset of your fund-raising efforts, you should have a goal to work toward. Sometimes you—as the person in charge of fund raising—will set goals. At other times the goal is set for you.

Try and have at least some involvement in setting the goal. You are the person who will be out there on the front line. You are the one in the best position to know whether a goal is realistic. If a goal is set too high, you stand a good chance of losing face if the goal isn't met—regardless of the reason. If the goal is too low, you won't be getting the maximum return from your efforts.

But won't that let you go way over the goal and look like a super fund raiser? Not necessarily, because once your campaign reaches its goal you'll be amazed at how quickly the donations stop coming in. One community chest effort we're aware of came to a screeching halt just a few thousand dollars short of its $100,000 goal when the local paper announced that the goal would easily be reached in a few days. Try for a realistic and reachable goal for your fund-raising campaign.

Volunteers

Most fund-raising efforts make use of volunteers to actually solicit the gifts. Unfortunately, working with volunteers is not always an easy task. The key to working with volunteers is to recruit the best ones possible, and then work carefully to get them involved in the spirit of your efforts. You might want to put together some basic information on the uses of the money being raised or on the people who will be helped by your organization. This will be of obvious benefit to the volunteer who is helping to raise funds. It's also important to supply volunteers with information on how to get larger gifts and how to communicate properly with people being solicited.

Ideally, you should have training sessions for volunteers. One important function of the training session is to instill enthusiasm. Volunteers will be much more aggressive and successful if they feel personally excited about what's going on in the organization.

Training sessions can also be used for simulations. Stage a mock solicitation using experienced fund raisers. By showing your volunteers how to deal with various situations, you'll enhance their chances for success and make them eager to try out some of the techniques for themselves.

There are, however, some problems involved with working with volunteers. One pitfall is the overeager, overbearing boor whom you would rather not send out to meet the public. The only concrete advice we can offer in this instance is to find a way to rechannel the enthusiasm of such people in a way that will keep them away from the public.

Perhaps such a person could be placed in an administrative position, keeping watch of results, or possibly sending out thank-you letters. In some cases, you'll have to bit the bullet and live with the eager-beaver type, hoping that he or she doesn't turn off too many people.

Perhaps you'll have to repair the damage after the fact. Figure 10-1 shows an attempt to set a donor straight after an "attack" by an overenthusiastic volunteer.

```
Dear

     Thank you for your November 14 letter regarding our phonathon
call and pledge form.  We sincerely appreciate knowing about the
problem!

     My purpose in writing is to apologize for the way the call and
the pledge form were handled.  We instruct our callers to ask for a
specific commitment, preferably with an increase.  We know that there
are many alumni and parents who, when called, cannot commit to a
specific amount for a variety of very understandable reasons.

     Perhaps our "prompting" of our callers left them (or at least one
of them) a bit over zealous.  Regardless, there is no reason to change
your preference for an unspecified amount to a specific pledge!  It is
especially embarrassing to have it happen two years in a row!

     Please accept our apologies!  As you requested, I have enclosed a
new pledge form with the amount left unspecified.

     Thank you for your concern.
                                              Sincerely,
```

Fig. 10-1. A letter of apology to soothe a donor after the donor has been approached by an overenthusiastic volunteer.

HOW TO REACH DONORS

Once your volunteers are in place and you have identified who you will be going after for money, you'll have to decide how to make the pitch.

There are several tried and true methods of reaching donors. Your choice of methods will depend on the time available, the number of volunteers, and the type of donors you are attempting to reach.

Mail

Mailing fund-raising appeals is an effective way to reach a large number of potential donors. When you're making an appeal to a whole community or to a large national membership, mail might be your best bet.

Your mailing piece should be appealing in appearance without seeming to be extravagant. Gold leaf printing on embossed paper could lead people to think that you're spending all the money you raise on your publications. On the other hand, you don't want a tacky and cheap-looking brochure. Experienced fund raisers know that donors are less likely to give money to an organization that appears to be in poor health.

Use the principles of good design and good writing discussed in chapter 2 and chapter 8. The brochure must tell your story and be visually appealing. Make your message clear and easy to understand. If you use photos, they should be striking, and they must relate directly to the theme of your copy. Keep the amount of copy to a minimum, and try to come up with a simple, effective lead or heading that clearly states your theme.

One of the most important things to include in a mailing piece is a mechanism to make it easy for your donor to make a gift. Depending on the design of your piece, you might want to enclose a *business reply envelope*, commonly called a BRE, with a place to fill in information. See Figs. 10-2 and 10-3.

Another method is to attach a *tear-off card* with which to make a pledge to be paid later. Other options include a toll-free number for a donor to call to make a pledge. If you have a toll-free number, be sure to have someone on hand to take the call day or night.

Phone

Phonathons are increasingly used as effective ways to raise money. Many colleges use this approach, and some of them have come to depend upon the phonathon as the sole means of reaching donors.

The advantage of the telephone approach is that the fund-raising message is assured of reaching its target. In effect, the donor is put on the spot, and it is difficult for him or her to put off a decision. If your callers are skillful, the donor

168   CHAPTER 10   FUND RAISING

THE DICKINSON FUND
A Million Dollar Milestone

BUSINESS REPLY MAIL
FIRST CLASS   PERMIT NO. 1   CARLISLE, PA
POSTAGE WILL BE PAID BY ADDRESSEE

NO POSTAGE
NECESSARY
IF MAILED
IN THE
UNITED STATES

THE DICKINSON FUND

Dickinson College

Carlisle, PA 17013-9984

Fig. 10-2. The front view of a business reply envelope.

Information about myself/family/classmates for publication in class notes
_____
_____
_____

Other information _____
Employer _____
Address _____
Telephone _____   Please make check payable to Dickinson College.
Job Title _____   Gifts are tax deductible.
Does your company have a matching gift plan?   ☐ Yes   ☐ No
Please enclose matching gift form, or for more details and forms, check with your company representative or personnel office.

PLEASE FILL OUT THE FOLLOWING INFORMATION:

Name _____   I/We enclose _____ .
Address _____   Please send me a reminder in ☐ December ☐ March ☐ June*
City _____ State _____ Zip _____   Credit this gift to:
☐ Check here if new address. Phone No. _____   ☐ My Class _____ ☐ Spouse's Class _____
My/our total pledge is $ _____   ☐ Friends of Dickinson
With my gift, I am pleased to become a member of the following   ☐ The Parents Fund _____
gift club: (name of child)   (class year)
          _____ Presidents Associates ($5,000+)   ☐ I would like to become involved in the Class Agent program
          _____ John Dickinson Society ($1,000)   Please send me information on planning a gift to Dickinson through:
          _____ Benjamin Rush Associates ($500-$999)   ☐ Bequests   ☐ Pooled Income Funds
          _____ Charles Nisbet Friends ($250-$499)   ☐ Annuities   ☐ Life Insurance
          _____ Gilbert Malcolm Fellows ($100-$249)   ☐ Unitrusts   ☐ Real Estate
          _____ Red & White Club (Under $100)

*__THE DICKINSON FUND FISCAL YEAR IS JULY 1 - JUNE 30.__

Fig. 10-3. The back view of a business reply envelope.

gets very few chances to refuse to contribute. The caller can deal with objections individually and tailor his approach to the individual donor.

The key to success in telethons is having well-trained callers. Training sessions can quickly turn raw recruits into enthusiastic and effective solicitors if, of course, the training is done properly.

Some organizations find it worthwhile to pay callers. Some use a flat hourly rate and others provide additional incentive by paying callers a percentage of the money they collect. If you choose the percentage method, be sure to base it on the money *actually received*, rather than the amount pledged. Not all pledges made via the telephone are honored when it comes time to write the check.

One standard method of running phonathons is to have volunteers all together in a large room, with one phone for each caller. There is a brief but thorough training session. Next, everybody starts calling. Food and drink are provided, and running totals are kept for each caller. This keeps callers competitive among themselves for the size of pledges and the numbers of donors. At the end of the session, prizes are awarded to the top callers. The idea behind this setup is to provide an atmosphere of excitement and competition as the group tries to reach a goal.

Phonathons can be successful, but they can also be expensive to run. This is especially true if your donors are spread out around the country. And there is always a certain amount of so-called *shrinkage*; pledges are made but not paid. Overall, the telephone can bring excellent results. However, the personal visit is generally considered more effective.

The Personal Visit

Because it involves a large time commitment, the personal visit should be reserved for fairly large donors. If you're looking for a sizable donation from a foundation or corporation, an in-person visit is appropriate. If there's an individual in a position to make a large contribution to your organization, it usually pays to make a special approach to him or her. It lets that person feel important. The personal visit also allows you to effectively ask for a specific amount.

Keep in mind that you might want to call on a "prospect" more than once. This way you can gauge the initial response and prepare to make an effective solicitation during subsequent visits.

Another consideration in the personal visit is choosing the right person to make the approach. The chief executive officer of a firm or organization often makes a very effective solicitor. Other possibilities include sending celebrity volunteers or well-known public figures. If not overused or wasted on "small fish," these techniques can significantly magnify the amount of the gifts taken in during your campaign.

Other Considerations for Reaching Prospects

Your most effective fund-raising efforts will probably involve combinations of the various approaches. Phonathons will often be preceded by a mailing. You might elect to leave a brochure following a personal visit. Personal letters are a very effective means of getting your message across. Modern word processing equipment (Fig. 10-4) can make it possible to personalize letters to far more people than you could reach by more standard methods.

The best-run fund raising campaigns carefully integrate media coverage to keep the public aware of what's going on. Here, you can follow the principles of getting into the media as described in chapters 3, 4, and 5.

Fig. 10-4. Modern word processing equipment is becoming a virtual necessity if you do large mailings. Among other functions, it allows you to individualize form letters.

APPEALS: HOW TO ASK FOR MONEY

Asking for money really isn't as unpleasant as most people think. If you keep a few basic principles in mind, you'll find that you can be very effective, and even have some fun in the process. Also, there's a terrific feeling of satisfaction in getting a large donation after a measure of hard work to convince your prospect that your organization is worthy of support.

Start out by convincing yourself that anyone who is in a position to do so should make a donation to your organization. If you assume that you're merely collecting money that is due you, you won't feel any hesitation in persuading your prospect to meet his obligation.

To persuade your prospect to write a check or make a pledge, you need to learn some tricks of the trade. The techniques suggested below have been recommended by seasoned fund raisers with proven track records. These hints work for pros and newcomers alike.

Be Direct

Let the prospect know right away that you intend to ask for a donation. People easily see through long "softening up" ploys. They don't need to have their time wasted. If you are direct, they won't accuse you of being deceptive about your purpose.

Tell Donors How Their Money Will Be Used

If it costs $5 a day to feed a family in India, then a $100-donation can keep a family in food for 20 days. Another effective appeal that follows this strategy states that for pennies you could save the sight of a child in an underdeveloped nation. Think of the good you could do for even $10.

Be Prepared to Suggest an Amount

Try to be realistic. If the donor has a giving record, use the last gift as your guide. But never ask for the same amount. Always aim higher. If it's a small gift such as $10, ask the donor to double it. The important thing is to have an amount ready to suggest. Don't be shy about asking for it.

"Last year, you gave us a $75-donation. If you were to increase that to a $100 donation this year, it would put you in our century club, and would make a significant contribution toward reaching our $100,000 goal."

Break a Suggested Donation into Smaller Units

A once-a-year gift of $100 works out to about $2 a week. This can be equated to less than the cost of one lunch. Try to show a donor how a small, weekly or monthly contribution can translate into a sizable donation to your organization.

Don't Give Your Prospect a Chance to Say No

If you start a conversation with a question such as "Will you be able to make a donation to our organization this year?" the prospect just might say no. You'll then be in the difficult position of trying to get him to completely change his position.

Suppose you instead say "Our organization is trying to get people to pledge money to help disaster victims. Many people we've contacted are pledging 50 cents a week, which adds up to a $25 donation. I'd like to put you down for that amount if we could."

Now, you've shown how easy the gift can be, and explained how it will be used. If there's still resistance, you can whittle down the amount. And you've reduced the chance that you'll lose the prospect altogether.

Try to Get Agreement to a Specific Amount

Let's say you're on the phone with a prospect and he says: "OK, you've talked me into donating, but let me think about the amount and I'll send it in later."

This can lead to a very small donation or to an unfilled pledge. When the prospect says he'll donate, this is the time for you to suggest an amount. Lead into it with, "It would be very helpful if we could put you down for a specified pledge. If you decide later to change it, you're certainly free to do so." You're more likely to get the money if the donor sees it as a stated amount of money which he owes to your organization.

As you gain experience in fund raising, you'll perfect the techniques that will work for you. The important thing to keep in mind is to be personable and sincere when approaching potential donors. You'll want to get to know your prospects well. Nevertheless you should be careful to avoid flattery and false praise. If your organization deserves support, you'll get it best by keeping people informed and aware.

If your fund-raising efforts are well planned and well organized—and you keep your eyes and ears attuned to finding sources of funding—you'll find great rewards in the effort.

Remember this final point. In many cases, people have a specific amount of money that they either give to organizations or donate to the government in the form of taxes. Your job is to make sure your organization gets its share of what the government doesn't get.

11
Public Relations for the Entrepreneur

WHEN YOU START A BUSINESS FROM SCRATCH, YOUR RESOURCES ARE, IN MOST cases, already strained. This means two things from the standpoint of the entrepreneur who needs to handle his or her public relations:

1. There is little money to devote to the public relations effort.
2. There is no excess personpower to whom you can assign public relations duties.

In short, you'll probably wind up doing it yourself on a shoestring—and that, of course, is the nature of entrepreneurship.

COST-EFFECTIVE PUBLIC RELATIONS FOR THE ENTREPRENEUR

Business statisticians repeatedly cite the fact that undercapitalization is the major cause of small business failures. However, let's temper that warning with realism: if you had unlimited funds, why would you be starting a business in the first place?

As stated and stressed elsewhere, PR is not now and has never been free; it always carries a cost in terms of investment of time and money, and as an entrepreneur, your time and money will both be in short supply. However, there are things an entrepreneur can do to ensure that his or her PR effort is not going to burst a budget already strained at the seams.

For the entrepreneur, the most important aspect of PR is usually publicity. As stated elsewhere in this book, there are many other objectives of public relations, including generating good will and building an overall image. For the start-up venture though, some inexpensive exposure is probably the most immediate goal.

This is usually the most practical and beneficial approach if there is some novelty attached to the business, such as a new firm which delivers gift baskets. If so, you might receive attention in the local press just because your idea is different, unusual, and falls into the "man bites dog" category. In other cases, publicity is also extremely helpful to the start-up firm with a *highly defined customer base*. If you are starting a temporary-help agency which deals exclusively with computer operations, publicity targeted directly to local computer-using firms can be of enormous help.

Be aware that local news media generally are interested in publicizing new business. You are valuable to the news organization both as a source of news and a potential buyer of advertising.

Procedures for securing publicity and good public relations for the entrepreneur do not vary greatly from the general principles presented throughout this book. However, there are some points which can prove particularly valuable to the start-up business person. Consider these ideas:

- An open house. Invite the public and the press. This is an especially valuable tool for merchants.
- Use local celebrities or dignitaries to promote your service, product or establishment whenever feasible. An open house is a good opportunity to exploit the celebrity. The VIP attracts attention and gives an implied or actual endorsement to your firm. Local political figures are often quite willing to share your limelight.
- Novelty events. Florists' shops can attract great attention by producing unusual flower arrangements for Valentine's Day. Any sort of business can consider floating a balloon. A new ice cream store might have a cow-milking contest. (Be careful that you do not violate local ordinances and check with your insurance agent about possible liability issues involved with holding your particular event.)
- Educational events. Real estate agents have generated good publicity and lined up future customers through "how to buy a house" seminars. Financial planners have done the same with sessions on investment strategies.
- Direct mail. Direct mail lets you target the most likely customers for your business. At its most basic level, direct mail involves buying or renting a list of likely prospects. (Look in your Yellow Pages under "Mailing Lists"

or "Advertising—Direct Mail" for list brokers.) You can also orchestrate your own direct mail campaign. If your business appeals to people who live in a certain neighborhood, for instance, you can arrange mailing of pieces by street or by ZIP code.
- Endorsements by satisfied customers. These can take the form of word of mouth or testimonials in written advertising.
- Free service giveaways. This type of promotion is especially useful when your service is difficult to conceptualize or easily explain. A computer consultant, for example, might be best advised to provide a free day of service so that a business can find out how valuable his or her service is and just what, exactly, the consultant does.

MARKETING FOR THE ENTREPRENEUR

Marketing is typically not the direct function of a PR person, but when the person doing the PR is the person who owns the company, both functions obviously go hand in hand.

What is marketing, then, and how is it different from public relations? Marketing usually means the function of *executing all the factors that stimulate sales, including definition and exploitation of a market.* Public relations plays a part in the marketing effort, usually the role of cultivating the interest of those who are likely to buy and producing persuasive literature.

It is essential to be aware that marketing is much more than simply selling. It involves the process of educating yourself about such factors as the income levels of potential customers, their geographic locations and distributions, their ages and interests, and the overall economic conditions of your community.

In large corporate environments, the marketing function is supported by a large and sophisticated research operation. While this is well beyond the capabilities of most entrepreneurs, some types of research are feasible.

Marketing research for the entrepreneur is usually a seat-of-the-pants affair, but it's an accepted business truism that some research is better than none at all. Consider, for example, the case of a prospective entrepreneur who planned to open a sandwich shop but did no formal or informal research into the potential market. She *assumed* that a restaurant serving only sandwiches would thrive in the downtown location she had selected, which was adjacent to an urban college campus. However, an experienced marketing executive, in a casual conversation at a social event, pointed out to her that students at the local college were highly unlikely to take advantage of that service. The reasons being they had a prepaid dining plan and because they very rarely had any occasion to walk down that particular street, even though it was near the campus. Also, it was apparent from the character of the current business in that area—a men's clothing store, an appliance showroom, and an insurance agency—that the site was not heavily trafficked by college students. The very nature of free enterprise would indicate that if that area had been promising to those who sell services and products to college students, it would have been exploited by now, since the college is well over a century old.

This is the type of seat-of-the-pants reasoning you'll have to develop if you handle your own entrepreneurial marketing and PR efforts. Perhaps the most salient point is this: Don't, as our prospective sandwich shop owner did, assume that your business will be a success because there's no competition. No competition often equals no demand.

The competition/demand equation is one which experienced marketers often apply to research in entrepreneurial start-up operations. You can take advantage of other basic principles in your combined marketing, PR and advertising efforts.

Take Advantage of Existing Material

One fundamental mistake of the marketing novice is the continual attempt to reinvent the wheel. An incredibly large amount of marketing information already exists. Mailing lists are a good example. As mentioned above, you can purchase or rent lists of customers likely to take advantage of your service.

Are you, for instance, in the construction trade? A mailing list broker in your area is certain to have dozens of lists of people likely to take advantage of your service.

Some resources are even free. Your local chamber of commerce probably has an extensive list of local businesses; these lists are sometimes grouped by product or service, and usually contain the names of specific officers in the firms.

Take Advantage of Your Public Library

Many books have listings from which an entrepreneur might benefit. There are published books which list manufacturers, manufacturer's representatives, publishers, doctors, and so forth. City directories, which list residents by address and occupation, are also useful in some marketing situations. Ask your librarian for help; he or she will be glad to steer you in the right direction.

Do Your Own Research

It's surprising how often this is neglected. Some research is relatively simple to undertake. For example, one merchant was distressed about the fact that he didn't know the locations from which his customers came. (He was in a heavily-trafficked area surrounded by several towns.) A marketing/PR professional who overhead the lament offered a simple suggestion: keep track of the ZIP codes on the sales receipts. Telephone exchanges are also grouped by location; keep them, too.

Be Observant

As Yogi Berra said, you can observe a lot just by watching. While the syntax was fractured, the observation is very valid. Watch what your customers do and listen to what they say.

One merchant forced to stay late to finish some bookwork was astounded to notice the number of people who drove into his parking lot in the evening, saw that the store was closed, and left. The merchant had assumed—a dangerous and not very incisive assumption—that he could reach an adequate supply of housewives in his suburban town with nine-to-five operating hours. But he neglected to consider that many couples who lived in this well-to-do suburb were able to live there only because each spouse held down a job. They simply couldn't get to his store during normal working hours.

Listen to Your Customers

Do they complain that your operating hours are too complex? Two or three complaints might represent widespread sentiment. While your hours might seem clear to you, you simply cannot expect customers to memorize your intricate opening and closing times. Also, do customers say, "I came on Wednesday but you were out to lunch?" Pay attention, because the one or two complaints might be indicative of hundreds of customers who left in frustration over the course of a year or two.

Ask Your Customers Questions

"How did you find out about us?" is a good place to start. Be aware, though, that people often cannot or do not give reliable answers, which leads to the next point: Try to inject some scientific accuracy into your questions. People are often reluctant to confront you directly with negative information. That's a pretty well-known human trait. So instead of directly asking patrons, "How was our service?" provide an anonymous questionnaire.

Don't Ignore Negative Feedback

Remember that marketing information you gather can be negative as well as positive, and NEVER ignore the negative feedback because it's unpleasant in its implications. In point of fact, your research may eventually indicate that your business is not going to make it. If so, remember this marketing adage: Your first loss is usually your cheapest loss. Better to abandon a sure loser than to pour additional thousands of dollars and years of effort into a failing proposition.

Marketing and marketing research is an ongoing function. A fact of life in the business world is that markets change constantly; failing to keep up with these changes is one sure way to doom your business.

Keeping a pulse on these changes is not a simple matter, but you can help your cause by reading, researching, and taking advantage of the expertise of others. Don't be afraid to ask for advice. Don't always take it as gospel, but carefully consider what people say about changing conditions, and keep up with the trade literature on your particular type of operation.

ADVERTISING FOR THE ENTREPRENEUR

As discussed elsewhere, advertising is a specialty that is largely distinct from PR, although advertising and public relations are geared toward the same purpose.

For the entrepreneur, especially the sole proprietor of a business, it is critical to remember that advertising alone cannot sell your service or product. In many cases, the best that can be hoped for is an initial inquiry; this is particularly true of businesses which involve complex contractual or individually arranged services, such as consulting firms. No one is going to buy a consultant's service from an ad alone. A great deal of follow-up will be necessary after the initial inquiry.

Entrepreneurial businesses vary in nature, which is one reason why advertising is not a one-fits-all proposition. Carefully consider the best option for your particular operation. Here are some guidelines:

Consider Print Advertising

For most entrepreneurial ventures, print advertising is the basic and most effective medium. Print is accessible to even the smallest business. Print advertising includes large and small newspapers, as well as pamphlets, flyers, and newsletters.

For the entrepreneur, durability is a major advantage of print advertising, as compared to radio or TV. The ad can be saved and handled; perhaps a coupon can be included.

Aim for Likely Buyers

Effective print and broadcast advertising is a function of how many *potential customers* can be reached and persuaded. It is particularly important for the entrepreneur, who is operating with limited cash reserves to remember that the goal is to reach those *likely buyers*, not simply to reach as many people as possible. If you own a cigar store, for example, your advertising will be wasted on teenagers.

The type of people you reach is a function of the medium's *demographics*. Demographics are statistical representations of a population. The aforementioned cigar store owner would do well to advertise on a medium which reaches many middle-aged males, such as during a radio broadcast of a baseball game. The owner would then reach the right demographic.

Sales people for various media can provide you with highly detailed demographic breakdowns of readers, viewers, or listeners.

Count on Numbers

It's important to point out that numbers are important. In essence, you'll get what you pay for in terms of raw numbers, because ratings for readership, viewership or listenership are pretty reliable. Usually, your advertising budget will be broken down in CPM, or "cost per thousand." (M is the Roman number for thousand.)

Ask the advertising salesperson for breakdown of your costs in terms of CPM.

Don't Forget Quality

A lower CPM doesn't always equal a bargain, because advertising is a *qualitative* as well as a *quantitative* buy. The CPM on a classical music radio station will generally be much higher than the CPM for a rock station. The reason: Listeners to classical music typically have much more money to spend than do rock-loving teens. So the owner of a Mercedes-Benz dealership would find it a false economy indeed to advertise on the local rock station because that station offered a lower CPM.

Evaluate Media's Strengths and Weaknesses

So, having made the assumption that buying advertising is a qualitative as well as a quantitative purchase, you now can shape your plans in some general direction. The choice of advertising vehicle, obviously, varies with your business. But you can now make some intelligent choices by evaluating the relative strengths and weaknesses of the media which compete for your advertising dollar:

- Print advertising's strengths include the tangibility of the ad, and the fact that newspapers stay around the house for a while.
- Magazines capitalize on this factor even more strongly; they may be kept and referred to for weeks and months.

- Coupons are a unique strength for print advertising; they can bring in customers and, since coupons are always coded as to the publication from which they came, they will give you an indication of the relative effectiveness of your advertising.
- Weaknesses of print include relatively high cost. Some newspapers and many magazines have an extremely high CPM. In addition, most daily newspapers are published in the afternoon and are typically read at night. Merchants who want to bring in customers that day for a particular sale can find that factor a problem. Also, remember that once a publication is in print, that ad cannot be changed until the next edition. This can be a major problem if there is an error, for instance, in an ad placed in a monthly magazine.
- Television has great emotional impact. It can be the premier persuader. It also reaches large diverse audiences, and for some advertisers this can be an advantage.
- On the minus side, TV is very expensive. The CPM may be low, but because TV reaches so many people the *total* cost is bound to be high for almost any ad. And in addition to purchasing the air time, you'll have to pay for production of the commercial, which is also usually quite expensive.
- One other problem with TV: The large, diverse audience mentioned above may not be an advantage for an entrepreneur with a highly specific product or service. You may be able to find a location in the broadcast day which ideally suits you, during a particular show perhaps, but in general, TV is a better medium for a mass-market type of advertiser.
- Radio has the advantage of relative affordability and the specificity of the radio audience. Most radio stations are fairly narrowly targeted in terms of the formats (rock, country, classical, etc.) and offer precise demographic categories to advertisers. Should you sell a product or service of particular interest to teenagers, for example, a local radio station targeting that audience can be a superb vehicle.
- A negative aspect of radio is that it is the least tangible of all media. It can't be seen or touched. This means, from a practical standpoint, that repetition is necessary. A one-shot ad in a local newspaper offering a list of store specials can be very effective because the reader can scan the list several times, searching for appealing items, and even bring the list to the store. But such a commercial on radio would lose much of its impact. It would have to be repeated many times in order to have any real effect. So don't count on buying one or two radio ads for *any* product or service, because repetition is always necessary for effective radio advertising.

How does one sort through all these options? One approach is to hire an advertising agency. Agencies usually place advertising on a commission basis, meaning that the media will rebate fifteen percent of the advertising costs to the agency. In some cases, advertising agencies do not add to the buyer's advertising costs, but agencies will typically add on fees to prepare materials for small advertisers. This is generally an equitable arrangement, because an agency would certainly lose money by planning and creating advertising for an advertising purchase which totals only a few hundred or thousand dollars.

When selecting an agency, be sure you know up front which services will be billed to you and which ones won't.

A final note relating to public relations, marketing and advertising for the entrepreneur: Always remember that any outlay of time and money in these areas must be geared toward producing a *specific* result. While that sounds painfully obvious, it is not a factor always adequately appreciated by the newcomer to the business world. Never advertise because you feel you should. Advertise because you have identified a market and want to reach it. Don't spend time and effort on garnering publicity unless that publicity can translate into profits. If fame is your goal, go into show business; if you want to generate profits, strive for publicity which will motivate potential customers.

12

How Much Does All This Cost?

"OUCH! LOOK AT THIS BUDGET! I THOUGHT THIS PR STUFF WAS SUPPOSED TO BE free." That's the actual reaction of a department head who finally added up salaries, postage, and photographers' fees—and decided he might have been better off taking out an ad.

No, PR is not free. Services cost money and so does staffing. The attitude that PR is designed to get something for nothing will usually backfire because next to nothing is invested. As a result little is gained.

Now, PR doesn't have to cost a fortune, but it's essential that some sort of budget be drawn up in advance so that you're not working on the end of a shoestring. If there's only a certain amount of money to be had, adapt the PR program to the budget. Review chapter 1 to get your priorities in order.

MONEY-SAVING TIPS

If necessary, discard the more expensive PR options in favor of the most cost-efficient ones. You don't have to sacrifice quality if the budget is low. Instead, do a good job on less ambitious projects.

Black and White Instead of Color

The elaborate full-color brochure might be scrapped in favor of a well-constructed black and white one. A good black-and-white brochure will always look better than a cheaply done effort in color.

Don't Waste Releases

Mailing lists can be pared down by asking the media who are receiving your releases if they use them at all and if they want to stay on your mailing list. A stamped, self-addressed postcard to be returned to you is about the least expensive way to go about it. Mimeograph the brief questionnaire on the postcard and insert it with the release. It might look like this:

DEAR EDITOR:
WE ARE UPDATING OUR MAILING LIST. IT WOULD HELP US IF YOU COULD CHECK THE APPROPRIATE RESPONSES.
Do you want to stay on our mailing list?
    Yes _____ No _____
Do we send you too many releases, too few, or just enough?
    Too many ____ Too few ____ Right amount ____

You might also include a question about how frequently press releases are used, but it's been our experience that editors are reluctant to establish a "quota" for PR people.

Mail Photo Availability Sheets

If you like to include photos with your press releases, consider sending a photocopy of the photo, along with a number where editors can call if they want you to send the prints. Cornell University's News Bureau has been using this technique since 1980, and has generously agreed to share the concept with us (Fig. 12-1).

News Bureau Science Writer Roger Segelken says that aside from cost-saving advantages (approximately 3 cents a copy versus 75 cents for the least expensive photo print; 25 cents postage for mailing a folded news release in a standard correspondence envelope versus at least 71 cents to mail a photo and a cardboard reinforcement in an oversize envelope), this technique gives an indication of release use.

Segelken also notes that he feels the photo availability inserts help the decision-makers in the media by giving them a feel for the story—or at least for the visual possibilities. Many news media, including television-crews, have been assigned to provide exclusive coverage of the topic after their editors have seen the photo availability insert, instead of relying on nonexclusive photos or film that could be provided by Cornell.

184 CHAPTER 12 HOW MUCH DOES ALL THIS COST?

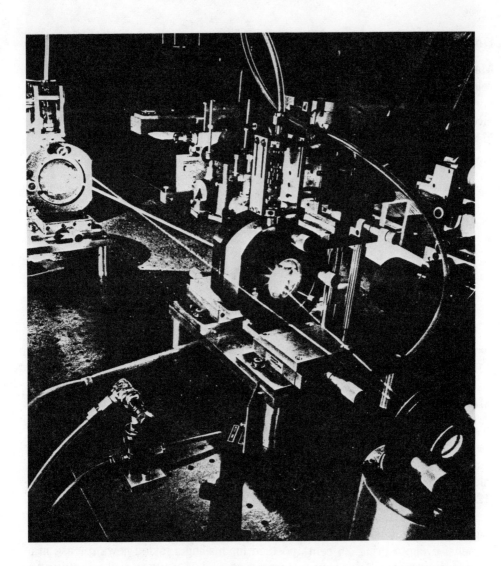

 Cornell University

News Bureau
110 Day Hall
Ithaca, N.Y. 14853

FEMTOSECOND INTERFEROMETRY. What appears to the human eye -- and to the camera --
to be a steady laser beam in a Clark Hall laboratory at Cornell University
is really a series of the shortest light pulses yet produced, an integral part
of a new technique called femtosecond interferometry. Photographs (color or
black-and-white) available from Cornell News Bureau, (607) 255-4206.

Fig. 12-1. A photo availability insert (courtesy Cornell News Bureau).

Photo Sizes

There was, at one time, a general editorial prejudice against 5-×-7-inch photos, but it appears to have faded significantly. The prints themselves are less expensive; remember that an 8-×-10-inch piece of photo paper is 80 square inches while a 5-×-7 piece is 35 square inches, which is less than half the size of an 8-×-10-inch photo.

By weighing your stationery and envelopes on your postal scale—an absolute requirement for a PR office—you can figure out a way to keep postage costs down by using 5 × 7s and nudging the weight of the release and photo down an ounce from the 8 × 10s. This can save you money on every envelope. Over a year or so, even small savings can really add up.

Every PR person has developed some favorite money-saving ideas. A membership in your local public relations society might be beneficial in picking up pointers on all aspects of PR, including money-saving ideas. The PR journals listed in chapter 1 offer some very practical money-saving tips; a subscription might easily pay for itself.

PRICES OF PRODUCTS AND SERVICES

One other way to save money is by shopping around for goods and services. Don't be afraid to send out bids on a project. To give you an idea of what you might wind up paying, we have prepared a very *general* guide. We've made an effort to get estimates from people familiar with prices in all parts of the nation, but this list will be far from definitive. It's only meant as a basic guide.

Technical restrictions in certain services can drastically increase costs. When a photographer tells you that a certain shot you want will cost double the standard rate, there probably is a good reason. Perhaps he knows that extra lighting or special processing will be involved. Don't be afraid to ask questions. Compromise on the more expensive options if that is possible.

Services

Photographer at Your Place. To bring in a photographer costs a minimum of between $60 and $80 per hour. Developing and printing costs will be extra. If you want to have some photos taken professionally, line up everybody and everything and hire the photographer for a whole day. It will be a much more efficient use of your funds.

Photo Lab Developing Film and Contact Sheets. Costs will be at least $5 for the film and $5 for the contact sheet. You get a better deal by shooting and developing 36-exposure rolls that almost double the number of photos for nowhere near double the price of a 20-exposure roll.

Developing Prints. You will usually wind up paying between $8 and $12 for an 8- × -10 print. If you have many prints made from the same negative, you'll get a price break, but there won't be a discount for many prints made from different negatives.

Work by a Graphic Artist. Usually the services of an artist cost upwards of $40 an hour. Having illustrations drawn will generally cost more.

Printing Brochures or Newsletters. The costs of printing brochures and newsletters depends on the size, paper, and layout. Giving approximate dollar figures would probably be misleading. Remember that color will usually cost three times as much as a comparable black-and-white publication, but a large number of photos will make the price of color printing jump dramatically. Separations must first be made and that can cost up to $350 per photo.

Hiring a Freelance Writer. Most freelance writers will ask upwards of $25 per hour. For some reason, clients who willingly pay hundreds of dollars for photos or artwork will balk at paying a writer $200 for ten hour's work. All we can say is that writing is very important. If you hire a freelancer you shouldn't scrimp.

Videotaping at Your Place. Many videotaping services will record on half-inch tape for about $150 for the first hour; you'll generally be given a price break after that. This is for videotaping for informational or instructional purposes, not for broadcast-quality television production. The costs of that are impossible to estimate because they depend on specific circumstances.

16-Track Studio Time. A sophisticated audio recording studio is where you can make complex productions for slide shows. The bottom-line costs will be about $75 per hour.

Products

35mm SLR Cameras. There's a wide difference between the list price of a camera and what you'll pay in a discount house or even a camera store. Almost any of the name-brand 35mm SLRs will do the job very well. Some will have individual features you'll find useful. A camera body—without lenses—will cost anywhere from about $175 to $500.

Lenses for 35mm Cameras. A standard lens, in the 50mm range, will usually come with the camera. If you break down the price, it will usually cost between $85 and $200. A 24mm lens might cost from $175 to $300. A 100mm telephoto lens might cost between $150 and $275 for a decent-quality model. You can certainly pay a lot more for any of the camera equipment listed, but super-quality equipment probably won't be necessary for your needs.

Tape Recorders. A cassette tape recorder is handy for recording radio actuality or simply dictating thoughts. The portable cassette players a PR person would use are not of the stereo variety. They are mono machines that might cost from $85 to $250.

Perhaps you will find it more useful to create your own chart. You can use the preceding headings as guidelines and include any products or services particularly important to your group.

13
National Media

YOU PROBABLY WON'T BE HAVING MUCH CONTACT WITH THE NATIONAL MEDIA. We're not trying to imply that beginning PR professionals don't have the ability to make national headlines. What we are saying, and what should be impressed on anyone who wants to make news, is that the national media have such a tremendous field to play that the odds will work against you.

This chapter touches lightly on the types of national media that are very difficult to break into. The more accessible types of national media receive a more detailed treatment. We'll give you an idea of the elements of news that are of national interest, and we'll discuss some hints on approaching these national outlets. First, however, let's define the ballpark.

TYPES OF NATIONAL MEDIA

Consumer Magazines. This category doesn't refer specifically to magazines such as *Consumer Reports*. The term refers to the kinds of publications consumers buy through the mail or off the rack. It covers an incredible variety of publications ranging from news magazines to teen magazines to hobby magazines.

Trade Publications. Trades form a large chunk of the magazine business. They aren't so well known as the magazines that appear on the newsstands. Trade publications are highly specialized and they appeal to professionals in various fields. Manufacturing, retailing, and education are three of the largest categories served by the trade press.

Wire Services. Services such as the Associated Press (AP) and United Press International (UPI) provide hard and soft news to newspapers, radio, and television. The AP and UPI also provide newscasts and news reports for radio stations.

Syndicates. Syndicates sell copy such as articles, columns, comic strips, and puzzles to all media, but most syndicated items appear in newspapers.

Broadcast and Cable Networks. Both radio and television have several networks that provide programming to local stations.

Major Newspapers. *USA Today* is a national newspaper. *The New York Times* and the *Washington Post* have such a great impact that they certainly can be considered part of the national media.

None of the above should be considered unapproachable. The national media want news, too, just as your local newspaper does. Unfortunately (from your standpoint), they have so much to choose from that it usually takes a great deal of effort—and hit-or-miss tries—to impress an editor who probably thinks he's "seen it all."

EFFORT VERSUS RESULTS

Is it worth it? That's a question that you'll have to decide. Yes, there is a great deal of prestige associated with coverage in the national media. For some organizations, national publicity will be invaluable. For others, it might not be worth the effort.

If you handle a product sold by mail order, there's no question that you'll want to pursue national publicity with zeal. But if your interests are primarily local or regional, national publicity might not provide what you need. Lest you think that we are belaboring a point, it should be pointed out that various public relations people of our acquaintance have become literally obsessed with getting an article in the *New York Times*. Their after-work hours are spent cultivating their "contacts," while their working day is centered around talking about the great "in" they have, and offering excuses for why they haven't made the *Times* yet.

On occasion, they do make the pages of that respected newspaper—often in a regional edition, toward the back. Clipping in hand, the PR person is likely to spend another week or two preparing reports about the coup.

Your time can be more wisely spent. If national exposure fits in with the overall goal of your PR program, devote an appropriate amount of time toward pursuing it. Be realistic in what you attempt, and keep in mind that the national media are "breakable" in various degrees of difficulty.

TOUGH AND EASY MARKETS

Coverage by the major TV networks is certainly on the most difficult end of the access scale. It is not a realistic goal for most people doing their own PR. There is very little time available in a network newscast. Sitting in the control room during a newscast (Fig. 13-1) gives a graphic picture of how the world's most significant news highlights are compressed into a few seconds of airtime.

Making the huge, nationally known newspapers is less difficult, but it is still a formidable task. If it makes you feel better, you can keep *The New York Times* on your mailing list, and someday a release might catch an editor's eye. Just don't bet the farm on it.

Syndicates and wire services see and reject an extraordinary amount of material daily. Nevertheless, either might be worth a try if you have a story of national interest. To study the needs and preferences of syndicates, simply pick up your local paper. An even better idea is to visit the public library and check some of the newspapers from out of town.

Also available at some libraries is the *Editor and Publisher Syndicate Directory*. It lists various syndicated columns and features handled by syndicates. If you can't find the book, it can be ordered from *Editor and Publisher*, 575 Lexington Ave., New York, NY 10022.

Fig. 13-1. TV network control room (courtesy Hartwick College Public Relations Office).

Another good reference to be found in almost all libraries and bookstores is the *Writer's Market*, published by Writer's Digest Books. *Writer's Market* has an informative listing of the various syndicates.

Wire services like hard, breaking news, but they use their share of soft news. In some ways, wire services function like syndicates, distributing feature material through the mail. But most of the wire service's function is to cover breaking news and feed it through transmission lines to the media.

Wire services also often offer regional reports. Wire services pick up a great deal of their material from local newspapers. Approaching the local papers is, in effect, the first step in trying to get something on a wire service.

CONSUMER AND TRADE MAGAZINES

Consumer magazines offer a more accessible avenue for a publicist. They eat up a great deal of material, and they always are on the lookout for interesting stories. Even though they fall into the general consumer category, many magazines are highly specialized. They aren't considered trade journals unless they contain material of a somewhat technical nature appealing to professionals. Some of the specialized consumer magazines deal with religion, home computing, fraternal organizations, antiques, aviation, and automobiles.

The trade press is also hungry for material, but of a more specialized variety. Remember, trade magazines are generally geared toward a profession. While a general-interest magazine about cars is a consumer publication, a magazine for car dealers is a trade publication.

If you can provide the appropriate type of specific information, you can crack an extremely profitable medium. If, for instance, the narrow market served by a particular trade journal consists of the kind of professionals who are typically your customers, a story in that journal will reach the exact group you want to reach.

It doesn't take extensive research to figure out which trade journals to approach. If you're involved in a specialized business, you might already be receiving several trade publications. Checking through your media guides will turn up other specialty publications that might be worth pursuing. The readership would be obvious; there's very little doubt as to who reads *Dental Management* or *Appliance Service News*.

Just because trade journals deal with technical areas, don't assume that they will accept amateurishly written material. Trade journals are among the best-written, best-edited publications. Please take a moment and read through the article reprinted from *Packaging Digest* (Fig. 13-2). Pay particular attention to the writing style and layout.

You probably can understand the thrust of the article even though you don't know a thing about packaging machines. This type of understandability is a plus

The third Precision labeler also has a rotary orienting mechanism that positions the containers by turning them up to 90 deg before entering the machine.

Meyer lists maximum container diameter of 4 in. and height of 7½ in. for the Type 5A. Maximum label size is 12½ in. long x 5 in. high. The machines require few change parts—just infeed screws and beaks and optional wipers and straighteners.

Slightly different needs were satisfied with Upjohn's purchase of its fourth Precision labeler earlier this year. The Model PPSF-D Type 5B was installed in April to serve the liquid products department. There it applies front, back and wraparound labels to round, oval and rectangular bottles. Most are glass, but again some plastic, in sizes ranging from 10 to 50 mL.

Operational advantages

Ed Doane, Meyer's Precision labeler product manager, explains how some of the equipment's operational features work to keep Upjohn's lines rolling. "A strong point of the machine is the combination of a changeable infeed screw, a clutch-brake-driven web path with double web-drive rollers and wipers that can be installed to apply a three-panel label."

According to Doane, the clutch-brake drive is extremely gentle to the web and is matched to the speed of other machine components by solid-state electronic controls. A single variable-speed potentiometer can adjust the entire machine.

Other adjustments required during changeover, including web table height and tilt, headgrip belt and wraparound position, are done via handwheels and require no tools.

Additionally, the web path has a simple layout to avoid entanglement, breakage and registration errors. "The label web path is nothing more than three sides of a rectangle, about as simple an arrangement as you can imagine," says Doane.

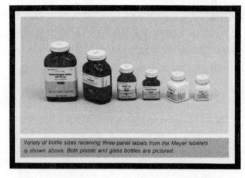

Variety of bottle sizes receiving three-panel labels from the Meyer labelers is shown above. Both plastic and glass bottles are pictured.

"We put further control on the web path by using a two-nip roller drive," he adds. These double rollers ensure that the web doesn't get out of time with the bottle, translating into reduced downtime to correct for registration problems.

It is obvious that versatility is important in Upjohn's labeling operations. Equally important is the ability to wipe down a three-panel label. "There are other types of pressure-sensitive labelers that can't apply a three-panel label," notes Benson.

Pharmaceutical packagers are increasingly looking to three-panel formats because of the growing amount of information required on each package. There has also been a trend towards the use of "space-saver" bottles that have a narrow front panel and therefore require more label area on the side panels.

Benson says the Precision's two-panel applications are also quite interesting because of "the unique way the leading edge of the bottle picks up the label."

Security measures

Another reason for Upjohn's switch to p-s labeling, aside from the production advantages, is security. "Because the pressure-sensitive labels come on a prepared roll, there's much less chance of getting a strange label than with a stack of labels," says Benson. And the Norwood hot-foil imprinter applies a crisp, readable lot number and expiration date to an uncoated section of the label.

The Precision labelers also sport an optional Lumat scanning device. This piece of equipment utilizes "smart" electronics to verify the presence of labels by detecting their luminescent ink. A small piston powered by an air cylinder rejects any unlabeled bottles.

Upjohn currently runs the four new machines on a single shift, with only occasional second-shift operation. The company is highly satisfied with both their current capability and future capacity. It also likes the minimal maintenance and the ease with which personnel can be trained to us them.

"We're quite pleased with the labelers," says Benson. "We also find them very cost-efficient because there's not much warm-up time required. You just throw a switch and they're practically ready to go. And there's no clean-up time needed either, so we've saved quite a bit on overtime."

More information is available from:
Geo. J. Meyer Mfg., div. of Figgie Intl., 4751 S. Meyer Pl., Cudahy, Wis. 53110.
Norwood Marking and Equipment Co. Inc., 2538 Wisconsin Ave., Downers Grove, Ill. 60515.

Fig. 13-2. A feature story in a trade journal (reprinted from *Packaging Digest* August 1982, Copyright 1982 by Delta Communications, Inc.).

for any article, even the most technical. Note that even though the article didn't define every term (assuming that readers of this specialized publication would know the basics), it did present the information in a logical, informative, manner.

Did you find that the writing style of the article was conversational? Did you notice that even though the article was about machines, *people* were featured—with liberal use of quotes? Were you also aware that the article had a beginning, middle, and end? That's what makes it a feature story. It's a good article in a high-quality magazine that reaches a perfect audience for the firm featured in the article.

In summary, don't ignore the trade press. If you work in a specialized field, it is often your easiest route to national exposure. But don't construe this as meaning that trade magazines will accept lower-quality material than consumer magazines.

APPROACHING MAGAZINES

Of all the national media, trade and consumer magazines will probably offer the best opportunity for someone doing their own public relations. How do you approach them? One way is to write a story and submit it yourself. Because magazines generally want feature stories, you'll want to become thoroughly familiar with the next chapter before attempting this. Including photos with the story will be helpful.

Before rolling a piece of paper into the typewriter, be aware that articles submitted blindly to magazines have a high mortality rate. Even general-interest magazines develop a specific *slant* appealing to a particular type of reader. If your article does not meet the editorial slant, it won't stand a chance.

Experienced magazine writers send a *query* first. A query is generally made by letter, and it explains the content and thrust of the proposed article. If the query letter catches the editor's eye, you might be given some guidance on what the editor would like to see in the finished product. The editor might agree to look at the article, but the editor will rarely make promises to someone he or she doesn't know.

There's another point you must consider before you submit an article; many magazines won't accept articles from public relations people. Generally, but not always, the larger consumer magazines will be least likely to accept a PR-generated article. Smaller consumer magazines and trade journals are more likely to accept articles written by a PR person. Even then the articles might be researched and extensively rewritten. Any magazine might, however, be interested in an outline supplied by the PR person. Such an outline could include quotes and facts.

Trade magazines are more likely to accept PR-written articles because their needs have quite a bit in common with what the PR person is willing and able to supply. Smaller consumer magazines might be more accommodating to PR people because they have smaller staffs and budgets and they appreciate the free material.

Publications do not generally pay for PR-generated material. It is usually considered unethical for someone paid to do public relations to receive payment for an article unless the publication is aware that it's a PR-generated piece and chooses to pay out of courtesy. We feel it is definitely unethical not to identify yourself as a public relations representative when submitting an article or querying a magazine.

Magazines, for various reasons, buy a great deal of material from free-lance writers. When a magazine assigns or buys a story, it is assumed that the writer does not have a vested interest. If the magazine accepts a piece supplied from a PR person, the editors take the information with the proverbial grain of salt. They do not assume that the PR is deceptive, but they simply realize that the PR person is employed or retained by the organization featured in the article.

This doesn't exclude PR-generated material from finding a home in magazines of any type. A magazine that doesn't print PR-written pieces might choose to follow up on a contact from a public relations person and assign a staff writer or free-lancer to cover the story. Contact between the editor and PR person can take the form of a press release, a fact sheet, or a telephone call.

You can opt to search out a free-lance writer to do the story and submit it to the magazine. If you supply materials, information, and photographs, the free-lancer might elect to seek out a magazine interested in the story. Alternately, you can pay the free-lancer yourself and submit the article as a PR-generated piece.

Locating free-lance writers is usually no harder than checking through the local Sunday newspapers. Many of the stories in the local supplements are written by free-lancers, and some newspapers identify the writers as free-lancers. You can call the writers directly, using the phone book, or try to contact them through the newspaper.

ELEMENTS OF A NATIONAL-INTEREST STORY

How do you decide whether the national media will be interested in a story concerning your group, firm, or organization? The answer isn't as simple as you might think.

The national media don't necessarily require a heart-stopping story. They require articles about topics that will have strong interest to a specific readership.

The same theory applies to consumer magazines and, to some extent, wire services and syndicates. Any story that has a strong interest to readers, viewers, or listeners will have a chance. This is especially true if it has an unusual slant. For example, some of the stories we have placed in national media were about:

- An "urban fossil hunter" who says fossils—even dinosaur footprints—can be found in building stones.
- A study that showed older people have as much ability to learn as younger folks.
- A professor of social work who says that myths about the elderly "con them out of" having sex.
- A poll that shows TV viewers worried more about censorship than violence on television programs.
- A nutrition specialist who pointed out that using iron cooking utensils can prevent an iron deficiency.
- A lawyer who contended that the elderly have an increasing need for legal protection and services, but are underrepresented.
- A special course for small-town police chiefs that is designed to help them cope better with matters such as presenting a budget to a town board or handling touchy public relations issues.
- A college course dealing with the business end of music, such as contracts and copyrighting.

The only common denominator to these stories is that they have something that makes the reader curious and willing to read on. All of the preceding stories required some digging and some creativity. Notice that most of the stories didn't deal with any really hard news.

Hard news, on a nationwide level, usually takes care of itself. If your organization has a major speaker, then your job as a public relations representative will involve letting the media know of the event and letting the speaker make the news. If your firm has a disastrous fire, it will make news whether you want it to or not.

If, like most PR people, you just don't have that much hard news, you'll have to generate some yourself. It can be done on the national, regional, or local level. The key to an interesting soft news idea is the angle. And the secret to presenting the idea is to learn how to write a feature story.

14

Feature News

A FEATURE STORY IS QUITE DIFFERENT FROM THE STANDARD PRESS RELEASE. quite simply, a feature story has a beginning, a middle, and an end. A press release is written in the standard inverse pyramid form. A feature story is what you are used to seeing in magazines. Feature stories almost always include anecdotes, that is, short narratives of an occurrence.

Feature stories are found in magazines and in newspapers. Some publications will accept feature stories from PR people, but some will not. Send a query letter before making a submission. Be aware that publications are always on the lookout for good feature items. Consider submitting an outline of the story or contact the editor and explain why you think you have a good idea for feature news.

THE STRUCTURE OF A FEATURE STORY

First, recognize how a feature story is constructed. Most, but not all, begin with an anecdote or quote.

> When Tom Martin, the department head, realized that jobs would have to be cut, he made an unusual decision. He fired himself.

—or—

> "I knew that one job would have to go," recalls Tom Martin, the department head, "but I also knew that no one in the department had any savings or outside income to fall back on. Except for me."

Most feature stories have a statement of theme that includes a sentence or two that tells what the story is all about. This statement of theme follows the opening quote or anecdote that has "hooked" the reader.

> Tom Martin knew that he could get by on his savings, and knew that he didn't want to go back to a job where he would have to fire people. He wanted to help people. So—four years ago at the age of 45—he entered medical school.

So now we know what the story is about: a businessman who doesn't like to fire people quite his job because he wanted to get into a helping profession. We also know that the rest of the story will deal with Tom's experience at medical school, the difficulties, if any, cause by his age, and so on. Because the theme statement mentioned that he entered medical school four years ago, we assume he is graduating, and expect that to be mentioned within the body of the story.

Unlike a straight news story, which is meant to be cut from the bottom and therefore gives information of decreasing significance as the story continues, the feature story has a definite ending—often a quote or anecdote.

> At his graduation, Dr. Tom Martin encountered a group of people he never expected to see standing in the reception line offering their congratulations.
>
> Dr. Tom Martin shook hands with each of the 25 employees in his old department.

See how it works? There is a beginning, a middle, and an end. If you were the public relations director of the medical school, you probably would have had little difficulty placing the story with various publications. You might have written the story completely (if you knew that the intended publication would consider a story from you). Or you could have prepared an outline that might look something like this:

- I: Four years ago, Tom Martin quit his job as a department head instead of firing someone else to satisfy budget cuts.

    Quote from Martin: "I knew that no one else in the department had any savings or outside income. Except for me."

- II: Martin entered medical school at age 45. He wanted to be in a helping profession, a job where he . . .

The outline doesn't have to be done in this form. Any sort of organized system will do, as long as it is constructed in the feature-story format. The following is an example of a published feature story along with explanations (in italics) of its structure.

The Robot Revolution Comes to WPI
by Carl Hausman
(Copyright 1982. Reprinted courtesy of the Worcester *Telegram*.)

Anecdotal opening . . . also, some description.

They don't look a thing like Artoo Deetoo, or any other mechanical personality in *Star Wars*.

Scene is set quickly.
Full names of organizations are used on first reference;
easier-to-read abbreviations are substituted later.

Instead, the industrial robots at Worcester Polytechnic Institute's Manufacturing Engineering Applications Center have an ungainly, ostrich-like quality. Their long-jointed arms (necks, perhaps) can reach forward and undertake a variety of tasks: assembly, welding, or operation of tools in stress failure tests. One recent demonstration at WPI involved a table-top robot pouring two cups of coffee—one black, one with sugar.

Now, the statement of theme;
what the story is all about.

The robots are on the WPI campus in a novel cooperative venture between the college and the Emhart Corporation of Farmington, Connecticut, a diversified firm, which has become known for its application of emerging technology to manufacturing operations.

"Its purpose" is the subheadline, added by the editor

Its Purpose

Staffed by WPI faculty and students along with Emhart engineers, the MEAC robotics laboratory is designed to develop applications of robots to specific Emhart plant operations, work out the problems and then get the system on to the Emhart line as quickly as possible. Meanwhile, WPI students get hands-on experience in the cutting edge of a new technology which, adherents claim, may be the key to revitalizing American industry.

First quote from expert; his full title is listed
Joint venture is described.

"The situation is advantageous to everyone," says Bennett E. Gordon, Jr. an associate professor of mechanical engineering at WPI and technical director of MEAC. "WPI gains access to expensive equipment it would be very difficult for us to obtain otherwise. Emhart benefits because they gain access to WPI facilities and faculty."

Note transition: "Because of the . . ."
refers directly to previous paragraph.

Because of the Emhart-WPI connection, Gordon says, "WPI is now one of the few institutions which offers hands-on experience in the field of industrial robotics."

Now, the story is given a more general, national scope. Relating your local story to major issues gives it more weight.

Its Time has Come

Robots in the labor force do, indeed, seem to be a solution whose time has come. A widening variety of manufacturers are now buying robots at unprecedented rates, and there's a growing attitude that American productivity is becoming a do-or-die issue.

A quote from another expert, directly commenting on theme of previous paragraph.

"I think industrial robotics is a great importance," contends Arthur Gerstenfeld, founder and co-director of MEAC and head of WPI's management department. "The whole question of improving productivity, of which industrial robotics is a part, is one of the most important factors in turning around the U.S. economy."

More major issues brought up. These show why the subject is important.

If there's ever been a doubt to the effectiveness of industrial robots, it has long since been dispelled by the Japanese. Japan is the worldwide leader in the use of robots, and has succeeded in applications of the devices to many types of manufacture. And, as if to rub American noses in the whole productivity issue, they do it largely with American robots and strategies.

Again, the quote serves as a transition, relating directly to the previous paragraph.

Japan's Success

"They read our textbooks," Gordon notes, "and much of their equipment was developed in the U.S." Gordon, who recently returned from a trip to Japan which involved an international colloquium on robotics and a tour of automated Japanese factories, points out that robots alone don't account for Japan's success.

More of the professor's qualifications are mentioned. Qualified interviewees give your story credence.

"There's a greater cooperative attitude among the technical and financial leaders in Japan, robots are generally accepted more easily, and there's a difference in management philosophy. Still, though, there's no reason why we can't implement the technology just as effectively. In fact, we should be capable of doing a better job, since much of the technology was developed in the United States. But if we don't implement this technology, we will become non-competitive with the Japanese."

Direction question livens up the piece, smooths transition to next topic: What can a robot do?

What exactly can a robot do to increase productivity? For one thing, it can be an assembly line's best worker, on its best day, 24 hours a day. It can handle routine assembly jobs without getting bored, or weld without being bothered by the heat and the flying sparks. And, in a very limited way, it can be taught to think.

Examples are important now. We're back to local issues, the crux of the article. National examples show why the college's experiments are important.

Senses Defective Part

Some robots, for example, can sense a defective part with their claws and toss it aside. The most advanced form of robot is programmed by computer, and can be readily reprogrammed to perform a different task. WPI is currently working on a project where a computer-aided design system, known as CAD, can be utilized to load a program automatically into the robot's memory. (Industrial robots are part of the computer-aided manufacture field, known as CAM; the common term used to designate automated design and manufacture integrated into one system is CAD/CAM.)

Interesting details, not really crucial to the piece

However, use of an industrial robot involves more than unpacking the crate and plugging it in. "After you've bought a robot, you have gotten only halfway to the point of having a functional system," Gordon explains. You still have to develop the computer program and the accessories that go into the system. With Emhart, for instance, we have to make sure that, after the robots leave here, they will integrate with other equipment in the plant."

Examples of projects at the college. Your stories should always include examples.

Testing Tools

An example of a WPI-Emhart robot project was a device to test Pop Riveter tools, which are made by Emhart. A robot called a PUMA 600 was programmed to operate the tool through thousands of cycles; this life-test will continue to the point of failure, which will be recorded and the robot automatically shut down.

Looking to the future is a common technique to begin wrapping up an article.

Future projects at the WPI robots lab include an arc-welding robot, scheduled to be delivered by the end of February. More advanced areas to be investigated by MEAC include voice input/output systems that will, in effect, allow the operator to talk to the robot and the robot to talk back. Gordon notes that in the future, an entire field of robotics will see an increasing emphasis on robots with advanced tactile devices, and even vision.

Philsophical issue also fits well into wrap-up

But where do humans fit into the scheme of future industry? "One of the myths about robots is that they will replace all humans," Gordon says. "Robots will certainly replace humans in hot, monotonous, dirty and dangerous jobs. But the result will be higher level jobs for workers, and an improvement in the quality of life."

Nice substantial quote for ending

Gerstenfeld concurs. "We really have no choice in the matter. It's pretty much the same situation as the original industrial revolution—we can either adapt or go backwards. But rather than putting people out of work, we can make the nation more competitive and, at the same time, create more jobs."

This story, by the way, was written at the suggestion of the college's public relations director, who knew that the local newspaper was interested in an article for a special section on engineering.

Feature stories don't have to be as long as the preceding example nor do they have to adhere to the formula. Most do, though, so it's probably a good idea to follow the set pattern at first.

News releases don't customarily follow the feature news format, but you can occasionally dress up your release with a featurish lead. Use this tactic only on soft news, not hard news. If you have any questions on the difference between the categories, refer to chapter 6.

Feature news can involve any number of topics. Product news can be handled in this manner; note how the Armstrong people use the feature format in product news (Fig. 14-1). Notice how the story shown in Fig. 14-1 has a beginning, middle, and end? That's the mark of the feature story.

The Armstrong story would be likely to appear in the home/lifestyle sections of Sunday newspapers. Try to identify the markets most likely to use your material and likely to reach the readers you want. Don't overlook weekly news-

ARMSTRONG WORLD INDUSTRIES, INC.   P.O. BOX 3001   LANCASTER, PENNSYLVANIA 17604   717/397-0611

FOR RELEASE: **ON RECEIPT**   CONTACT: Robert C. de Camara
Armstrong Press Services
Ext. 4752

HOW HIGH IS YOUR 'FLOORING I.Q.'?

(Part II)

Rotovinyl floors are comparatively flexible and lightweight and are suitable for do-it-yourself installation. Inlaid vinyl floors are not. The very heftiness of the inlaids makes them difficult for amateurs to work with.

Plus, rotovinyls, unlike inlaids which are made in 6-foot widths only, are available in 12-foot widths as well. In many cases, seaming--one of the more ticklish tasks for the amateur--is unnecessary.

One of the easiest installation methods for d-i-y'ers is known as Interflex and is relatively new. But the number of floors that can be installed this way is growing rapidly.

The advantage of Interflex is that it doesn't require spreading adhesive all over the surface to be refloored. Instead, you merely fasten down the new floor at the sides of the room and at seams.

Also, Interflex-installed floors can go down over old problem-floors that otherwise would have to be covered with plywood underlayment--an expensive and tedious extra step.

- MORE -

Fig. 14-1. A product news item formatted as a feature story.

- 2 -

Another welcome innovation is a Trim and Fit kit that overcomes the d-i-y'ers main concern about working with sheet-vinyl materials: the worry of not obtaining a good fit or of ruining the material.

For the first time, the Trim and Fit kit assembles all the elements needed to make a paper room-pattern, transfer the pattern to the flooring material, and cut the material to room size.

A no-wax surface may be had with either inlaid or rotovinyl floors. In fact, these days comparatively few sheet vinyl floors for use in homes don't have a no-wax surface.

But all no-wax surfaces are not alike. There are essentially two kinds: vinyl and another, even tougher surface that goes by various trade names such as Mirabond.

Both kinds protect the floor's pattern and color and both make floors easier to clean. But a vinyl no-wax floor (that is, one with a vinyl surface, as opposed to Mirabond) needs periodic applications of polish to maintain a high gloss.

On the other hand, a Mirabond no-wax floor will keep its "like new" look--without polishing--far longer than a vinyl no-wax floor. Eventually, even the extra-durabond Mirabond surface might lose some of its luster in areas of heavy traffic. If this should happen, a special floor finish is available to touch it up.

The tile picture is much more varied and interesting than it was just a few years ago.

Cork and rubber tile are no longer domestically manufactured and asphalt tile is made strictly to order in limited quantities for commercial use (mainly to replace damaged or worn tiles in older buildings).

- MORE -

Fig. 14-1. Continued.

- 3 -

Vinyl-asbestos tile is still widely sold but its popularity, nevertheless, has declined markedly since the advent of newer, better-looking and easier to maintain no-wax tiles.

Now, many of the same features found before only in sheet vinyls are available in tiles: attractive designs, no-wax convenience, spill- and stain-resistance.

Most tiles sold today for residential use are the type known as "self-adhering" or "self-sticking." These are the ones with the adhesive on the backing. So-called dryback tiles (without adhesive) are of interest mainly to builders of economy housing.

Self-adhering tiles are still probably the easiest of all floors for the do-it-yourselfer to install. All you do is remove a paper from the back of the tile to expose the adhesive, position the tile on the floor and press down. Most rooms are a half-day job, or less.

The first major advance in the recent tile revolution came with the introduction of no-wax tiles. Next came tiles with vastly improved designs that, for the first time, faithfully simulated the appearance of natural or handcrafted materials like brick and ceramics.

The latest development is "parquet" squares (12 by 12 inches) and planks (different sizes) that look like expensive hardwoods. These vinyl "parquets" and planks are self-adhering, no-wax, easy to clean and can go down in places you wouldn't dare put real wood (like basements). Plus, their hardy vinyl wear surface resists staining and water-spotting.

As you would expect, these new tiles, "parquets" and planks command a premium price. For example, it costs about $325 to do an average-size 9 by 12-foot room in the top-priced plank (if you install it yourself).

- MORE -

Fig. 14-1. Continued.

- 4 -

    Still, that's less than you'd spend to do the same room in the best grade of sheet vinyl, requiring professional installation.

    Finally, the floor you buy should come with a guarantee that covers the full cost of material and labor (if you paid for professional installation) for one year from the date of purchase. The guarantee should provide additional but lesser coverage for the second and third years.

    With a guaranteed brand-name product from a reputable local store, you can be pretty sure your flooring purchase will live up to expectations, especially since you've taken these few minutes to educate yourself on the subject. Good shopping isn't just luck.

# # #

Fig. 14-1. Continued.

papers that often use feature stories. They might be less reluctant to run a PR-generated feature.

To summarize, feature stories take a different form than straight hard news. Instead of the inverse pyramid, they have a beginning, middle, and end—and they use anecdotes. A feature story will usually be longer than a press release, but it doesn't have to be a specific length. Although newspapers use feature stories, the feature story format is what we're accustomed to seeing in magazines.

All the print media use feature stories, but some will not use PR-generated features. A call or query letter will determine this. A query also is used to determine if the publication is interested in a specific story. You should specify that you are doing PR for the group, organization, or firm when pitching the idea to the editor.

If a publication you want to reach does not use features from PR people, you can suggest an idea for a feature story. You can also submit an outline of the proposed story. Just make sure it fits the feature story type of organization.

Suggesting ideas to editors is often quite productive. They are looking for good ideas. Remember that having a writer do the story will save you a great deal of work. Although it's perfectly permissible to send out feature stories to a number of media—just like mailing out your standard press releases—it can often be more productive to call or write a letter, offering the story exclusively.

50 FEATURE IDEAS

You'll have to come up with some ideas before talking to an editor. Don't call and ask him to "do a feature on us." Have some ammunition, so you can say "We have a story with a very interesting slant here. Our new manufacturing technique involves lasers, which are used to . . ."

Feature ideas come in all shapes and sizes. All shown in the last chapter, seemingly insignificant items can make even national news if they have an angle that makes them different and arouses the reader's curiosity. Keep in mind that a feature idea will almost always be more tantalizing if there is a possibility of good photos to accompany the story.

The following 50 feature ideas won't all apply to your group, firm, or organization. Actually, none of them might, but they'll provide a springboard for you to start thinking of your own ideas. Some are purely of local interest. Some might not really reflect directly on your organization, but they will at least keep the company name in the news.

1. Interesting hobbies practiced by your personnel. It's a rare organization indeed that doesn't turn up a skydiver, musician, or karate expert (Fig. 14-2).
2. Unusual remodeling or refurbishing efforts done by your organization.
3. Special programs offered by your organization and interesting people who participate. An example is an annual ethnic food-cooking competition. If you don't have unusual programs, you can always invent one.
4. Advice from any expert in your organization relating to topics of public interest. Your comptroller might comment on personal investment, for instance.
5. How your organization makes special provisions for the handicapped.
6. Views of any of your employees who have lived in a nation that's currently making news.
7. A profile of someone in your organization who knows a famous person.
8. Technical specialists in your organization offering guidance to consumers buying high-tech products. A staff photographer, for example, might have some interesting comments on buying a camera.
9. Achievements of your organization members, especially in sports. You might find out a foreman was once a good professional fighter.
10. A significant and interesting segment of your organization such as a hospital burn ward. Approaching an editor with this idea will be far more productive than asking for a feature on the hospital. Does your hospital or volunteer group conduct mock disaster or emergency drills? They usually provide good photo opportunities and are a natural feature for the local paper (Fig. 14-3).

Fig. 14-2. Chris Dakas, a part-time karate teacher who has traveled to Okinawa several times to continue his studies, has been featured in local publications several times. His accomplishments reflect well on him and, by implication, on his employer, the city police department.

11. Someone in your organization who is undertaking an unusual project, such as a cross-country motorcycle trip.

12. People in your organization who perform unusual jobs, such as pilots or animal keepers in a lab.

13. Any interesting manufacturing process, and particularly those dealing with high-technology items such as computers or lasers.

14. Your firm's security director giving advice for homeowners on protection against burglars.

15. Anything dealing with personal health.

16. Unusual children of employees. Is an employee's daughter an Olympic-class skater?

17. A profile of your night-shift workers. This idea might spur an editor into doing a broad article on night-shift workers, including (of course) your firm.

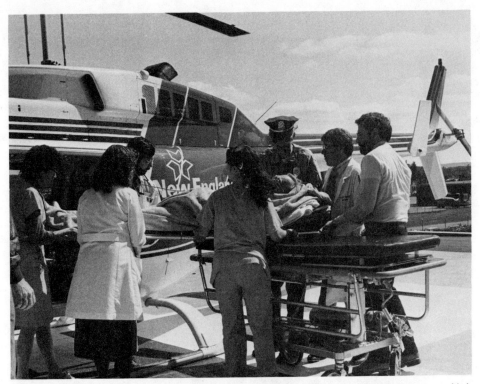

Fig. 14-3. Disaster and emergency drills are excellent photo opportunities (courtesy University of Massachusetts Medical Center Public Affairs Office).

18. A profile of someone who has worked in your organization for 40 years. What were things like when he or she started?
19. Someone in your organization who helps young people; a minister, perhaps, who heads a youth group.
20. A profile of a high-ranking woman in your organization and her views on women in the workplace.
21. Your chief fiscal officer commenting on why a recession is coming to an end or why it is not coming to an end.
22. Your safety director or a physical education instructor giving hints on summer or winter sports safety.
23. A personnel director commenting on career changes.
24. A museum gift-shop director offering some unusual Christmas gift ideas.
25. A profile on anyone in your organization who receives an honor, work-related or not.
26. A day in the life of your biggest VIP.

27. Any woman in your organization who lifts weights (you'd be surprised).
28. Energy-saving tips from the person responsible for your organization's energy-saving program.
29. How your organization deals with a downturn in the economy (valuable if you rely on contributions).
30. Unusual uses of computers in your organization. Does your political candidate keep his schedule on a computer? Does your museum have a computerized inventory?
31. A professor of English commenting on legal mumbo jumbo in contracts and consumer agreements.
32. The unusual history of your headquarters. Was the building once used in the Underground Railroad? Was it the city's first barber shop? Does it have any special architectural significance? See Fig. 14-4.
33. People in your organization who have made dramatic career changes.

Fig. 14-4. This interesting photo shows how a modern factory can work very efficiently in a century-old plant (courtesy Nypro, Inc.).

34. A CPR training program at your institution that will make it a "cardiac safe" environment. If you don't have such a program, you can start one. If may pay off in more than just good public relations.
35. The food service specialist in your organization explaining food cost-cutting measures.
36. Any unusual educational course offered by your organization.
37. Exercise or fitness programs offered within your organization (Fig. 14-5).
38. Interesting activities of retired members of your organization.
39. Recollections of veterans in your organization who witnessed famous battles. Pitch this well before Veterans Day.
40. Details of how your firm saves energy, fights pollution, etc.
41. A profile of someone in your organization who does extensive volunteer work.
42. A story on any interesting or unusual way your organization interacts with the neighborhood. Do neighbors bring snowed-in workers coffee? Do workers help in security surveillance in the neighborhood?
43. Unusual talents of people in your organization. Does your accounting manager have the lead in the local community theater?
44. Any employee in your organization who has overcome great obstacles such as a physical handicap.
45. Travels by members of your organization. This could be adapted—with your help—to a feature piece that a member of your organization sells to the local paper. Make sure to get the name of the organization logically worked into the story. This might not have any direct benefit, but it will get you some exposure.
46. Profiles of foreign visitors to your organization.
47. Anything happening at your firm or organization that appears to be part of a national trend.
48. Research at your organization. This is especially appropriate if it deals with energy or some other hot topic.
49. How your firm prevents injuries on the job.
50. Anything that relates to new methods of doing business: working at home, employees on a four-day week, firms that have employees vote on policy matters, etc.

Now start thinking on your own ideas. Perhaps your organization is so interesting that a story about it can stand alone. Most organizations need a little creativity to get their people and ideas before the public.

50 Feature Ideas 211

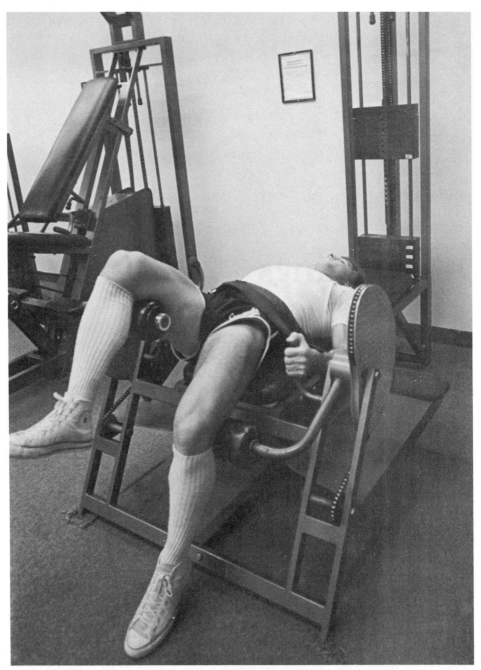

Fig. 14-5. Fitness training facilities often make interesting photos or feature articles (courtesy Holy Cross College Public Affairs Office).

15

Other Things You'll Need to Know

WE MIGHT SEEM A BIT PRESUMPTUOUS BY IMPLYING THAT ALL THE OTHER things you'll need to know to undertake a PR effort are condensed into this chapter. We're not trying to give that impression. What we do want to get across is that by reading the preceding chapters you should have picked up about all the basics needed to get started with a public relations campaign. Now, let's consider some of the other areas you might need to know about at some point.

SLIDE SHOWS

A slide presentation can be very effective, but all too often it's marred by the expectation that assembling a few transparencies and ad-libbing the narration is all that's required. This type of approach results in a slapdash effort that can do more harm than good.

The starting point in putting together a slide show is to establish what its purpose will be and what sort of message you want to communicate. Once that's defined, it is usually helpful to write a description of the show. This helps to crystallize your thinking and keeps things organized. Next, draw up a script. It's usually better to write the script before taking photos. That way you'll know exactly what photos you will need, and you will save effort and expensive film.

The simplest form of a slide show is a series of slides with a script. The script is read aloud (or used as a guide to ad-libbing) as the slides appear. A typical script might look like this:

Slide #1. Short of students in classroom. Narration: This is where it all begins . . . the classroom of the Acme Instructional Institute.

Slide #2. Closeup of student using equipment. Narration: What we're going to show you is the way in which our advanced program of hands-on, technical study can . . .

More sophisticated slide shows will involve producing an audio track on a cassette. Producing an audio track with music, narration, and other effects will require the use of highly complex mixing equipment, such as the 16-track studio shown in Fig. 15-1.

A prepared audio track will usually include synchronization tones that will automatically advance the slides for you. You'll need a special unit to play the tape and transmit the synchronization pulses to the slide projectors. If you go to the trouble of preparing an audio track, you might want to use two slide projectors. This will allow you to smoothly dissolve between the two images. To do that, you also will need a dissolve unit and a tape playback device such as those shown in Fig. 15-2.

Fig. 15-1. A control board in a 16-track recording studio.

214 CHAPTER 15 OTHER THINGS YOU'LL NEED TO KNOW

Fig. 15-2. A Wollensak AV-33 dissolve unit (left) and a Wollensak 3M 2851 visual sync tape recorder.

As far as the slide projectors are concerned, you might want to mount them on a rack similar to the one shown in Fig. 15-3. This aids in aiming the projectors and makes the setup easier.

Slide shows can become quite complex and expensive. The dissolve unit and tape playback unit shown in Fig. 15-2 costs about a thousand dollars, and the slide projectors will cost about $300 each. And we haven't included the cost of producing the show in that tally.

Another drawback to slide shows is that some people object to carting around the necessary equipment. One way around this is to use a self-contained unit that will show a one-projector program without the need for a screen. The Singer Caramate 3300 sound-slide projector, shown in Fig. 15-4, is quite popular. At approximately $500, it would be significantly smaller investment as well as a smaller load.

Another option becoming increasingly popular is to have the slide show transferred to video tape and played back through a video cassette recorder (VCR). The unit shown in Fig. 15-5 is a heavy-duty industrial model, and it sells for about $1500.

Home model VCRs have become increasingly popular and good quality units are widely available for between $250 and $500 (see Fig. 15-6).

Videotape playback capability is especially useful if you have available or plan to have available television programs for presentation. You can also elect to have the slide show transferred to filmstrip. An audio-visual production agency will often have the necessary equipment to do slide-to-video or slide-to-filmstrip transfers.

Fig. 15-3. Two Kodak Ektagraphic slide projectors mounted on a convenient stand.

The slide show, in any form, makes an excellent addition to a speech or presentation—if all goes as expected. A bungled slide show can truly prove embarrassing. If you are at all able, take an audio-visual technician along when you give the presentation. If you can't obtain the services of a technician, be sure to have some extra bulbs on hand. Also bring along extension cords and adapters to plug

216 CHAPTER 15 OTHER THINGS YOU'LL NEED TO KNOW

Fig. 15-4. A Singer Caramate 3300 sound-slide projector.

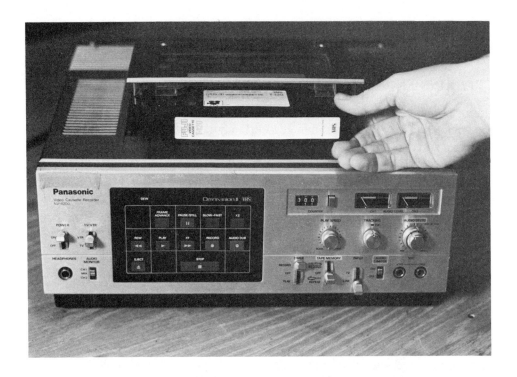

Figs. 15-5 and 15-6. Video cassette recorders.

a three-prong plug into a two-prong outlet. You'll never know what you'll encounter when you take the slide show on the road.

SPEAKING ENGAGEMENTS

Service organizations such as Rotary clubs and Kiwanis clubs are almost hungry for guest speakers and programs. It's certainly not too difficult to track down a member and find out if they'd be interested in your program.

You will find a slide show quite handy, and you also might want to have some other visual aids such as charts or posters. Don't attempt to read your speech word for word. The Public Speaking 101 technique of putting thoughts on index cards and ad-libbing is still just about the best method of putting together a speech. Keep your speech short. Definitely keep it within the guidelines given to you by the person running the meeting.

PROMOTIONAL GIMMICKS

Devices such as inscribed key holders or cigarette lighters might not be appropriate for some organizations; you'll have to decide that for yourself. These types of devices can create a favorable impression among the people you give them to, and will keep your name in front of a segment of the public.

Many specialty and novelty firms produce these types of gimmicks. Often the manufacturer's name and address is somewhere on the novelty item so you should be able to track down manufacturers of items you find appealing.

EVENTS

Special events don't have to be exclusively for the media; you might want to have an open house, a homecoming weekend, a fund-raising dinner, or an appearance by a celebrity. The event might, of course, still attract media.

Once again, we repeat our warning about calling a "press conference." If there is any doubt about whether the announcement or speaker is important enough to guarantee press coverage, alter the nature of the event. Try to integrate the press coverage into an event that will go on regardless of whether the press shows up or not. An event staged specifically for the media can prove embarrassing if no members of the press show up.

Parking

Make sure that there will be enough parking spaces, and arrange some sort of management plans for the traffic. If a great many people are expected, it might be helpful to notify the police department.

Preparing the Site

If the event is to be held in a place other than your organization's headquarters, make sure you have complete permission to use the site. Check to determine if some sort of permit is necessary if the event will be held in a public place.

Plan logical seating arrangements. You might want to set up a special section for press (photographers will want to stand). Although most TV crews will have adequate battery power, it never hurts to have some heavy-duty extension cords plugged into a large circuit.

Have Backup and Safety Plans

In some cases, you might want to have medical help on hand; at least have a list of emergency telephone numbers. Think in terms of safety. Check that cables are taped down or strung across the ceiling, out of the way. It's also a good idea to determine if your insurance will give you adequate protection in the event of an accident on the premises.

Think about rain dates for an outdoor event. You won't be able to make adequate plans on a Sunday afternoon when the rain is falling and people are asking you when to reschedule. Put together backup plans in case a speaker doesn't show or is late (politicians are notorious for this).

Keep Literature on Hand

Having a printed handout will be very beneficial. It will be especially useful if the event involves fund raising.

In summary, the most important aspect of staging an event is attention to detail. Assume that things can go wrong and anticipate problems. Murphy's law applies quite specifically to special events.

DISPLAYS

Many communities have display cases at such places as airports and banks. These displays are often free, and they can give you some wonderful publicity.

Even though the display area might be furnished at no charge, you'll have to come up with the display. It probably will be well worth the investment to get an artist to help construct the display. Very few things suffer by comparison as much as a seedy display that is right next to a well-done one.

On a smaller scale, you can often put your posters or newsletters on bulletin boards. Public libraries are good locations for this.

BUYING ADVERTISING

Sometimes you just won't be able to accomplish what you want through "free" publicity. It might be simpler and less expensive in the long run to buy an advertisement rather than churning out press releases that don't get printed. Truly commercial ventures, of course, will have to be promoted mostly with paid advertising. Remember that an ad can say virtually anything you want to get across (within the limits of taste and the law) and isn't subject to the alterations of editorial people. By the same token, an ad is taken for what it is—an ad—and generally isn't given as much credence as editorial coverage.

You might want to use advertising to supplement your PR efforts in publicizing an event where it is crucial that you get a good turnout. If you are a member of a profit-making organization, the marketing people will usually handle the advertising. But in nonprofit organizations, the job of planning and buying advertising might fall to you. It isn't necessary to be an expert in media to buy advertising, but it helps. If you buy a great deal of advertising on a regular basis, it might be worthwhile to work with an advertising agency.

An agency will help package your message in the most persuasive form, and it will buy advertising space and time based on sophisticated measurements of the various audiences. Advertising agencies often work on commission from the media from which the advertising is purchased. For small accounts, a retainer will be charged to the client.

The advertising agency can be particularly helpful in determining with which medium you should place your advertising. Nevertheless, the majority of readers of this book probably will be dealing with local (versus regional or national) advertising. In the case of local outlets, you'll probably have a very clear idea of where you want to place your ads. The most difficult part of the decision might be the choice among using television, newspapers, or radio.

Television Advertising

If your budget is strictly limited, TV will probably be out of reach. Television advertising, when it is well done, is very effective, but it costs a lot of money. Aside from the cost of production, the rates for playing the commercial will be high.

Newspaper Advertising

Newspaper advertising will almost certainly be accessible to people doing their own public relations. In newspaper terminology, you'll be buying *display advertising* as opposed to *classified advertising*. By getting the terms straight right away, you can avoid a mix-up on the first telephone call to the paper.

The newspaper's sales representative will present you with a variety of options. The prices of newspaper ads are based on size and placement. Instead of requesting specific placement, you can choose to buy *run-of-paper* (ROP) advertising. In this case the newspaper people will determine placement of the ad.

Newspapers commonly offer different rates to profit and nonprofit concerns. The rates are expressed on a *rate card*. When looking at a rate card, be aware that there often are discounts for advertising bought in combination with morning and evening papers (when both are owned by the same firm) and discounts for purchases of several ads.

Newspaper advertising is especially useful for fairly complex items such as a series of events to be held on one day. It's also useful if you have a coupon or address to write for additional information. Remember that you will need quite a bit of lead time to get a display ad made up and placed in the paper.

Radio Advertising

Radio can reach a great deal of listeners at a bargain price. Along with this, radio has the advantage of hitting a specific target audience. If you want your message to reach teenagers, there is bound to be a station in your area that caters to that group. You can even buy a time slot that hits your target audience most effectively. In many radio markets, for instance, more teenagers listen in the evening hours than at other times.

Radio carries many speciality shows. The owner of a Polish bakery might prefer to advertise on one of the polka programs so common on Sunday mornings. An advertiser might also prefer to have a product identified with a certain radio personality. That can be accomplished by programming most commercials on a specific show.

Radio advertising is sold according to a rate card that bases the cost of ads on time and placement. The most expensive time will be so-called *drive time* in the early morning and late afternoon. The term drive time comes from the large number of commuters who are in their cars and listening to the radio. Drive time is radio's equivalent of television's prime time.

Specifying time slots will cost you extra. The least expensive way of putting ads on is the *run-of-station* (ROS) formula. Station personnel will place your ads in a variety of time slots at their discretion. Radio stations will almost always specify a minimum number of *spots* that you can buy. The spots will generally be 30 or 60 seconds.

You have several options in the way your advertising will be presented. One way to place an ad is to write up the copy—usually with the help of the station's account representative—and have the announcers read it live. This gives some identification with the various announcers on duty through the day. A variation of this is to furnish the announcer with a fact sheet that lists the important details, but not in narrative form. The announcer ad-libs the commercial. A good announcer can really give you your money's worth with a fact sheet.

A poor announcer, though, will make you wish that the commercial was pre-recorded. If you have one favorite announcer you'd like to do the spot, he or she can record it once and it will be played back on tape machines every time it runs. This method will have to be used if you have sound effects in the commercial.

Sometimes a standard commercial will feature a *music bed*. In this case, some of the commercial will be a music segment and the announcer will read live copy. This allows some flexibility for changing sale items.

A produced commercial, with music or sound effects, will entail some additional expense, but it will also give you exactly the sound you want.

Other Media

Magazines sometimes offer special sections. Museums will usually want to place an ad in many of the regional tourism magazines. Organizations offering summer camps might want to advertise in special selections, such as those in the *New York Times Magazines*.

CHOOSING MEDIA

You will rarely find yourself in a position where you have a clear-cut choice as to which medium you will use to promote your PR effort. Generally, you will gratefully accept whatever media attention comes your way.

However, there may be occasions when you target particular media for public relations. As discussed elsewhere in the chapter entitled *Public Relations for the Entrepreneur*, advertising is targeted in quite a specific fashion.

Here are some general characteristics of the relative strengths and weaknesses of various media as those strengths and weaknesses relate to a PR effort.

Radio

Radio is not a medium which typically uses much feature material or human interest stories. In our experience, radio is generally not worth pursuing for these purposes.

Advantages of Radio Coverage. If you do achieve placement of a news story on radio—and radio does hungrily need news, as opposed to human interest—that story will probably be repeated many times during the day. Another benefit of achieving radio coverage is that segments of the population who are not avid readers of newspapers are more likely to *hear* your story. College students, for example, are well-reached by radio.

Disadvantages of Radio Coverage. Radio stories are very brief, and may not make a memorable impact on the audience. Also a disadvantage is the fact that there is more potential for misunderstanding the story on radio than in other media. (The reason is that the listener does not have visual cues, as in television, and cannot go back and re-read a portion of the story, as with a newspaper.)

Be cautious about seeking radio publicity if there is a possibility that a misunderstanding could be damaging to your organization.

Television

TV is often a difficult medium to crack, since there is a lot of news to be presented in a small time period. One peculiarity of TV coverage that may work to your advantage, though, is that stations are becoming more sensitive to viewership in outlying portions of their coverage area. However, such stations usually cannot designate a large number of staffers to the effort. So if you are making news in one of the less-served areas of your TV station's coverage territory, and can make it convenient for the reporters to cover the story, you may receive more than your share of publicity.

Advantages of TV Coverage. A great deal of prestige is attached to TV coverage. It confers an immediate celebrity status on those interviewed.

Disadvantages of TV Coverage. TV deals with the "sound bite," the quick, pithy response. Complex issues are usually not best presented on television, and therefore there is some potential for misunderstanding of your spokesperson's position. You also need to utilize a competent media spokesperson in order to tailor the message to the medium.

Newspapers

Newspapers are interested in a wide range of stories, including a great deal of feature material. Because newspapers typically have larger news staffs than other media, and because many of those news departments are specialized, i.e., travel, business, etc., you have a better chance of getting coverage if your organization falls within those realms.

Advantages of Newspaper Coverage. Newspapers, and also magazines, are more durable than TV and radio. This means that you can easily place clippings in a scrapbook, show them to other members of your organization, and use them for future reference. If placement of a story is a major coup for you, demonstration of your coup will be much easier with print media. Also, remember that newspapers typically seem to cast people inexperienced with the media in a more favorable light than does television, making newspapers a good choice for the newcomer to PR. Appearing on a television interview is difficult and stressful, and is a skill only developed through practice. Learning through mistakes, incidentally, can be a painful process.

Disadvantages of Newspaper Coverage. There are few cons to appearing in print, although the durability of the print medium can prove an embarrassment if the story is negative or incorrect. An incorrect story on radio can be changed by the text hour's newscast, and a TV story can be fixed during the next newscast. But a mistake in print hangs around for the duration of the publication, and even if a correction is made, the correction won't appear until the next day and it may not be noticed, anyway.

HOW TO CONTACT AND DEAL WITH A REPORTER

Effective media relations are often based on how well public relations people can make contact with reporters and editors, and once that contact is made, how well PR practitioners can communicate in a positive, persuasive way. It is often quite difficult to overcome the reluctance of the working media to sit down and talk with public relations people. For one thing, members of the media are usually very busy. Secondly, many reporters have had a bad taste left in their mouths by previous dealings with inept PR practitioners.

There are no realistic formulaic approaches which will work in all circumstances, but some general guidelines will help you break through initial barriers. With those guidelines in mind, don't be reluctant to take the plunge and set up some appointments. Keep these points in mind:

1. The overriding concern of meeting with a reporter is that you must not waste anyone's time. This means that the idea for the meeting should be presented in such a way that the reporter knows the get-together is going to be brief. Let the journalist know during your first phone call that you would like only a few minutes to present some story ideas *that might be of interest to the reporter*. Say, "I have some story ideas which might work very well for your weekly business column." Never say, "We really want some publicity for our business and I want to get you to write about us."

2. Having assumed that you will make it a short appointment and will present only information useful to the reporter, you can also take the approach of presenting information about experts in your organization who can provide information for future stories. You may, for example, reap dividends by speaking with a reporter for a business journal and briefly presenting the backgrounds of several economics experts on the faculty of your university, stressing each member's ability to speak to a specific news-related topic.

3. Another method to gain entree to media representatives is to create a formal situation in which a newsmaker, such as the CEO of your organization, or your political candidate, is introduced to the reporters and editors over lunch, or in a meeting, or during a session of a newspaper's

editorial board. (An editorial board is the meeting of management and editorial writers during which positions on various issues are debated and determined.) In situations such as this, it is always important to be prepared to discuss some specific areas or issues of current public importance. It is also critical that your newsmaker be a legitimate VIP; editors and reporters won't want to spend time with someone who is not a legitimate newsmaker.

4. Be sure that there is a reason for meeting with the journalist rather than just sending the material through the mail. Unless there is a good rationale for your presence, don't push for a meeting. If you can see some benefit in a face to face conversation, try to set something up; otherwise, be content with mailing a press release.

5. One way to gain entree is to ask for "five minutes" with the reporter. It is difficult for anyone to turn down such a modest request. But be prepared to stick to that time limit.

6. Be gracious if you are turned down in your request for a meeting. Remember, deadlines can be very pressing and the reporter may simply not have the time. Always leave the door open so that future arrangements can be made. Say, "I understand . . . the next time I'm in town I'll call again."

7. Also, be prepared to have appointments cancelled at the last minute. This is not a delightful experience, especially if you've travelled some distance, but often the reporter simply has no alternative. Reporters don't really make their own schedules; editors and events do.

8. If you want to meet with a member of the media in a distant city—say, if you are travelling to New York from Ohio—never tell the reporter with whom you wish to meet that the meeting is the sole focus of your trip. Because of the scheduling problems mentioned in point #7 above, journalists are very reluctant to take the chance of being responsible for ruining your entire trip. Say, "I'm going to be in New York on Tuesday, and wondered if you might have five minutes . . ."

9. Don't make your initial meeting a lunch. Hold off on making lunch dates until you know the reporter or editor fairly well, or unless you are introducing a major newsmaker to reporters and editors. Most journalists are reluctant to commit themselves to an extended period of time with someone they don't know. Aside from that, many reporters are compelled by ethical codes to pay for their own lunches, so they won't even gain a free meal from the experience.

PREPARING A PRESS KIT

What goes into a press kit? That's not an easy question to answer, because the term has a different meaning among individual PR practitioners. And in any event, the goals of preparing a press kit differ, as will the contents. But in general, a press kit is defined as *a collection of information designed to serve as a reference for the media*. It usually contains a press release, photos, brochures, biographies, and other relevant information, as seen in Fig. 15-7.

A press kit is usually used as a handout during a major event (Fig. 15-8). Sometimes, a press kit is given to reporters as a general reference for future stories; although it is doubtful as to how many kits are kept in this circumstance.

As an example, sports public information directors typically prepare a press kit which contains rosters, photos, and general information on the team and the team's schedule and win-loss record. In this example, the press kit is distinct

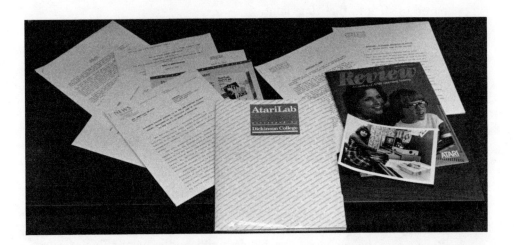

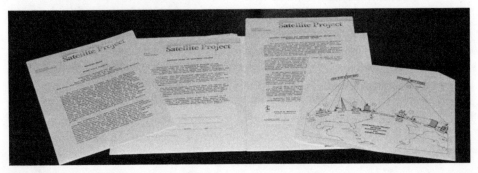

Figs. 15-7 and 15-8. Typical press kits.

from a press release in that it contains a *variety* of information, intended as background for a major story.

In essence, the organization of your press kit depends on your individual needs, so the following list is not meant to be a prescription of what is necessary. Evaluate your own requirements and choose from among the options.

- *Press release*. If the kit is handed out at a major event, there will almost always be one major press release included; that release sums up the event. Sometimes, PR directors will staple the summary press release on the front of the two-pocket envelope holding the press kit materials.
- *Photos*. The photographs are usually portraits of the newsmakers involved, or photos or artists' depictions of a physical object, such as a new product or a building to be constructed.
- *Backgrounders or biographies*. It's a good idea to provide a succinct history of your institution, as well as detailed biographies of the VIPs involved. The organizational history is more important than you might suspect; it has been our experience that reporters are more likely to attempt a story about an organization if they know full details of its background. That background includes: date of founding, information on the principals of the company, and details of the products or services produced.
- *A text of the speech or a summary of the remarks to be made during the event*. Providing a copy of the speech makes coverage much simpler for reporters; they can do some writing in advance and concentrate on producing other aspects of the story during the speech. Be sure to *embargo* the text of the speech, meaning that you indicate clearly that the text cannot be released until after the speech is made.

    Incidentally, caution your speaker to stay relatively close to the text of the speech. Otherwise, reporters will be placed in the embarrassing position of possibly reporting inaccurate information. You will make enemies in the press corps if this happens with regularity.

    Sometimes, current events will mandate that the speaker make a departure from prepared remarks. There's no reason why he or she can't cue the press to this: "Let me depart from my planned remarks for a moment to comment on today's ruling by the Supreme Court." That's a perfectly appropriate tactic, one which may save embarrassment for everyone.
- *Schedules of activities*. This is particularly important for a political candidate. Incidentally, if there is any doubt as to whether an event is open to the public and/or press, be sure to make that absolutely clear in the schedule. (For example, a speech in a downtown park is obviously open to press and public, but what about a "meeting with Senator Smith"?

Don't leave any doubt as to whether that meeting is a public or private affair.)
- *Phone numbers of contacts.* Always include a number where someone who can provide more information can be reached.

USING REPRINTS

If a newspaper or magazine runs a particularly flattering story about your firm or organization, ask the publisher for permission to reprint the story. You can use the reprint as a handout or a mailing piece.

FINAL THOUGHTS

During your own public relations involves experience as well as knowledge. Because you've just about finished this book, it seems safe to say that you've accumulated enough knowledge to get started and handle the job quite competently.

There will be problems, of course. One of the most frequent problems will be people in your organization who have no understanding of the nature of press coverage and expect to see news about the organization in banner headlines—every day. In Appendix D, an experienced public relations expert demonstrates how he handles that situation.

Speaking of experience, be aware that almost all veteran PR people have picked up a lot of theirs the hard way. Throughout this book, we've tried to pass along information that will allow you to benefit from the experience—and mistakes—of others.

Everybody makes mistakes. Honest mistakes are easily fixed, but mistakes arising from duplicity or deception are not. Moral issues aside, a straightforward approach to getting your message across will reap some very practical advantages. You'll stay out of trouble if you follow Mark Twain's advice.

"When in doubt," he wrote, "tell the truth."

Appendix A
Sample Press Releases

THE FOLLOWING SAMPLE RELEASES ARE INTENDED TO BE USED AS GUIDES, NOT as multiple-purpose, fill-in-the-blanks formula stories.

Key points of the releases are listed on corresponding pages. By noting the general format of the releases, and the way the key points are worked in, you can quickly get a good idea of how your releases should be laid out.

Notice that the releases are all written in the third person form, as opposed to the first person form. In other words, the organization is always referred to as "the organization" instead of "our organization," and the releases are written using quotes from the principal figures instead of having the principal figures write directly as in, I feel that the proposed . . .

This is the standard way to write a press release. If you feel compelled to make a personal statement in the first person, the letters to the editor sections of daily papers are more appropriate. Incidentally, don't overlook letters to the editor; they can be very persuasive and might get your message printed when a press release won't.

Keep in mind that these samples are for purposes of illustration. They don't necessarily indicate the proper length of a similar release. Your releases will probably be longer, but it's our feeling that a release kept to one page will often stand a better chance of escaping the editor's pencil. Also, the editor just might be swayed to using a shorter press release because he knows it won't need extensive shortening.

ANNOUNCEMENT OF AN APPOINTMENT OR PROMOTION

1. The release shown in Fig. A-1 has a dateline which indicates the point of origin of the story. Some people use datelines on press releases and some don't. In general, a story that will be sent out of town has a dateline, while a story distributed locally won't. Newspapers don't dateline stories within their home cities.

2. If you use a dateline, note that the addresses given in the body of a datelined story are assumed to be within the place of the dateline. If there's no dateline, the city must be identified. Always be sure that all addresses are referenced directly (Anywhere Blvd., Los Angeles) or within the dateline.

News From Hypothetical

The Hypothetical Organization
1280 Typical St.
Los Angeles, California 90007
(213) 000-0000

FOR IMMEDIATE RELEASE

CONTACT: Lee Massey

NORRIS APPOINTED GENERAL MANAGER OF HYPOTHETICAL

LOS ANGELES ①-- Martin P. Norris has been appointed general manager of the Hypothetical Organization.

Norris, who lives at 1141 Anywhere Blvd.②, will be in charge of all operations of the Hypothetical Organization at the local headquarters and at the two subsidiary plants in Nevada and New Mexico. He will report directly to Hypothetical's president.

An employee of the Hypothetical Organization since 1967, Norris, 44, previously held management positions with several manufacturing firms, including Ohio Mills and Maryland Electronics, Inc. Norris started his career at Hypothetical as a personnel assistant, and was promoted to director of personnel in 1974. He was named assistant general manager in 1979.③

Norris holds a bachelor's degree from Case Western Reserve University. He received the 1981 Outstanding Manager Award from the National Management Council. Norris has been active as a volunteer for the Red Cross and the Boy Scouts of America.④

\#

Fig. A-1. Note the dateline.

3. It's a generally accepted procedure to give a capsulized summary of the appointee's work history. Your release might go into greater detail.
4. The reader wants to know something about the appointee's educational and personal background.

Another, and perhaps better, way to handle an announcement of an appointment or promotion is to quote the person who made the appointment, usually the chief executive officer. We left the direct quote out of the story purposely so that you might compare the effect with subsequent releases that contain quotes.

ANNOUNCEMENT OF AN EVENT

1. Always give the complete date and time for an event (Fig. A-2). It's helpful, too, if you can give the event an official name or title. An official name or title can be capitalized.
2. Don't forget the address. Save the editor the time spent checking to see if the event will be held at the same address as on the stationary.
3. Don't be reluctant to describe the event in detail or to list the program. You could get more detailed than this example.
4. The most common mistake in an announcement of an event is leaving out the price, if any, and whether it is open to the general public. The editor really must know this.
5. Another, old-fashioned way to end a release.

Announcements of events are probably the most frequent type of press release. They are relatively easy to write, but don't be lulled into carelessness. Fouling up a date or time can land you in a world of trouble. Triple check everything!

News From Hypothetical

The Hypothetical Organization
1280 Typical St.
Los Angeles, California 90007
(213) 000-0000

FOR IMMEDIATE RELEASE

CONTACT: Alex Foley

HYPOTHETICAL ORGANIZATION TO HOLD CHRISTMAS CONCERT

The Hypothetical Organization's Annual Christmas Concert will be held Tuesday, Dec. 23 at 7 p.m. ① in the main auditorium at Hypothetical Headquarters, 1280 Typical St. ②

Featured entertainers will be the West Coast Mastersingers, a group of 50 male vocalists who will present a program of traditional holiday carols along with Christmas music from the classics. On the program will be works by Bach and Mozart. ③

Admission to the 90-minute concert is free and is open to the general public ④

-30- ⑤

Fig. A-2. Announcement of an event.

ANNOUNCEMENT OF EARNINGS

1. Figure A-3 shows a fairly standard way of announcing earnings.
2. Here's a case where you use attribution. We recommend use of attribution whenever possible. Note how much more authoritative the release seems when someone is quoted directly. Also note that the title is capi-

News From Hypothetical

The Hypothetical Organization
1280 Typical St.
Los Angeles, California 90007
(213) 000-0000

FOR IMMEDIATE RELEASE

(MAILED 10/1/82)

CONTACT: Jean Latimer

HYPOTHETICAL ORGANIZATION REPORTS LOSS IN THIRD QUARTER

Sales and earnings for the third quarter ended Sept. 30 were down compared to the same period last year,① according to Vice President for Sales Ralph F.X. Sullivan.② However, Sullivan said, profits are expected to rise when $10 million in new government contracts take effect Jan. 1 of 1983.③

Sullivan said the Hypothetical Organization reported earnings of $2.1 million on sales of $22.3 million for the quarter ended Sept. 30, down from earnings of $2.5 million on sales of $22.9 million for the same period one year ago.

The organization's lackluster performance stems from an overall weakness in the economy, Sullivan said.④ He noted, though, that no layoffs are anticipated and that money continues to be spent for development of new products and services. Sullivan said that increased profits from the upcoming government contracts may result in hirings of as many as 200 new employees.

The Hypothetical Organization manufactures abrasives used in industrial applications.⑤

-END-⑥

Fig. A-3. Announcing earnings.

talized because it comes *before* the name. If it comes after the name, it would not be capitalized.
3. There's no reason why you can't inject some optimism into an otherwise gloomy release as long as what you say is true.
4. The reader will have asked himself "Why are profits down?" Provide an answer whenever there appears to be a question dangling.
5. It's always a good idea to specify exactly what the group, firm, or organization does.
6. Another way to end a press release.

Readers of financial news are pretty sophisticated about profit and loss numbers. There's no point in trying to fool them with tricky numbers; be straightforward.

OBITUARY

1. Never, ever, leave any doubt as to the date of death in an obit. Don't rely on a date at the top of the release. Put the date of death right in the copy. See Fig. A-4 on page 234.
2. The age of the deceased always must be included in an obit.
3. Cause of death is not always included, but we think it should be.
4. Some history about his affiliation with the company is appropriate.
5. The final three paragraphs are pretty standard obit material: memberships, war history, education.

Obits are a common responsibility of PR people. The speed with which you will need to furnish an obituary to the press will quickly point out the necessity of maintaining biographical information of VIPs in your files.

A PUBLIC INTEREST STORY

1. A timely "hook" helps catch the reader's—and the editor's—attention. See Fig. A-5 on page 235.
2. Is it really necessary to define weather stripping? If there's any doubt at all, define the term. Remember that your audience is very broad, and all the members won't be as well-informed as you are.
3. It's important to mention your expert's qualifications.
4. Give an example to show that he has really accomplished what he's talking about.
5. This ending is similar to a feature news ending. It finishes up a story with a satisfying "thump."

News From Hypothetical

The Hypothetical Organization
1280 Typical St.
Los Angeles, California 90007
(213) 000-0000

FOR IMMEDIATE RELEASE

CONTACT: Linda Day

JOHN P. TYLER, HYPOTHETICAL CHIEF EXECUTIVE, DIES AT 66

John P. Tyler, president and chief executive officer of the Hypothetical Organization, died today (Oct. 5) at Lexington Memorial Hospital. He was 66. Taylor had suffered a stroke on Oct. 3, and died without regaining consciousness.

Tyler was president of the Hypothetical Organization since 1965. Prior to joining Hypothetical, he was senior vice president of Melrose Products, Inc., of Anytown, New York.

He is survived by his wife, Amy, two sons, and five grandchildren.

Tyler was a member of the First Congregational Church. He was a was a member of the Brotherhood International Fellowship, Inc., and a trustee of the United Giving Fund of Greater Los Angeles. He was a director of the Gifford Museum.

Born in Los Angeles, Tyler attended public schools in the city and enrolled at UCLA. His attendance at UCLA was interrupted by service in the United States Navy during World War II, where he served as an officer aboard the battleship U.S.S. Massachusetts.

Following the war, Tyler returned to UCLA and was graduated with a bachelor's degree in 1948.

-END-

Fig. A-4. An obituary.

News From Hypothetical

The Hypothetical Organization
1280 Typical St.
Los Angeles, California 90007
(213) 000-0000

FOR IMMEDIATE RELEASE

CONTACT: Martin Vanderbilt

WEATHERSTRIPPING CAN CUT FUEL BILLS, SAYS HYPOTHETICAL ENGINEER

With rising fuel prices and record cold predicted this winter①, a Hypothetical Organization conservation specialist notes that homeowners can cut their energy bills substantially by the simple, inexpensive technique of weatherstripping -- placing insulating materials in cracks found around doors and windows.②

"Cracks around a typical window can let in as much cold air as an eight-square-inch hole," said Elwood T. Maple, director of engineering for the Hypothetical Organization. "But a dollar's worth of weatherstripping can reduce that significantly."

Maple, who is in charge of the energy conservation program at the Hypothetical Organization③ notes that weatherstripping alone cut fuel consumption 20 percent last winter at the Typical St. headquarters.④

"It doesn't take any particular skill to apply weatherstripping, and the directions are usually right on the package," Maple said. "The big advantage is cost: The materials for weatherstripping are very inexpensive. In most cases, weatherstripping can pay for itself during two weeks of cold weather. After that, the rest of the winter is gravy."⑤

-END-

Fig. A-5. A public interest story.

Stories that apparently serve the public interest can serve your interest too by showing that your organization is concerned and capable.

NEW BUSINESS OPENING

1. Never leave any doubt as to the time or place of an event associated with an opening. See Fig. A-6.

News From Hypothetical

The Hypothetical Organization
1280 Typical St.
Los Angeles, California 90007
(213) 000-0000

FOR IMMEDIATE RELEASE

CONTACT: Monica Thomas

TV PRODUCTION FACILITY TO OPEN ON TYPICAL ST.

The Hypothetical Television Production Studio will open Sept. 15 at 1280 Typical St. in Los Angeles. There will be a public open house at 2 p.m. that day.① A studio tour will be given and refreshments provided.

Studio President Julius Lawton says② the facility will be used for production of television commercials and instructional videotapes.

Lawton, who was a producer at CBS for ten years before becoming an independent producer three years ago,③ says he noted a need for a small but fully equipped studio in the downtown Los Angeles area.④

"Many of the people and organizations who might want to have videotapes and commercials produced just can not afford the prices charged by larger studios," Lawton says. "But our studio has been set up specifically to meet the needs of the smaller clients. We can provide the services they want at a more reasonable rate than studios with larger staffs and bigger facilities."⑤

-END-

Fig. A-6. Announcement of the opening of a new business.

2. Notice the word *says* is used instead of *said*. *Says* is acceptable in lighter, soft-news material because it gives the copy some spark by being in the present tense. You'll notice most magazine articles are written in the present tense. Beware of using *says* in controversial or hard-news items. What someone "says" yesterday will not always be what he "says" tomorrow.
3. Qualifications give credibility to the business.

News From Hypothetical

The Hypothetical Organization
1280 Typical St.
Los Angeles, California 90007
(213) 000-0000

FOR IMMEDIATE RELEASE

CONTACT: Martin Webster

A recent auto wreck which claimed the lives of two city men -- and resulted in ① a suspended sentence to a driver involved in the accident who was convicted of driving while intoxicated -- shows that reforms are needed in the state's drunk driving laws, said Timothy L. Nolte, chairman of the Hypothetical Safety Organization. ②

"I feel that everyone in the city was shocked by the recent tragedy on Anyplace Blvd., " Nolte said. "And the slap on the wrist given the drunk driver added to the outrage. It is time that judges and legislators wake up to the fact that stricter laws and tougher enforcement are needed to stop the carnage on the highways of our state."

Nolte is calling for the establishment of a city-wide commission to draft new legislation aimed at deterring drunk driving. ③

The Hypothetical Safety Organization is a non-profit group established in 1972 to educate the public in various aspects of safety. The organization has 250 local members. ④

-END-

Fig. A-7. Position statement.

4. This answers the dangling questions of why he thought opening a TV studio was a good idea.
5. More about why the studio is needed. This is really a bare-bones treatment, but it's probably all a small business will get.

The opening of a new business is often the first task to occupy a newcomer to PR. Open houses held in conjunction with a business opening are a good idea. It might be better to schedule the open house from 2 P.M. to 4 P.M. so as not to scare off people who might not be able to make a specific tour at exactly 2 P.M..

STATEMENT OF POSITION

1. The temptation here is to say "only a suspended sentence." Avoid this kind of editorializing in a press release, unless it's contained within a direct quote. See Fig. A-7.
2. Notice that the chairman is doing the talking. The assumption is that he represents the organization.
3. The statement of position is bolstered by an actual request for action. The call for the city-wide commission, if it's a legitimate and important item, might have been a better way to lead the story.
4. It helps to give some background on the organization. This lends the statement of position some credibility.

The statement of position often gets good play in the media. It helps greatly if you have had some previous contact with editors and reporters so that they know your organization is legitimate and responsible.

NEW PRODUCT NEWS

1. This story (Fig. A-8) is obviously intended for national distribution, hence the dateline. If there's doubt about the need for a dateline, be on the safe side and use one.
2. It seems wise to avoid the temptation to put an adjective such as "revolutionary" here. Try to show why a new product is revolutionary, rather than saying it is.
3. Quotes add credibility to new product news.
4. Why does anyone need this product?
5. Make sure to put something about availability of the product in a release such as this. If the product genuinely interests the public, they will want to know where to buy it.

The key to getting news about a product out lies not so much in writing a brilliant release as knowing exactly where to send it.

News From Hypothetical

The Hypothetical Organization
1280 Typical St.
Los Angeles, California 90007
(213) 000-0000

FOR IMMEDIATE RELEASE

CONTACT: Louis Krantz

NEW LAWN SEED GROWS IN NEAR-TOTAL SHADE

LOS ANGELES ①-- A new ② lawn seed which will grow grass in areas of near-total shade has been introduced by the Hypothetical Organization, manufacturer of Hypothetical Seeds.

"The new Heavy Shade Grass Seed represents a breakthrough in seed technology," said Marvin R. Elliot,③ director of research for the Hypothetical Organization. "The product actually is a mixture of seeds, especially developed for low-light situations."

Development of the formula for the new seed mixture, according to Elliot, involved collecting samples of grasses found growing in South American rain forests.

The newly-developed seed mixture will be of special help to homeowners in the Northeast,④ Elliot says, where a combination of cloudy weather and the prevalence of heavily-treed lots often makes lawn growth sparse. Previous seed mixtures, Elliot said, were not able to maintain thick growth in heavily shaded areas.

Hypothetical Heavy Shade Grass Seed is available at all Hypothetical Lawn and Garden Shops nationwide.⑤

-END-

Fig. A-8. New product news.

FACT SHEET

1. Don't forget to include *all* the basic information. See Fig. A-9
2. Since this is not meant to be published verbatim, such direct instructions are permissible.

News From Hypothetical

The Hypothetical Organization
1280 Typical St.
Los Angeles, California 90007
(213) 000-0000

FOR IMMEDIATE RELEASE

CONTACT: James Nolan

HYPOTHETICAL BUILDING DEDICATION: FACT SHEET

The building to be dedicated today cost $14 million to build, and was under construction for nine months.

The new building will house the Hypothetical Organization's research laboratories. ①

Work to be carried out in the new building will include research into the development of new plastics compounds for the packaging industry.

Hypothetical President Allen G. Crenshaw will officiate at the ground-breaking ceremonies at 11 a.m., Tuesday, July 15. (Crenshaw will be available for interviews at 9 a.m., July 15, at the site, and will also be available after the ceremony) ②

The new building, at 1281 Typical St., is directly across from company headquarters.

-more- ③

Fig. A-9. A Fact Sheet.

3. If there's more to your release, indicate it. We haven't included another page of the fact sheet, but we did include the *more* to remind you.

Fact sheets are very useful to the news media but, for some reason, they are underused by public relations people.

Appendix B
Broadcast Style

IT'S NOT NECESSARY TO WRITE PRESS RELEASES INTENDED FOR BROADCAST media differently from those sent to the print media. Broadcasters expect to rewrite the news in broadcast style.

Nevertheless, you will want to write in broadcast style when you are putting something out specifically for the broadcast media. Public service announcements or narrations are two examples.

Rather than overload you with complex samples and analysis, we'll pass along a few simple tips that you will easily be able to apply to your writing.

- The most obvious difference between writing to be read on the printed page and writing to be read out loud is that out-loud writing is conversational. If your writing doesn't sound natural when read aloud, rework it until it flows naturally.
- About 20 to 25 words is the top limit you'll want to put in a sentence to be read aloud. If the sentence is too long, look for a natural place to break it into two sentences.
- In broadcast, attribution is usually put first. "John Jacobs said that there is a notable lack of concern about the issue," rather than "There is a notable lack of concern about the issue," John Jacobs said.
- Direct quotes are not used very often in broadcast writing; generally, paraphrasing is used. Of course, the comments are still attributed to the speaker.
- You must always strive for clarity, clarity, clarity! The listener cannot go back over what's been said and read it again.
- Avoid contractions such as *didn't*. Its too easy for the audience to mistake it for *did*.

Appendix C
Model Release

FOR COMMERCIAL USE OF SOMEONE'S PHOTO, YOU SHOULD ALWAYS OBTAIN A signed model release. We're going to hedge a bit here and recommend that you see the attorney connected with your group, firm, or organization to get information on the type of release best suited for your type of business and the laws of your state. Having said that, here's an example of a release form that is commonly used:

Date _____

    I HEREBY CONSENT to the use by _____, for the purpose of advertising or trade, of my name and/or a portrait, picture, photograph or moving pictures of me and/or recordings of my voice, or any reproductions of the same in any form. I agree that such portrait, picture, photograph of me and plates and/or negatives connected therewith shall remain the property of _____.

Signed _____ Witness _____

Appendix D
Put It In the Paper!

UNFORTUNATELY, YOU ARE LIKELY TO HEAR THAT REQUEST—OR ORDER—MANY times in your PR career. Here's how Fred Broad Jr., president of Vermont Fund Raising Counsel, handled the situation in a memo to staffers of an organization he once advised.

Understanding the Press

"Gee, we ought to put that in the paper!" Have you ever heard anyone say that? Have you ever said it yourself? Those of us who work in the areas of publicity and promotion hear it often, perhaps several times a week. With about the same frequency we also hear the other side of it, "Why didn't you put that in the paper?" It seems to me that one of my little essays might be appropriate on this subject. This one is titled "Understanding the Press." The word "Press" is used to denote all forms of communications media, written, film, audio or electronic. Though I shall deal specifically with what is today often called "print media" but which was formerly known as the newspapers, the principles are the same for all of them.

The first thing to understand is that the only people who "put things in the papers" are the *editors*. We can send in press releases, and usually do, or have, reporters can write stories, photographers can take pictures, but only *editors put things in the papers*.

The next thing to understand is that there are a number of factors that determine what is "put in the papers" and what is not. The fact that we think an item is important is not one of them. Newspapers, and other communications media, are first and foremost profit-making business. When they cease to be this, like the *Washington Star* and the *Philadelphia Bulletin*, to name only two great ones, they go out of business and stop publication.

All newspapers operate on a fixed formula of percentages of space devoted to advertising and to news. While this may vary from paper to paper, it usually runs about 60% for advertising and 40% for news. The size of each issue of a newspaper is based on the amount of advertising that has been sold for that issue. The number of pages in any issue is thus approximately 40% additional space for news over what has been sold for advertising, realizing of course, that it has to come out in an even number of pages—you can't leave one side of a page blank. For example, if there has been space equivalent to 12 pages of advertising sold for a particular issue, then there will be space equivalent to 8 pages available to the editors for news and you will have a 20 page paper. Since editors always have more news available than there is space available to print it, this means that there is always competition for the news space.

To determine what is going to get the available news space, the editors ask two questions about any given item. First, "Is it news?" and second "Will it sell papers?" If the answers to these questions is "Yes" in both cases, then the item will undoubtedly get printed. If it is "yes" to only one of them, then there may be a 50-50 chance. If it is "no", or "maybe" or any degree less than a firm "yes", the chance of that item making the paper are fairly slim unless the editor for some reason has some extra space to work with, or the competition is not so keen. This naturally means that there is considerable subjective judgement on the editor's part in answering these questions. Why different editors think the way they do, of course, can only be answered by them. If the editor's judgement on these things makes a profit for the newspapers, then the publishers are happy, if not, then they get a new editor.

What is news? *It is what an editor thinks is news*. Also, we must remember that there is a considerable time factor involved. Something that may have been news one day, when it did not beat the competition for the space, may no longer be news by the next day, even though there may be space available then. Everyone thinks his story is important, but the editor must decide which of three stories gets the space when there is only room for two.

What sells papers? Unfortunately the answer is all too often "lurid sensationalism." Editors do not care who buys papers as long as they sell lots of them. Remember, advertising rates are based on circulation, just as TV time rates are based on ratings.

What can we do to try to improve our chances of "getting things in the papers?" I suppose the first thing is to understand what the editor is up against and try to think like an editor. Another thing to remember is that quality, not quantity, on a consistent basis pays off in the long run. If you get the reputation of flooding the papers with pages of inconsequential verbiage, most editors are not going to get beyond the name at the top of the release. The ideas that "if we send in enough stuff," or "if we put enough pressure on them," some of it will get printed, are absolute nonsense. In fact, it will work just the other way.

Newspapers are published under deadlines so there is usually pressure to get copy ready for each edition. Knowing what a newspaper needs and supplying it with copy that requires the least work to make it ready for the typesetter is always helpful. For example, an editor has decided your story deserves printing. He can give it four column inches. The story runs six inches. What does he do? In nearly every case he will simply chop off the last two inches. He does not have time to re-write press-releases. Therefore, the writer who knows this will put the important items at the top. Always write stories in the order of decreasing importance.

These are only a few instances of things one should know in order to understand the press. I could go on ad nauseam, and some of you may think I already have, but this illustrates the point. The public information person who gets the reputation at the paper of always sending in good copy, well written to require the least effort for publication, and dealing with significant topics, and who does not burden the editors with reams of inconsequential trivia, will be the one who has the highest incidence of publication. Remember, the papers, and other media, owe us nothing. They will do what they can to help us as long as we don't make it too difficult for them. So, when we tend to get upset because something we sent it did not get printed or did not seem to get the attention we thought it merited, try to understand it from the paper's point of view. Good understanding and cooperation on our part will usually result in cooperation and understanding from the papers.

WHAT MAKES THE NEWS?

Who determines what goes into the newspaper, and what is most likely to make news? Kenneth J. Botty, editor of the Worcester *Telegram* and *The Evening Gazette*, addressed the issue in his weekly column, *Editor's Report*, reprinted here with the permission of the *Worcester Telegram*.

2B   Sunday Telegram   October 24, 1982

Editor's Report/
Picking from the daily news menu is difficult

By Kenneth J. Botty
Editor

"Who decides what story goes where?"

A woman asked that very good question the other day at a coffee with the editor session. We tried to answer it as fully as possible but the truth of the matter is that story selection and placement, on these and other newspapers, is an involved and complex problem. It is a dragon which might be faced and slain each day, each edition, and when you step over the carcass of one, you know just as certainly as the clock on the wall will keep ticking, that another one will come lumbering into view over the next rise.

A number of editors contribute to the process and a lot of the groundwork, especially for Page 1 content, is done at a daily news conference. The managing editor presides at this session and, typically, reviews the stories brought up for Page 1 consideration by the editors who attend the meeting.

The news editor, for example, will bring up the most important stories on the wires and a couple of them may be marked for Page 1 attention. The city editor, in charge of the local reporting staff, will discuss what the city-side reporters are working on that day and may offer one or more stories for possible use on the front page. The chief of the regional desk will run down a list of the best offerings from the newspaper's bureaus and offices. Also contributing are other departments such as sports and Accent or Family Today. The photo department is very much a part of the scene and the editors learn what stories have accompanying art, what photographs are coming and what are considered to be the best bets for Page 1 display.

The meetings are informal and the discussion, if it does nothing else, establishes something like a baseline against which the continuing flow of news will be evaluated.

It is not at all unusual, for example, for decisions reached at 6 or 7 p.m. to be re-examined and completely changed because of late-breaking news that is judged to be more significant.

Competing for Space

In a very real sense, every story in the newspaper competes against every other story for a headline and position in a particular edition.

What makes one story more important than another? There are no easy or simple answers to that question either. Generally, stories with the greatest potential impact on the greatest number of people receive primary consideration. A story, for example, saying that auto insurance rates in Massachusetts were going to increase by 20 percent would be a very good bet for Page 1 use because it would affect everyone who owns and operates a car in the Bay State. Other stories may be selected for a variety of reasons, because they have international importance, because they reflect the human condition, because they illuminate and explain something of interest to most readers or, simply, because they have an angle of unusual interest that prompts intense reader involvement. These are usually referred to as "talk-about" stories, the ones that are discussed the next day in the home, the office and at lunch.

Understand that no sane newspaper man or woman claims infallibility. We judge the flow, put one story up against another, give careful consideration to its significance to our readers, its impact, its import, its meaning, and then designate its position in the day's paper. No one expects every reader to agree with every editing decision. Indeed, if we were to invite 100 people in from the street, present them with several hundred stories, and ask each to design his or her own front page, the results would undoubtedly resemble a patchwork quilt. It would illustrate that each of us brings a different perspective to the news of the day.

Readers Are Editors

Actually, every reader is free to be his or her own editor. That is one of the very real strengths of the print medium. You can read what interests you and ignore the rest if you so choose. Most people, in truth, do exactly that. Some turn first to sports, some start with the crossword puzzle, others head directly for the comic page, others read the paper front to back and some start on the last page and work their way forward.

We spread it out for you every day, and in the last analysis it is you who decides what you want. A daily newspaper has to be all things to all people and, given the incredible range of human taste, the difficulty of picking from the daily news menu becomes apparent.

Which is why so many of us are addicted to the business.

Index

A
active voice, 20
actualities (radio), 54-57
adverbs, 20
advertising, 159, 178-181, 219-222
Aldus PageMaker, 154-155
angling press releases, 70
annual reports, 8, 144, 232
aperture, 86
artists, graphic, cost of, 186
attribution, 68

B
biographical information, 227
black and white vs. color, 92, 146, 182
brainwashing, 3
brochures, 140-144, 159, 162
budgeting, 182-187
business correspondence, desktop publishing, 163
business reply envelopes, fund raising, 167-168

C
camera-ready copy, 139
cameras, 76, 186
captions or cutlines, photos, 117-118
catalogs, desktop publishing, 159
celebrity appearances, 174
classified advertising, newspapers, 220
cliches, 21
color vs. black and white, 90, 146, 182
columns, 29
computers (*see also* desktop publishing), 73, 151-153
concise writing, 12, 69
contact (proof) sheets, 94-95, 185
contractions, 20
contrast in pages, 158
coupons, 180

D
darkrooms, 96-106
definition and meaning, writing, 16-17
demonstrations, writing using, 19-20
depth of field, 85-87
desktop publishing (*see also* computers), 65, 67, 73, 151-163
  applications for PR, 158-163
  computers for, 152-153
  graphic design with, 157-158
  printers for, 155-157
  software for, 153-155
details in writing, 19
developers, film development, 100
development officers, 164
direct mail campaigns, 174

display advertising, newspapers, 220
displays, 219
drive time, radio, 52
dubbing, video, 35

E
editing, 18
embargo text of speech, 63-64
endorsements, 175
enlargers, 97
entrepreneurial PR, 173-181
  advertising, 178-181
  cost-effective plans for, 173-175
  marketing, 175-178
events, 4, 41-43, 63, 174, 218-219, 227, 231
exclusives, 30
exposure (light) meters, 87-89

F
f-stops, 82-84
facilities and equipment, 7
fact sheets, 239
feature news, 12, 196-212
film, photographic, 89-90, 96-106, 185
fixer, film development, 100
flash bulbs, 92
flyers, desktop publishing, 159, 161
fonts (*see* type style and sizes)
forms, desktop publishing, 160
framing, photo composition, 114
fund raising, 164-172

G
gimmicks, promotional, 218
giveaways, 175
goodwill, 2, 5
graphic design (*see also* publications, layout of), 126, 157

H
hard news press releases, 59
headlines, 64, 128, 141
human interest stories, 29, 61, 233-236
humor, 21

I
image creation or reinforcement, 2, 6
in-house publications, 3, 8
information, checking accuracy of, 69
internal communications, 3
inverse pyramid writing style, 12-13

J
"journalese", 12
justified print, 130

K

key slides, television, 41

L

layout (*see also* graphic design), 126, 157
leads, 12
lens, 76-82
letterpress printing, 144
liaison officer, 9
lies, 9
local interest stories, 28
looking space, photo composition, 107, 109

M

magazines, 144-146, 178-180, 188, 191-194, 222
mailing labels and lists, 71-73, 167, 183
marketing, entrepreneurial, 175-180
media
    advertising, evaluating strengths and weaknesses of, 179
    dealing with, 9-10
    directories of, 7
    getting coverage from, 9
    national coverage, 188-195
    overplaying stories to, 10
    selection of, 222-224
model release, photographic, 242
mouse, desktop publishing, 153

N

national coverage, 188-195
negative publicity counteraction, 3, 9, 177
negatives, 90, 97
networks, broadcast and cable, national coverage, 189
new business openings, 174, 236
new product news release, 237
news bureaus, 2
newsletters, 138-140, 159
newspapers, 22-23, 223, 224, 243-245
    advertising in, 178, 179, 180, 220
    contacting for publication, 31-33
    national coverage, 189
    operations of, 23-27
    story selection by, 27-31
non-profit organizations, fund raising, 164

O

obituaries, 233
offset printing, 144, 148
open houses, 174

P

paragraphs, 14-16
phonathons (*see* fund raising)
photo availability insert, 183, 184
photo composition, 106-117
photography, 9, 29, 30, 74-121, 206-211, 227
    cameras for, 76
    captions or cutlines for, 117-118
    color transparencies, 94
    contact (proof) sheets, 94-95
    cropping, 136-138
    darkrooms and film developing, 96-106
    depth of field, 85-87
    developing costs, 185, 186
    directing attention into photo, 108, 110
    exposure meters for, 87-89
    f-stops, 82-84
    film selection, 89-95
    flash bulbs, 92
    framing, composition and, 114
    lens for, 76-82
    lighting for, 93-94
    looking space, 107
    mailing photographs,, 119
    model release, 242
    patterns and striking views, 113-114
    people in, 108, 111-112
    photo availability insert, 183, 184
    photo composition, 106-117
    photo size, cost savings in, 185
    photographers, fees for, 185
    press packets using, 120-121, 183-184
    proportional scale use for reducing, 134-136
    publications, calculating space for, 133
    selective focus in, 114
    shutter speeds, 84-85
    storage and organization, 119-120
    telling story with, 115
    thirds rule for composing, 106-108
    vertical vs. horizontal format, 115-117
picas and point size, 126
position, statements of, 63, 237
press conferences, television, 41
press packets, 42, 120-121, 226-228
press releases, 2, 3, 8, 58-74, 227, 229-241
    accuracy of information in, 69
    addressing to specific persons, 73-74
    angling for specific publications, 70
    attribution, 68
    broadcast style, 241
    checklist for, 5
    definition of, 1-10
    desktop publishing and, 65, 67, 73
    determining type needed, 4
    distribution of, 32-33, 70-74
    fact sheets for, 239
    format of, 59
    hard news, 59
    layout and production aides, 65-67
    photographs in, 74, 183, 184
    pronoucement guides in, 65
    publications dealing with, 7, 8
    radio, 51
    samples and fill-in-the-blank type, 74
    soft news, 61
    writing skills for, 63-70
press-type, 65-67
printers, 149-150, 155-157, 186
printing process, 144-150
promotional gimmicks, 2, 218

promotions or advancements, 63, 229-230
pronouncement guides, 65
pronouns, 17, 21
proofreading, 17
propaganda, 3
public affairs offices, 2
public information officers (PIOs), 2
public service announcements, 35, 36, 44-45, 53
publications, 122-150
   anchoring corners in, 129
   annual reports, 144
   balance, 130
   brochures, 140-144
   columnar style, 128
   contrast in, 128
   cropping photos, 136-138
   headlines, 128
   justification, 130
   layout, 126-138
   magazines, 144
   newsletters, 138-140
   points and picas, 126
   printers shops, 149-150
   printing process, 144-150
   proportional scale use, 134
   space vs. copy available, 130-136
   trade, national coverage, 188
   type style and size for, 122-126
   typeset vs. camera-ready copy, 139
   visual emphasis, 128
publicity, 5, 174

Q
quotations, 19

R
radio, 48-57, 222, 223
   advertising in, 180, 221
   drive time, 52
   press releases to, 241
   producing finished releases (actualities) for, 54-57
   public service announcements, 53
   station operation of, 48-50
   story selection by, 50-52
   syndication of, 56
   talk shows, 53-54
reference libraries, 18
rehearsing, 17, 21
reporters, contacting and dealing with, 224-225
reprints, 228
rogue paragraphs, 14
rotogravure printing, 144
rough drafts, 17
run-of-paper (ROP) advertising, 220
run-of-station (ROS) advertising, 221

S
safelights, 100
schedules, 227
seasonal events, 29
second person pronoun, 21
Segelken, Roger, 183
selective focus in photographs, 114
sentence length and style, variation in, 21
shutter speed, 84-85
sidebars, 28
slide shows, 212-218
soft news (*see* feature news)
software, desktop publishing, 153-155
speaking engagements, 63-64, 218, 227
statements of position, 63, 237
stationery, desktop publishing, 160
stop bath, film development, 100
stylebooks, 69
syndicates, national coverage, 56, 189

T
T-Max film, 92
talk shows, 45-47, 53-54
tape recorders, 56, 187
target audiences, 5, 8, 177-178
tear-off cards, fund raising, 167
telephones, 56, 167
telephoto lens, 78-80
television, 34-47, 223
   advertising in, 180, 220
   event planning and coverage by, 41-43
   press conferences, 41
   press releases to, 241
   public service announcements 44-45
   station operations, 34-41
   story selection by, 39-41
   talk shows, 45-47
timers, photographic, 98
trade magazines, national coverage, 188, 191-194
transitions between paragraphs, 15-16
transparancies, color, 94
Tri-X film, 92
tripod, 91
type styles and sizes, 122-126, 157
typesetting, 139, 149

V
Ventura Publisher, 154
vertical vs. horizontal photo formats, 115-117
videotape, 35, 186, 214, 217
volunteers, fund raising, 165

W
white space, 158
wide-angle lens, 80-81
wire services, 35, 40, 189
writers, cost of, 186
writing skills, 8, 11-21, 63, 69
WYSIWYG software, desktop publishing, 155

Z
zoom lens, 81-82